Re-interpreting Brecht: his influence on contemporary drama and film

Des roten Barden Soll

Zeichnung: Wigg Siegl

„Nu machen Se geene Mährde, Genosse Brecht. Dichten Se mal 'n schneidches Marschlied für unsere neie demogradsche Volgsarmee."

A cartoon from the West German journal *Simplicissimus* (February 1956) showing Brecht astride a muzzled Pegasus. The circus performance reveals the Western view of Brecht's relationship to the Communist state.

Re-interpreting Brecht: his influence on contemporary drama and film

Edited by
PIA KLEBER
and
COLIN VISSER

University College, University of Toronto

Published by the Press Syndicate of the University of Cambridge
The Pitt Building, Trumpington Street, Cambridge, CB2 1RP
40 West 20th Street, New York, NY 10011–4211, USA
10 Stamford Road, Oakleigh, Victoria 3166, Australia

First published 1990
First paperback edition 1992

Printed in Great Britain at
the University Press, Cambridge

British Library cataloguing in publication data

Re-interpreting Brecht: his influence on contemporary drama and film.
1. Drama in German. Brecht, Bertolt, 1898–1956
I. Kleber, Pia II. Visser, Colin
832′.012

Library of Congress cataloguing in publication data

Re-interpreting Brecht: his influence on contemporary drama and film /
edited by Pia Kleber and Colin Visser.
p. cm.
Includes index.
ISBN 0 521 38140 1
1. Brecht, Bertolt, 1898–1956 – Influence.
2. Theater – History – 20th century.
3. Motion pictures – History.
I. Kleber, Pia. II. Visser, Colin.
PT2603.R397Z8525 1990
832′.912–dc20 89–35684 CIP

ISBN 0 521 38140 1 hardback
ISBN 0 521 42900 5 paperback

CE

FOR ANNE, ED, AND DAVID MIRVISH

Contents

Contributors

MANFRED WEKWERTH 1951–6 studied with Brecht at the Berliner Ensemble. 1956–68 Principal Director with the Berliner Ensemble under the Artistic Directorship of Helene Weigel. 1968–77 directed plays and films in Europe and abroad. 1975–88 Artistic Director for the Institut für Schauspielregie in East Berlin. 1977 returned to the Berliner Ensemble to become Artistic Director, where he continues to direct major productions of Brecht and Shakespeare. Since 1982 President of the Academy of Fine Arts of the German Democratic Republic. Author of works on the theatre of Bertolt Brecht and of theoretical analyses of his own work in the theatre.

JOACHIM TENSCHERT 1952–6 Assistant to the distinguished critic, Herbert Jhering, and Research Fellow at the Academy of Fine Arts of the German Democratic Republic. 1958–70 Chief Dramaturge and Director at the Berliner Ensemble. 1970–7 directed plays by Brecht and conducted workshops in England, Australia, Cuba, Japan, Austria, and Sweden. In 1977 he returned to his position as Chief Dramaturge and Director at the Berliner Ensemble. Professor of Directing at the Hochschule für Schauspielkunst 'Ernst Busch', in East Berlin.

ROLF ROHMER Professor, Theaterhochschule 'Hans Otto', Leipzig. 1969–82 Rector, Theaterhochschule 'Hans Otto', Leipzig. 1982–4 Artistic Director, Deutsches Theater, East Berlin. 1979–83 President, International Federation for Theatre Research. 1984– Chairman, International Executive Board of the World Encyclopedia of Contemporary Theatre. Extensive publications on German drama and theatre, and on theatre in the German Democratic Republic.

KLAUS VÖLKER 1969– Dramaturge, Schauspielhaus, Zürich; Theater am Neumarkt, Zürich; Basler Theater; Bremer Theater; and Schillertheater, West Berlin. Collaborated with Directors such as Peter Stein, Horst Zankl, Hans Hollman, Luc Bondy, Nicolas Brieger, Adolf Dresen, Peter Zadek, and Hans Neuenfels. 1980– Professor of Theatre at the Free University, West Berlin. Translations from French to German include works by Alfred Jarry, Boris Vian, Raymond Roussel, H.-P. Roché, Jean-Paul Sartre, Jacques Copi, and Jean Genet. Extensive publication on Brecht, Beckett, Wedekind, O'Casey, Yeats, and Synge. Co-editor of the collected works of Bertolt Brecht (*Gesammelte Werke Bertolt Brechts*), 1967.

JOHN WILLETT Became fascinated by Brecht's work in the late 1930s, started writing about it after the Second World War, met him in 1956 and has subsequently translated, edited and taught Brecht in four continents. Selected the 1986 Neher exhibition and helped animate Eisler performances and recordings, notably *Die Massnahme* in 1987–8. Publications include: *The Theatre of Bertolt Brecht* (1959), *Brecht on Theatre* (1964), *Art and Politics in the Weimar Period* (1978), *The Theatre of Erwin Piscator* (1979), and *The Theatre of the Weimar Republic* (1988). Editor, with Ralph Manheim, of the Methuen editions of Brecht's plays, poetry, and prose.

BERNARD DORT Graduate of the Institut d'Etudes Politiques de Paris and of the Ecole Nationale d'Administration. Doctorat d'Etat ès Lettres (1971). Professor at the Sorbonne, Université de Paris III–Sorbonne Nouvelle (Institut d'Etudes Théâtrales). 1983– attached to the Ministry of Culture; Professor at the Conservatoire National Supérieur d'Art Dramatique, and Literary Counsellor to the Théâtre National de Strasbourg. Contributed to the dissemination of the knowledge of Brecht in France through his numerous publications on the subject, and through his editorship of periodicals such as *Théâtre populaire*, and *Travail théâtrale*.

PAUL WALSH Graduate, Graduate Centre for the Study of Drama, University of Toronto. Instructor at the University of Toronto and the University of Minnesota. Book review and special projects Editor, *Canadian Theatre Review*. Theatre and dance Critic. Research Assistant, Uppsala University, Sweden.

MAARTEN VAN DIJK Teaches drama at the University of Waterloo, Ontario. Extensive experience in acting and directing. Publications in contemporary and eighteenth-century drama, theatre, and theatre history. Has performed and directed Brecht in Canada and New Zealand.

MARTIN ESSLIN Head of radio drama at the BBC from 1963 to 1977. He has been teaching at Stanford University since 1977. Author of *Brecht – a Choice of Evils* (1959; 4th edn, 1984). Most recent book *The Field of Drama* (1987).

KAREN LAUGHLIN Associate Professor of English, Florida State University. Her essays on contemporary playwrights, dramatic theory, and feminist theatre have appeared in *Modern Drama*, *Women and Performance*, *Latin American Theatre Review*, and *The Apalachee Quarterly*.

RENATE MÖHRMANN 1977– Professor at the Institute for Theatre, Film, and Television of the University of Cologne. Her publications on women film-makers in the Federal Republic of Germany, on women on stage, and on the theatre history of Berlin include *Die andere Frau* (1977), *Die Frau mit der Kamera* (1980), and *Die Schauspielerin* (1989).

THOMAS ELSAESSER Senior Lecturer in Film and English at the University of East Anglia. Author of *New German Cinema: A History* (1989) and of essays on film theory, film genre, authorship, and film history in numerous collections and anthologies. Has published in *Screen*, *Sight and Sound*, *October*, *American Film*, *Wide Angle*, *New German Critique*, *Discourse*, *Cinetracts*, and other journals.

ERIC BENTLEY His writings on Bertolt Brecht are now collected in two volumes: *The Brecht Commentaries* (Grove Press, 1981), and *The Brecht Memoir* (PAJ Publications, 1985). His Brecht records remain in print with Folkway Records and his *Brecht–Eisler Song Book* with Music Sales Corporation. He is General Editor of the Grove edition of Brecht.

Acknowledgements

We wish to thank particularly Christopher Innes for his unfailing advice and assistance, and Carol Robb and Cyrilene Beckles who painstakingly prepared the typescript, coping goodhumouredly with the frequent revisions and corrections. We thank, too, Sarah Stanton of Cambridge University Press for fostering this volume from its inception, and Mary Baffoni for giving the text her close attention.

This book grew out of the International Conference and Theatre Festival, BRECHT: THIRTY YEARS AFTER, which was sponsored by the University College Drama Programme, and held at the University of Toronto in the Fall of 1986 to mark the thirtieth anniversary of Brecht's death. Our especial thanks are due to the Canada Council, the Social Sciences and Humanities Research Council of Canada, the Government of Ontario Ministry of Citizenship and Culture, and the Goethe Institute of Toronto, who made it possible to assemble the scholars and theatre practitioners whose work has been gathered together in this volume.

Pia Kleber and Colin Visser

I

Introduction

PIA KLEBER

On the cover of its issue of 11 February 1956, the German satirical journal *Simplicissimus* featured a cartoon depicting a circus tent, with Bertolt Brecht wearing a laurel wreath and sitting on a muzzled Pegasus. The ringmaster holding the horse's leash is Walter Ulbricht, then head of state of the German Democratic Republic (GDR). In the caption he is ordering Brecht to compose a striking marching song for the new people's army. The cover, a wickedly malicious birthday present – Brecht had turned 58 the previous day – epitomized the Western view of his relationship to the Communist state. But the controversies surrounding Brecht were not limited to his ideological opponents. Half a year later the Marxist critic George Lukács delivered a speech at Brecht's funeral which was meant to lay controversies to rest. Aimed at reconciling Brecht's theories with Aristotle's concept of catharsis, a point upon which Brecht and he were diametrically opposed, Lukács's eulogy embodied yet another misunderstanding, typical of the many that occurred during Brecht's lifetime.

Three decades after Brecht's death his stature takes on increasingly mythic proportions, yet his reputation fails to reconcile either the critics of his own generation or those of the generation that followed him, who are approaching his work for the first time. But is not Brecht's entire *oeuvre* based on contradictions and on his desire to stir up controversy and doubt? One might even imagine the familiar smirk on Brecht's face as he contemplates from beyond the grave the continuation of these debates. The lively discussion at the International Theatre Festival and Conference, BRECHT: THIRTY YEARS AFTER (October 1986, Toronto, Canada), the International Symposium

BRECHT AND THE PARADIGM CHANGE (December 1986, Hong Kong, China), and the International Brecht Dialogue 88, ART AND THE ART OF LIVING (February 1988, Berlin, GDR) indeed demonstrate that interest in Brecht is still very much alive.

A glance at the *MLA International Bibliography*, and at the lists of newly published books on Brecht presented in *Communications*, the journal of the International Brecht Society, confirms this observation; it also illustrates the difficulty of keeping track of all publications on Brecht. Certain events or historical data, however, have triggered interest in specific areas. A spate of recent biographies and the opening of the FBI and CIA files on Brecht might be responsible for the fact that many critics have developed an unhealthy fascination with Brecht's private life. The thirtieth anniversary of his death in 1986 and his ninetieth birthday in 1988 provoked a re-evaluation of his theory and practice with a strong emphasis on Brecht the director, and prompted countries throughout the world to re-examine Brecht's relevance to the present.

The collection of essays in this book records material first introduced at the Conference BRECHT: THIRTY YEARS AFTER. Presented by some of the most prominent Brecht experts, including representatives from both East and West Germany, whose conflicting interpretations have not hitherto been gathered together in a single book, these analyses offer a unique opportunity to examine the differing views of Brecht's impact in various countries and in specific areas such as acting, directing, feminism, and film. It also tries to remedy some of the serious misunderstandings of the complex work of Brecht, caused by the fact that many critics have severed Brecht the playwright and poet from Brecht the theorist and theatre practitioner.

While the essays are grouped under certain rubrics, these groups do not represent divisions so much as complementary aspects of Brecht's work. The evaluation of Brecht's impact in his own country, the GDR, initiates the discussion. Manfred Wekwerth, who worked closely with Brecht and who since 1977 has been the Director of the Berliner Ensemble, the company founded by Brecht in 1949, is ideally suited to bridge the gap between theory and practice since he is himself both theoretician and practitioner. In dealing with certain Brechtian notions, Wekwerth attempts to establish Brecht's own sense of them in 1956, thus restoring to a pristine meaning terms dimmed by three decades of misuse. Joachim Tenschert, a dramaturge with the Ensemble and a frequent co-director with Wekwerth, contributes an account of the development of the Berliner Ensemble after the death of Brecht. He invites us to consider whether Brecht's thesis that staging methods, interpretation of plays, and the structure of the repertoire must constantly change (since history itself is in a state of evolution) has been borne out in the work of his own company. Rolf Rohmer concludes the first section of the volume, which has been given over to representatives from East Germany, by analysing the importance of Brecht the playwright in his own country, and by examining the problems encountered by later playwrights faced with the difficulties of assimilating the influence of so overwhelming a predecessor.

Three broader studies of the importance of Brecht in the Federal Republic of Germany, in England, and in France succeed the first group. Klaus Völker, whose biography of Brecht was published in 1976, seems to concur with the general view held by theatre practitioners in the FRG that Brecht presented a simplified view of reality and that the closed form of his parables does not provide adequate opportunity for interpretative variety. However, John Willett and Bernard Dort agree that Brecht still has a living contribution to make to the theory and practice of the theatre, despite the differing reception of his work in England and in France.

As a further corrective to the long-prevailing overemphasis on Brecht's theoretical writings, the two sections that follow deal with specific aspects of Brecht's acting techniques and staging methods and with performance studies of two Brechtian productions – Benno Besson's *Hamlet* (1979) and the Royal Shakespeare Company's production of *Mother Courage* (1983). The object, however, has not been to present a unified view of Brecht's work. Rather, the opposing views on acting and blocking expressed by Martin Esslin and Maarten van Dijk, and on adaptations by Esslin and Paul Walsh, establish the dialectic that can be initiated between a generation of scholars contemporaneous with Brecht, and a new generation eager to investigate once more the practical implications of Brecht's methodology. To limit Brecht's impact strictly to the theatre, however, would be to do him an injustice: essays follow that examine his influence on contemporary feminist writers and on film, on which he has made a profound impression. Eric Bentley concludes the volume by challenging one of the themes that has unified the collection of essays: the notion of influence.

All three contributors from the GDR, Manfred Wekwerth, Joachim Tenschert and Rolf Rohmer, suggest that the work of Brecht has to be reread, and re-interpreted for a society subjected to radically altered circumstances. Indeed, while Brecht wrote to increase self-recognition and to promote change in a capitalist society, the GDR is now faced with the realities of a socialist society. One can either argue that what has been achieved is the best of all possible societies, a *fait accompli*, or submit the new society to a Marxist analysis, which treats reality critically and reveals its contradictions. Choosing the latter alternative, Manfred Wekwerth poses seven questions about Brecht's key concerns: changing the world; *Gestus*; pleasure; reason; *naïveté*; distancing/identifying; breadth and diversity of realism. These terms are being redefined in the light of the changed social conditions in the GDR. It is a timely and salutary reminder that such controversial terms are themselves part of a process of change and re-evaluation, rather than a static shibboleth.

Identifying the phrase 'changing the world' as the main issue in Brecht's theatre, Wekwerth argues that Brecht's focus is particularly relevant to challenges posed by the scientific and technical revolution which society has to master. He bases his analysis on Marxist theory and refers to Brecht's concern with collectivity. The changes in the means and conditions of production in socialism enlarge the sphere of human possibilities. The recognition and resolution of individual differences in needs, abilities and pleasures not only 'lift the individual to universal status but also stabilize the collective', since, with that recognition and resolution, the possibility of the exchange of what the one individual needs for what the other produces increases. Wekwerth thus proposes as a reading of the phrase 'changing the world' (a reading which would be meaningful in a socialist society) the demonstration that the prerequisite for the free transformation of *all* is the free transformation of *each* individual.

But the free transformation of each individual is seen by Wekwerth in relation to the collective. This is precisely the point Heiner Müller challenges in plays like *Mauser* (1979). He believes that the subjection of the individual to the collective might lead to the fossilization of the present *form* of the collective, particularly in a society like the GDR whose terms of socialism are now firmly established. Müller has proposed a dialectic between history and the individual, since, as Elizabeth Wright aptly argues, 'the historical necessity of obtaining the subject's consent (*Einverständnis* in Brecht's sense) clashes with the desire of the individual for emancipation, where the full realization of socialism is uncertain or impossible'.[1]

Rolf Rohmer elaborates on the problems that the younger generation of playwrights in the GDR faces in accepting Brecht's work. 'Concerned with present-day problems, with the complicated issues of contemporary social reality', these young people 'demonstrate a constant hope and desire for change'. They are 'interested in plays that deal with specific issues, with intense situations and conflicts, and which deal with these openly'. Clearly the use of the fable or parable, which entails distancing and generalization, does not fulfil this demand. After 1933, Rohmer argues, Brecht had to accommodate the various points of view and different understandings of tradition held by the anti-Fascist democratic United Front made up of the most diverse socio-political groupings. Their sole point of agreement was the fight against Fascism. Moreover, Brecht did not have the opportunity in exile to try out his plays on stage and test the audience's reaction. The result was the literarization of his theatre both in theory and practice. The price he paid for this was the upgrading of the importance of the fable. It was concentration on the use of the fable which effectively prevented Brecht from reworking his earlier plays. But the fundamental problem for younger playwrights is not the difficulty in revising Brecht's material, but the implicit nature of messages in the parable form. It is Brecht's form itself that they reject in their search for a more explicit and direct communication with the audience. Müller shares this view. In a conversation with the philosopher Wolfgang Heise, he characterizes Brecht's parables as extemely closed and calculated, and therefore difficult to break open. But, he argues, 'that's precisely what keeps plays alive for the theatre, that at one time one stratum is at the surface and then in another situation and in another generation, the next one comes to the surface.'[2] Only by such deconstruction can the text work again. Müller accuses Brecht of judging and theorizing about his experience too quickly. What stays in the mind is not the experience but the judgement. In order to reveal the contradiction between 'judgement' and 'experience' one has to 'expose the essential reality [*Realitätskern*] of his [Brecht's] experience with experiences of today'.[3] Müller and Völker both see Brecht's *Fatzer* fragment as more suited for such a deconstruction, because it is 'an unfinished play, a play without solutions, a play which asks painful questions and is open to question' (Völker). Völker considers the production of the *Fatzer* adaptation by Heiner Müller, directed by Manfred Karge and Matthias Langhoff in Hamburg in 1978, more successful than the staging of Brecht's *Fatzer* fragment at the Berlin Schaubühne under the direction of Frank-Patrick Steckel in 1976. Despite his criticism of Steckel's production he maintains that the play 'deserves to be produced with all its contradictions'. It is interesting to note that the Berliner Ensemble produced the *Fatzer* fragment in Heiner Müller's adaptation to celebrate Brecht's ninetieth birthday (10 Feb. 1988), particularly since Völker claims that 'the experimental exploratory period of the Berliner Ensemble effectively ended with the 1964 production of *Coriolanus*'. Such a statement might be dismissed as just another West German prejudice. Yet John Willett, who notes that the West German theatres 'have gone off Brecht during the last decade or more', also argues that 'the East Germans (including the Berliner Ensemble itself) no longer have anything infectiously new to say about him'.

Joachim Tenschert rejects this opinion and asserts in his essay that the Berliner Ensemble constantly rereads and re-explores Brecht's work 'to find messages for the world of today and of the day to come'. Endorsing this trend, the production of *The Caucasian Chalk Circle* (premièred 1976), which the Berliner Ensemble presented as part of the Toronto Conference as their North American début, indeed constituted a rethinking of the play and of its earlier staging by Brecht in 1954. The completely different set design – the revolve had been exchanged for a sloping stage – was probably physically as beautiful as von Appen's creation of 1954. The hard lesson, however, which Brecht taught the 1954 audience by clearly distinguishing the good from the bad, had been softened, even blurred. In that production the rigid expressions of the masks of Brecht's ironshirts showed the rigidity of people who have become unquestioning instruments of the powerful, while Simon did not wear a mask; his face remained free, like Grusha's. The ironshirts of the 1976 production wore only nose make-up, exactly like Simon. They were more realistic and human and thus less rigid. Since there was no physical distinction between them and Simon, the audience could infer, rather like the three gods in *The Good Person of Szechwan*, that one needed only *one* good person to justify the existing world order. It was a rethinking of the play, but it was also a concession to the audience, and something of the seriousness of the parable was lost.

Völker is as critical of the Brecht scene in the FRG as he is of that in the GDR. He claims that the only West German *mises en scène* of Brecht's work worth discussing, after Peter Stein's famous production of *The Mother* (1970), are Manfred Karge's *The Mother* (1982), Alfred Kirchner's *Saint Joan of the Stockyards* (1979) and his *Mother Courage* (1981) – all three staged in Bochum – and Jürgen Flimm's *Baal* in Cologne (1981). The common features shared by the Kirchner and Flimm productions are modern settings and direct references to contemporary political situations. Such 'strained topicality' in production methods, however, is one of the nine points John Willett makes in outlining the main obstacles, as he sees them, which have to be overcome to achieve a vital Brecht in Great Britain. 'Those directors', he continues, 'who are frightened that Brecht's political message isn't topical enough for today often try to work in "contemporary" references in the form of slide projections or video material or even changes of text and setting. In our country, where the German experience between 1919 and 1945 has uncomfortable lessons for us, this blurs Brecht's point. As with Shakespeare, either the man has something to say to us or he hasn't; and you can't improve matters by dressing the play up differently.' Manfred Wekwerth also takes a stand on this subject in his section on 'reason' by declaring it 'nonsensical' to adapt plays to the most recent stage of historical understanding, for the basic assumption would be diametrically opposed to Brecht's concept of 'historicizing'. He shares Brecht's confidence in the intelligence of the spectator and believes that the stories 'in their historical and poetic concreteness . . . can be transferred by the audience to other times and situations'.

The post-Brecht theatre practitioners of West Germany seem to have as little confidence in the thinking ability of their public as the

East German ones, and both share a common goal of more direct communication. At least in the GDR there is a reaction to Brecht. In the FRG and France one hears only of a Brecht-fatigue (Brecht-*Müdigkeit*). Völker explains that Western artists and intellectuals 'retreat into more private and aesthetic domains with the general failure of political hopes and ambitions'. They consider Brecht now as much a classic as Goethe and Schiller. 'The Brecht-fatigue', comments Werner Hecht, the director of the Brecht-Zentrum in the GDR in his 1988 article 'Wie mit einem Klassiker umgehen?', 'is connected with a Western theory-fatigue in general, which not coincidentally also manifests itself in a general Marxism-fatigue.'[4] This not only agrees with the view of Völker, but is underlined by Bernard Dort. On the one hand it seems to be natural that the generations after Brecht reject his example in order to define their own position, even while always using Brecht as a reference point. On the other hand Brecht's reception in both Germanys has always fluctuated with the current political climate. The conservatism in the FRG and the Glasnost phase in the GDR, which openly permits the search for forms adequate for a new social order, confirm this trend. There is, however, another stumbling block which discourages theatre directors from taking on the challenge of re-assessing Brecht. Peter von Becker points out in his article 'Wer hat das Recht am Brecht?' the enormous problems of getting permission from Brecht's publishers and heirs to stage Brecht in any revisionary form.[5] The required guarantee of *Werktreue* (faithfulness to the text) prevents precisely those stagings which break the play open in order to bring layers to the surface that were hidden at the time they were written: the prerequisite, according to Müller, for keeping the plays alive. Brecht himself always considered his epic plays as a transitional form which had to be challenged and changed in order to remain continuously subversive.

According to Bernard Dort's essay, the decline of interest in Brecht within French theatre circles parallels that of their West German colleagues. He also sees this as a 'result of the cultural climate and of changes in ideology. One can speak of the return of repression, the repression that has occurred since this theatre first put to the fore its civic, political, and even revolutionary mission.' He blames the entire French intellectual climate. There is a connection to be found between the mistrust of the East and West German theatre people in their audiences' abilities to judge for themselves, and Dort's description of the present situation as a 'rejection of the idea that thought is capable of changing the world'. Even Giorgio Strehler, whom Brecht once hailed as the best possible director for his plays, seems to have lost the ability to present Brecht in a revolutionary way that would instigate in the spectator the desire for knowledge and the pleasure of discovery. His third production of *The Threepenny Opera* (1986) was aesthetically extremely beautiful, but this beautiful extravaganza, and the reliance on established theatrical devices, robbed the play of any true political potential. Dort attributes the failure of Strehler's staging to two factors: firstly, that the director dealt with it as if it were a classic – though it is not yet a classic and Dort questions whether it will ever be one; and secondly, that Strehler presented the work as if it were self-sufficient and 'had only to be true to itself'. The failure of Strehler's *The Threepenny Opera* is, however, a question of staging and not of text. A concert given by Sting and Gianna Nanini in Hamburg in 1987 in which they sang songs from *The Threepenny Opera* was able to evoke a sharp political edge through their unorthodox and fresh way of presenting the texts, which brought out that excitement and pleasure combined with political awareness for which Brecht had hoped. Sting's interesting approach seems to echo Willett's account of the present Brecht reception in England, where there is 'no falling-off in the volume of productions' even though the same wave of political conservatism found in France and the FRG swept over the United Kingdom. On the contrary, the productions have 'meanwhile so improved (on the whole) as to persuade even the sceptic that our theatre is now able to make something of Brecht'. Willett believes that Brecht is now being seen in England 'as a direct riposte to the each-man-for-himself, weakest-goes-to-the-wall ethic of Mrs Thatcher's sub-Reagan government'.

Like Tenschert, Völker and Dort, Willett too refers to Max Frisch's remark about Brecht being reduced to a classic, and declares this idea to be 'patent rubbish'. He explains the specific attitude towards Brecht in Britain by identifying Brecht's ups and downs less as 'changes in his reputation and theatrical status' than 'changes in our grasp of his achievement. In Britain he has always been both seminal and boring depending on how he is presented and understood; and what goes up and down (but on the whole more up) is our ability to understand and present him'.

Despite the differing analyses given by Dort and Willett, they see their respective theatres threatened by the same dangers: particularly by what Willett calls 'self-importance', and Dort calls 'narcissism'. The famous Brechtian theory of ensemble work has yet to replace the traditional ego trips, whether in acting, directing, or design.

Both share the opinion that neither France nor Britain is yet able to convey the full impact of Brecht's work. Dort considers it necessary to come to terms 'if not with the totality of his work then at least with fragments or selected moments from them', with 'his concept and practice of the theatre, and a general idea of its function'. Willett speculates that poetry, music and design provide keys for a deeper understanding of Brecht. 'There are poems of Brecht's', he states, 'which encapsulate so much, and move so economically from the small specific object to the great human issues, that they are almost unbearable to read aloud. This is where the study of his deeper relevance for our own time has to begin.' The newly published East German discs, featuring the performances of Hanns Eisler himself, Robyn Archer's recordings made for EMI with Muldowney, John Harle and the London Sinfonietta, and David Bowie's RCA record of five songs from *Baal* bring, Willett says, 'the most vivid and attractive part of Brecht's theatre out of the special realm of Berlin exotica, making it relevant rather to our own musical and poetic concerns'. The incorporation of music in plays has to be dealt with thoughtfully, however. The failure of the 1983 RSC production of *Mother Courage*, directed by Howard Davies, is attributed by Maarten van Dijk in part to George Fenton's musical score, which 'aimed for atmosphere instead of meaning', making the songs a 'seamless part of the action'. In contrast the Théâtre du Soleil's use of music in its highly successful production of Hélène Cixous's *Sihanouk* was in full sympathy with Brecht's practice (Dort).

Dort also praises Ariane Mnouchkine's direction of *Sihanouk* for exemplifying the Brechtian style of acting, through which the actors presented 'a series of comportments, which might be contradictory' instead of constructing a character. 'Sihanouk . . . could at one moment be as playful and light hearted as a comedian in the silent cinema, and at the next he could be as contorted and self-absorbed as a product of Actors' Studio: he played one *and* the other. He would be at one moment a fully realized imp and then a Buddhist Priest.' The way Mnouchkine's actors showed 'how they comported themselves, carrying each *Gestus* to its conclusion, without allowing one to contaminate the next', astonished the spectator and thus compelled him 'to understand and contemplate' the contradictory behaviour of the characters. Dort's analysis of this contemporary director's work confirms Walter Benjamin's assumption that 'Brechtian acting is a series of comportments. It is both concrete and discontinuous'. This was not so in the RSC *Courage* production. The music, the superficial design and indistinct blocking seemed to have prevented the actors from presenting 'each scene for itself' and as a result they missed the meaning of many crucial points of the play (van Dijk).

Martin Esslin takes a vigorously opposed attitude to Dort's and van Dijk's claim that a critical, dialectical style of acting 'would provide social, political and ideological insights which would prove powerful incentives for the audience to press for radical changes to the society'. He questions whether an epic style of acting can show that human nature changes through changing social conditions any more convincingly than the Court theatre style it superseded. On the other hand van Dijk postulates that this technique has 'a simple practical advantage for the working actor and director' independent of what one may think about the ideological implications attributed to it. Although Brecht expected insights and further conclusions from the spectator, he did not insist on them: he was not so naïve as to believe seriously that one of his plays would be able to transform the spectators into followers of socialist humanism. And, indeed, Esslin's demand that a director should find the right style of acting for each individual work is in total agreement with the practice of the Berliner Ensemble as outlined by Ekkehard Schall and Benno Besson:

Character, morals, style are of no interest in a production. A Brecht production does *not* start out with a style; the style emerges during rehearsals in the sequence of situations, in which attitudes are assumed and then played. The process has to be justified, not the character.[6]

Brecht pondered, felt, considered things in a remarkable manner. It was a sort of standard he gave. Each took what they wanted. But it was not an inheritance. (Walsh)

The only constant component Brecht and his disciples share is a dialectical way of thinking. In his practical work Brecht was concerned with the relationship of text and *mise en scène* rather than with the relationship of theories and production; it is a basic misconception of this first principle which has stunted so many subsequent approaches to the staging of his works.

Paul Walsh's documentation of Benno Besson's mounting of *Hamlet*, in which Besson cast the comic actor Asko Sarkola in the role of Hamlet, seems to exemplify Esslin's definition of a distanced acting style which has been 'practised from time immemorial' and therefore cannot claim to produce unique ideological and political effects (Esslin). The reason for Besson's choice of the comic actor, however, was, Walsh suggests, precisely to elucidate both 'the historical sources and the social consequences of Hamlet's dilemma' by means of exaggerated gestures. Besson's approach to the *Hamlet* production apparently also contradicts Esslin's comments on the type of adaptation approved by Brecht. A Brechtian staging of *Lear*, Esslin argues, would provide 'the socio-historical background', show what conditions obtained in primitive feudalism and establish that 'Lear is merely a product of his time'. Yet Besson can be shown to have held to Brecht's aim of retaining for future generations the '"original freshness, the element of surprise . . . the newness of productive stimulus" that are the hallmarks of classic plays' (Walsh). He attempted to resolve contradictions between our historically new thought and the haunting demands of past and present experience. Mnouchkine's and Besson's productions both confront the problems of our time by a 'double detour', as Dort calls it. One travels via Cambodia and Sihanouk, the other via Shakespeare, to dramatize 'materials that are painfully contemporary' (Dort). In contrast to the sentimentalizing of the RSC *Courage* production, which made the decision *for* the audience, Besson's 'desentimentalized treatment of the fable and its legendary characters' allowed the audience 'to cut through the cult of personality and see the story from the perspective of our own present and possible future' (van Dijk and Walsh). According to Walsh, 'Besson brought the events of the play to bear on the character of Hamlet rather than allowing the play's most famous and persuasive character to dominate the audience's response.' This particular Brechtian staging revived the original vitality and power of the text by the 'disruption of expectations in a rich application of the dialectics of *Verfremdung* ["alienation" or "distancing"]', a concept whose validity is disputed by Esslin, and was ignored by Howard Davies's *Courage* production (Walsh). The two analyses of the *Hamlet* and the *Courage* productions confirm a widely held opinion that the desired effects of Brecht's theory are seldom found in the practical realization of his own plays, at least as they are produced at the present. This brings us to the paradoxical situation of a 'Brecht-reception without Brecht', as described by Andrzej Wirth.[7]

Besson's approach to classical texts and Mnouchkine's staging of Cixous's play correspond to the treatment of dramatic material by both American feminists and such British writers as Caryl Churchill. Karen Laughlin classifies the 'historicizing' of dramatic events as one of the three principal aspects of Brecht's theatre aesthetic which American women playwrights found useful in developing their own feminist theatre. This device provided them with the tool to re-examine history from a woman's perspective and also to reveal 'the social and political forces at work in shaping women's destinies'.

Both American and British feminist playwrights have attempted not only to write double roles like Brecht's Shen Teh/Shui Ta into their scripts, but also frequently use multiple and cross-gender or cross-race casting. Myrna Lamb has a pregnant man beg his female doctor to 'abort a fetus that has been implanted in him against his will', while Megan Terry and Jo Ann Schmidman 'cast both men and women in the roles of the female prisoners and the prison matrons' in their docudrama *Babes in the Bighouse* (Laughlin). The aim of this alienation effect through cross-gender or cross-race casting is to raise consciousness about the conditioning of social roles and dominant ideologies in both the actors and the audience. Another alienation effect in Martha Boesing's *River Journal*, as in Besson's *Hamlet*, is the use of masks. Boesing invites the spectator to examine the social conditions which have caused the characters in her play to adopt 'these alternate identities' while the designer of Besson's *Hamlet* production, Ezio Toffolutti, suggests that the mask forces 'the actor to express his role . . . with the whole body, attaining a more concrete representational mode' (Laughlin and Walsh). The audience is thus forced to break with 'habits learned from film and television of reading individuals entirely through facial expressions rather than through interactions and relationships'.

Karen Malpede's belief that 'the shock of recognition unites audience and actors, and each group is simultaneously moved towards an emotional understanding of the next world action' (Laughlin) is similar to Heiner Müller's, as outlined in his conversation with Heise.[8] He postulates 'learning through shock', a central point in Brecht's theory which has not yet been sufficiently explored. By the term 'shock' Müller understands 'the moment of truth, when one sees in the mirror the image of the enemy'.[9] This is not unlike Malpede's suggestion that 'the audience . . . is meant to see the act of understanding . . . the new truths she or he has uttered' (Laughlin). Wolfgang Heise defines the Brecht/Müller concept of shock as both 'eliminating distance and creating distance within one event and through one event'.[10] He recognizes the relationship between destruction and productivity as a true Brechtian dialectic.

Laughlin points to various similarities which can also be found in other successors of Brecht, male or female – Heiner Müller, Benno Besson or Ariane Mnouchkine, to name just a few. After all, Brecht wanted to provide a model for the changeability of the world and to raise awareness of role playing and its underlying causes. It is therefore almost inevitable that revolutions of any kind may find the material and methods they need in Brecht. But that does not guarantee that everyone who wishes to present Brecht is committed to struggle against all oppression. Nor does it mean that everyone who uses the epic mode is interested in calling upon the audience to be productive in any way. More than one critic has pointed out that the epic idiom 'has become the universal language of contemporary theatre, irrespective of its ideological origin'.[11] Thomas Elsaesser makes the same observation about film: 'Not all the Brechtianisms in postwar cinema . . . are true to the spirit of Brecht, and among those who have claimed him for their work, fewer inherited his questions than copied his answers . . .'

A link can also be found between the use and understanding of Brecht by feminist playwrights and the West German women film-makers discussed by Renate Möhrmann. They all share a belief in the changeability of society by means of critical and political theatre work or film-making. In the early seventies female film directors still fought the same cause of oppression as Brecht did, since at that time they saw 'the roots of women's oppression in the capitalist system rather than in patriarchal conditions' (Möhrmann). Caryl Churchill has demonstrated how this transition can be accomplished since her socialist feminist analysis examines the relationship between patriarchy and the economic system.[12] Brecht's preoccupation with collectivity, discussed by Wekwerth in this volume, equally concerned the women's cinema in both production and reception (Möhrmann). Collectivity in production meant changing the entire structural organization in theatre and the whole production apparatus in film. Speaking of his involvement in filming *The Threepenny Opera*, Brecht stated that he saw in cinema a unique opportunity for such a 'refunctioning' (*Umfunktionierung*).[13] Völker attributes Peter Stein's as well as Peter Zadek's achievements in this respect to Brecht, who sought 'not to supply the production apparatus without . . . changing that apparatus' (Völker and Elsaesser). Elsaesser reminds us that Brecht himself had, 'in the early 1930s, practised a strategy of interventionism (*eingreifendes Denken*) in just about every debate and through every existing medium of cultural production'. In his theatre, Peter Stein followed precisely this principle in creating a model of co-determination with his ensemble at the Schaubühne in West Berlin: everyone was to have a say in the way the theatre was to be run. A statute of co-determination regulates the internal democratic processes of the Schaubühne. The task was to emancipate the actors from their traditional roles as mere tools of the director. They all came to Berlin from various theatres where hierarchies had stagnated and working conditions had become corrupt in order to produce a different kind of theatre. Collective work also constituted the base for the extraordinary achievements of the Théâtre du Soleil in France.

In film the same process can be observed since one of the problems avant-garde film-making had to confront in the 1970s was that its relationship to politics also meant engaging 'more actively with the diverse apparati of production' (Elsaesser). West German film-makers seemed to be very susceptible to this side of Brecht, 'being directly involved in institutional battles and strategic decisions', so that intervention in the apparatus and 'not merely supplying it with a product' became one of the most Brechtian aspects of the new

German cinema, 'crystallizing around the representation of the working class, of working-class subjects (*Arbeiterfilme*), and the strategies and compromises these entailed' (Elsaesser). This choice of subject applies to both genders, as the first international women's film seminar in Berlin in 1973 proved. 'The everyday life of female workers, with the organization of strikes, the demand for equal pay, and the problem of women's double burden' were the problem areas discussed in the presented films (Möhrmann).

Despite the fact that Brecht involved himself in film-making, he had several reservations about cinematic techniques which he believed imposed only a 'rigid fixation of the spectator's point of view'. His impact on film is nevertheless undeniably strongly felt, even though different countries have adopted his theories in different ways (van Dijk and Elsaesser).

Most of the seven aspects questioned by Manfred Wekwerth in the opening paper of this volume are discussed independently by contributors, in areas that range from playwriting and directing to film-making and theorizing. And yet Eric Bentley challenges the notion of influence altogether. At first glance it may seem surprising that the questioning of the premises of the other papers comes from someone who knew Brecht personally, because his essay is reminiscent of the younger generation for which distance seems to be a necessity. (Bentley, after all, turned to playwriting too.) These writers commit a kind of *Vatermord* in order to be free to do what *they* want, which has its own irony because the young Brecht had himself done exactly the same thing by insisting he could not find anything good in any of the theatre of his time. Bentley proclaims that 'disciples have to find the energy to become rebels'. It seems the 1980s produced a lot of rebels, specifically against Brecht's so-called mature plays, and their closed form of the parable. As mentioned before, there is a consensus amongst scholars and theatre practitioners that Brecht's early works, like *Baal*, *Fatzer*, *Brotladen* or the *Lehrstücke*, are more accessible because Brecht did not present them as a finished unified whole but as fragments, which leaves these particular texts in a more fluid, open-ended state. The concert by Sting and Nanini or *The Seven Deadly Sins of the Petit-Bourgeoisie* by Pina Bausch (performed at Wuppertal in 1976), however, reject the notion that Brecht's plays have lost their relevance for our time.[14] Rather, they confirm one's suspicion that the performing arts in general have been unable to emerge from under Brecht's theory – or the heavy interpretation of it – in order to find new ways of staging which would produce the stimulating and productive tension between text, visual and auditory elements necessary to keep the plays alive. It would be interesting if innovators like Bob Wilson, who has already collaborated so extensively with Heiner Müller, Brecht's recognized heir, or Tadeusz Kantor could be allowed to experiment with Brecht's texts, break them open and reveal the richness and complexity of those plays, whose multi-faceted subjects remain all too relevant today.

The fact that many contributors to this collection have chosen to discuss various elements and not Brecht as a unified entity should be a reminder that his legacy is not a closed system of theory and practice. Brecht's ideas are scattered as fragments amongst all his writings from the diaries, production notes, theoretical essays, interviews and poems. He himself considered his writings as transitory and not as a bible to be followed unquestioned by his disciples. As Heiner Müller said as far back as 1980, to use Brecht without criticizing him is treason.[15]

Theatre practitioners might follow the examples of film-makers or feminist writers and extract from Brecht's theory and practice what is most relevant at the time. The time now seems opportune to challenge his whole work anew to discover ideas which may have become hidden under the cumulative strata of scholarship. Heiner Müller, as we have seen, singles out Brecht's theory of 'learning through shock'. Brecht demands distance from oneself in order to live the shock which is a necessary prerequisite for the very process of learning. 'One has to teach the people to be frightened at themselves in order to give them courage.'[16] According to Müller, one has to find the shock centre of every story, situation, or character and to find the means to present it to the spectator as such. Only such a shock centre can develop into a centre of strength, which produces the necessary energy to overcome fear. Fear can be vanquished only by confrontation, not by suppression.[17] This theory unquestionably challenges the Aristotelian notion of catharsis and leads us back to Georg Lukács's eulogy. The catharsis in Brecht's concept of shock, however, has nothing to do with a psychological purgation but produces rather a very complex activity to liberate oneself from fear.

Lukács wanted the world to be shown as 'potentially whole, hoping to inspire the revolutionary reader with utopian hope and faith', whereas Brecht shows the world as 'fragmented and infinitely transformable so as to force the audience into a continuous process of rewriting it'.[18] It is a challenge which his work throws out to scholars and theatre practitioners alike.

2

Questions concerning Brecht

MANFRED WEKWERTH

Brecht has taught us well how to practise and discuss theatre: so well, that people have been known to use Brechtian language to dismiss him. Brecht's theatre has become so widespread that at times we don't even notice him. Wherever you look, something is getting 'alienated'. *Gestus* (we still do not have a plural for it) is so rampant at rehearsals that it has to be restrained from degenerating into mere gesticulation. Out of every theatre programme that used to restrict itself to background material now peeps the 'causal nexus'.[1] 'Changing the world' is no rarity either. When recently a lighting technician called out to me that he was alienating the light – and pushed a pink gel in front of a spotlight – I told myself it was time to talk about Brecht again. Or, to alter a famous quotation slightly: We've been changing the world long enough; once more it has become a matter of interpreting it. It is not wrong concepts that are dangerous, but imprecise ones; untruths do less damage than half-truths. And conceptual destruction is more destructive for Marxism than for other theories since it robs it of the concrete vitality which is precisely what makes it both true and attractive.

It is not the absence of change but its bewildering abundance that has left many theatres timidly questioning whether they can still help to change the world. In particular, when illusions such as the one that theatre could confidently change the world *all by itself* failed to work out, some of us replaced them with other illusions: the illusion, for instance, that theatre can simply abdicate from changing the world. And whenever cogitation is replaced by hesitation, gumption by presumption, analysis by alarm: enter mysticism and its most easeful form – pessimism; so that history has to conform to whatever our opinion of it happens to be, and the question of how to perform the world is solved by forever performing one's self.

And yet, as a source of models of real and imagined human interactions, the theatre has the irreplaceable ability to illuminate *what* is performed by *how* it is performed, in that for the duration of the play a person can be contrasted with himself, and directly and visibly experienced as both subject and object. The Theatre of the Absurd was able to live out its two decades because inaction on the stage can be a moving experience, if it is performed as an event: one of the fundamental capabilities of the theatre. What is there to prevent us then from presenting human deeds – in facts and conflicts, in achievements as in defeats, happy and sad – especially where they seem to be avoiding conflict with each other? It is almost comical to note how where revolution is most successful – that is, most lasting – it is least noticed. Changes are obliterated from our everyday consciousness the more they are a part of our everyday life. It is probably because the challenge to theatres was never so permanent as now that it is so seldom noticed. And many problems of the theatre seem so large because they are presented as so small – as mere theatrical problems. To ask the larger questions, when the smaller ones are pressing; to keep ideals in sight even in less than ideal circumstances; to design lives, when it seems a matter of mere survival; to insist upon the greater peace, when we don't yet have the lesser peace; to yearn for difficulties, as a challenge to overcome them; to wrest a growing comprehension of the world from its growing unfathomableness; to see making increasing distinctions not as a curse but as mankind's work; yes, even to treat despair not as a desperate end but as a beginning of productive doubt; to take each general agreement not as the end of historical change but as an urgent occasion for criticism; and, in order to keep both spirit and initiative fresh, now and always to speak of the future not as 'legitimate' but as 'highly probable' because, always, 'as much truth gets through as we carry through' – surely all this is what Brecht meant when he declared that the most beautiful and urgent mission for art in the closing years of the twentieth century is to strengthen the human will to live. This was surely what was meant by his suggestion that we not speak any more of his theatre as 'epic theatre', nor as 'dialectical theatre', but as 'philosophical folk-theatre'. He must have been attracted by the irreconcilable contradiction set up between pure (and therefore false) philosophy and simple (and therefore false) folk-theatre. For Brecht, in his last years, was interested in both: philosophy and entertainment. Philosophy makes it possible for theatre to entertain people, in the future as well as today. And entertainment makes possible the 'stress-testing of concepts [i.e. philosophy]', so as to achieve those apparent simplicities that induce complexities. Without philosophy and without folk-theatre, the theatre easily falls into the noncommittal depths of 'creeping empiricism' (Lenin); or, worse yet, it swings between 'the high-flown misery and the trite' (Engels).

It is time to speak of Brecht. Yet nothing is more difficult than stepping forward into an earlier state of mind. And so we must put some questions. Not to Brecht but to ourselves. And not about the new (the 'innovative', as it is always called in theatre circles) but about the long-acknowledged.

1. CHANGING THE WORLD

The key to Brecht's theatre is the changing of the world, and that desire to do so which it is the theatre's task to organize. By this Brecht meant first of all the transforming of social relationships – what he referred to as social overhaul. After the overhaul of society which occurred in the German Democratic Republic, Brecht spoke, particularly in his last years, of the transformation of the world, which had become even more urgent because of the possibilities and necessities of the dialectical process. 'The theatre of the scientific age', he wrote, 'is in a position to make dialectics into a source of enjoyment. The unexpectedness of logically progressive or zigzag development, the instability of every circumstance, the joke of contradiction and so forth: all these are ways of enjoying the liveliness of men, things and processes, and they heighten both our capacity for life and our pleasure in it.'[2]

In the German Democratic Republic, changing the world through the theatre is often used only as a poetic metaphor or 'an accomplished fact', as if social change had already occurred. Or as if the changes, as they now occur, were hardly possible to enact in the theatre any more since any gain in productivity would have to be paid for with the loss of overview and thus of human perspective.

Nevertheless, the scientific and technological revolution that is now under way is the greatest breakthrough in and overturning of the powers of production that has ever occurred in human history. It distinguishes itself from all previous transformations in that not only is a man's arm stretched but his mind gets involved too. As with the stone axe, one can build a house or strike a man dead. And the question 'curse or blessing?' must be replaced by the question 'regression or mastery?', because there is no such thing as standstill for mankind. Increased refinement or oblivion are the fundamental alternatives for human development.

We may ask whether the changes resulting from the scientific and technological revolution are what Brecht meant when he spoke of how 'changing the world' would follow a complete social overhaul, so that the world is constantly being changed by people's cumulative life's work. Certainly – that would seem to be basic. Yet the world gets changed by today's capitalism too, in some places more than by socialism, though of course at a cost to humanity. Its technology drains the vitality of labour out of the production process; but the people, who for the sake of increased production are removed from the work process, are also consumers – deprived of the increased volume of produce. The technology of capitalism does not change the simple ground rules of its social relations. *They* would have to be changed if this world is to be changed. For Brecht always viewed 'changing the world' in the context of revolutionary activity.

The question remains of how we in the German Democratic Republic can, under new social conditions, understand and display the concept of 'changing the world' as a revolutionary behaviour. It must surely be through our mastering society's advance, which more than ever depends upon mastering the scientific and technological revolution. But what is new in that revolution is its inherent dialectic: that it has made possible for us previously unknown developments of the individual subject, and that, on the other hand, it could itself have become possible only through a previously unknown development of the individual subject. How can this dialectic, which turns upon the extension of 'the subjective factors', also become a turning point for the theatre? In short: What can the theatre itself change, if it wishes today to change the world?

Following Brecht, we have identified the collective as of first concern in changing the world. A theatre that seeks to change the world must above all, after Fascism's systematic destruction of collective activity and thinking, awaken people's courage and capacity for collectivism. It becomes necessary once again to clarify collective attitudes, impulses, and precepts. People must rediscover what, before the Nazi barbarism, counted as the common good of the labour movement. If one realizes that Engels's *Anti-Dühring* was in its time printed as a serial novel in the journal *Vorwärts*, one can imagine what has been lost. The first performance of *Mother Courage and her Children* in Berlin in 1949 was intended – apart from all its artistic achievements – as a withdrawal cure for those who still had the false pathos of 'a people without room' ringing in their ears. Sparse staging was a passionate weaponry against murderous passions. Brecht knew that this could only be the beginning of his theatre, the aim of which is not the withdrawal but the blossoming forth of human beings. Once these social necessities had for the most part been learned in the theatre (and learned with pleasure too), the sphere of social possibilities also revealed itself. If we say that in socialism the overhaul of the means and conditions of production always simultaneously enlarges the sphere of human possibilities as it relates to 'the universality of needs, abilities, pleasures, productive strengths' for individuals, then 'changing the world' must now also include – after the biggest imaginable change in society and the achievement of equal social opportunity – the working out of individual differences in terms of needs, abilities, and pleasures. Since the recognition and accommodation of people's differences not only lift the individual to universal status but also stabilize the collective, it can be said that 'necessity' grows into 'exchange':

> If individual A has the same needs as individual B and gets a return on [*realisiert*] his work under the same circumstances as individual B then no relationship exists between them . . . Both need to breathe; air exists as their element for both; [but] this doesn't bring them into any social contact . . . Only the distinctness of what they need and what they produce makes possible an exchange and their social equality within it; this genuine diversity is therefore the prerequisite for their social equality within the act of exchange.[3]

Now, isn't it the wide-reaching idea of the collective, with its much greater 'mass power' (which we are supposed to develop in the theatre), to 'further intensively the reproduction' of the world – that is, to change it? And shouldn't we also, in the theatre, follow Stephan Hermlin's suggestion that we read this passage from the Communist manifesto forward and not backward? 'The old bourgeois society, with its classes and class conflicts,' it reads, 'will be replaced by an association in which the free development of each will lead to the free development of all.'[4]

Couldn't this widening of the sphere of human possibilities, this open-endedness, make it possible for a theatre concerned with changing the world to take on a changed function: that of performing those possibilities? Could it not demonstrate not only human conduct as the ensemble of social relations but also social relations as an ensemble of concretely individual people? It could describe the future not by fleshing out established historical concepts but by interpreting history as what it really is: 'nothing other than the process of people pursuing their objectives'.[5]

Once we have enriched society through acting out and making known individual needs, and enriched the individual by making known new needs, we find that in fact the rich man is a needy man too: 'The rich person and the needy person are equally the living expression of a single totality.'[6]

Increasing and organizing differentiation in the presentation of people and their relationships with each other subtly develops in the community the strength which it needs for larger change. This is theatre as a consciousness which does not merely picture the world but produces it: as Lenin remarked, 'Human consciousness not only reflects the objective world but also creates it.'[7]

What we are talking about here is performance that uses reality not merely as the external performing style, 'realism', but rather as its real content; 'trial-and-error' as play in search of the new where one least suspects it; and individual self-discovery as a community project which starts with the assumption that individuality exists because other individuals exist. 'One equals no one,' writes Brecht in *Man Equals Man* (1926). 'Anything less than two hundred at a time is not worth mentioning.'[8] And in 'Me-ti': 'Only when everyone stands on the same step can you tell how different they are.'[9]

Hasn't a 'theatre overhaul' taken place? Could this overhaul be a key for a theatre in which free change for one individual is the condition for free change for all?

2. GESTUS

In his discussions with Hans Bunge, published as *Ask More about Brecht*, Eisler said: ‘Yes, the *Gestus* is one of Brecht’s brilliant discoveries. He discovered it, just as Einstein discovered his famous equation.’[10] If what Eisler maintains is true, why hasn’t it ever been investigated? Do scholars and theatre people make a detour around Eisler’s formulation because they consider it one of his typical exaggerations? A biographical note: Brecht always talked while writing; he couldn’t help but think that thinking was simply a way of behaving. When he wrote something – whether lyrical, dramatic, or scholarly – he performed it aloud for himself, as if he were saying it to someone else in order to bring that person into a concrete situation: to teach him, encourage him, make him curious, abuse, question, distract him, shut him up, surprise or insult him. Is this just Brecht being odd or ill-bred, or could it be an occasion for far-reaching suppositions concerning interventive thinking? Or we might ask ourselves: just how does theatre work? In ill-informed theatre circles they are talking again about ‘verbal’ effect as distinguished from ‘visual’ effect, or of ‘literary language’ that is ‘relieved from its traditional central function’ to make room for ‘visionary experiences, disturbances, necessities’.

It seems time then to speak of the *Gestus*, upon which indeed language, movement, gesture, silence, objectivity, and the visionary too, are based, in that it places all of these in a concrete situation between persons. There is here an encompassing, genuine materialism of the theatre, if one takes it as a premise that in society human relationships *are* materialism. By means of a ‘gestic acting style’ everything done in the theatre would reveal human activity, since that style always demonstrates a relationship. And isn’t the gestic style of performance *itself* this human activity, in that it shows everything in a definite relationship to the audience, setting out to astonish them, make them angry, plead with them, sharpen their hearing, invite sympathy, and bring out their protest?

Isn’t *Gestus* above all the ‘language’ of the theatre? We all know that when an actor gets his line wrong it often goes unnoticed by the audience if he follows through with the right *Gestus*. We all know that the word ‘fine’ (*schön*) can take on different meanings: for example, when someone is approached about whether he is willing to lend some money and answers 'fine' this differs from when a father whose child has broken a window says, 'Fine – just fine.'

Whole plays change their meaning when shown in another *Gestus*. We think of Brecht's suggestion that we ask of *Faust*: 'Why doesn't Faust marry Gretchen?' The *Gestus* thus presented to the audience avoids the prop of unavoidability or excusableness, and puts questions concerning a great injustice, setting criticism of Faust the person within circumstances which let him be seen not only as a truth-seeker but also as a criminal. The 'critical posture' towards what is shown, which Brecht wanted from his audience, is impossible without the powerful, basic *Gestus* of wonder. What actually happens on the stage is not our only standard of evaluation. Faust doesn't marry Gretchen, Othello strangles Desdemona, Courage loses her children; but in tandem with these events we consider how things could have happened differently: Faust marries Gretchen, Othello lets Desdemona live, Courage holds on to her children. The *Gestus* 'why must it happen that way and not another?' mobilizes not only insight but also the pleasure of self-discovery, of continuing the story – the self-confirmation of an active person, of the way he consciously lives, which is also what constitutes a human being in the theatre. Eisler transcribed the gestic to music. Gestic music, gestic speaking, gestic silence, gestic movement, gestic gesture, gestic writing, gestic metaphor – these are the elementary founding principles of theatre (and not only theatre) which create a relationship between people and their objective, be it discovery or pleasure, thought or play. What consequences, one wonders, does this hold for an aesthetic, and for the theatre itself, which till now has been misunderstood as 'language art' or 'scenic art'? What consequences does it hold for theatre schools, where one still always speaks the word 'fine' finely?

3. PLEASURE

Let us therefore cause general dismay by revoking our decision to emigrate from the realm of the merely enjoyable, and even more general dismay by announcing our decision to take up lodging there. Let us treat the theatre as a place of entertainment, as is proper in an aesthetic discussion, and try to discover which type of entertainment suits us best.[11]

These statements, from the beginning of *A Short Organum*, were hardly noticed, certainly much less than others, yet here is probably the deepest and most fruitful insight formulated in Brecht's work: the fundamental role in art of human enjoyment. Here Brecht lifts theatre to the level of Marx's formulation regarding enjoyment in *Grundrisse*.[12] There has nevertheless been scarcely any investigation of the function of pleasure in Brecht's work. People prefer to cling to old formulations, in which Brecht banned the 'culinary' from the theatre; or the 'teaching-play' theory, in which aesthetic matters are minimized for the requirements of teaching, at least for the actor. To this day scholars and theatre people, when they speak of Brecht and his theatre, assume the primacy of edification over amusement, clarity over emotion. To this day, an 'aesthetic' chases breathlessly and vainly after 'fine art' as though it were a peculiarity of sugar to be sweet, while we overlook the fact that in enjoyment, as one of the highest human activities, the beauty and richness of art find their explanation: the self-affirmation of the human being, independently and inquisitively becoming acquainted with his own vitality and so making himself more productive as a person. Couldn't the role of pleasure make the function of Brecht's theatre and indeed all contemporary theatre – whether its subject be serious or amusing, instructive or playful – more complex and at the same time more concrete, in that the effect of this theatre is measured not only by the communicated content and form but also by the increase in humanity's capacity for enjoyment? Indeed, one would think that that is where its main business lies – which means nothing but that needs are most often satisfied through art when new ones are awakened. The awakening of curiosity, thirst for knowledge, capriciousness, anger, happiness, sadness, courage and exuberance is at the same time an extension of people's capacity to enjoy, and their capacity to change, which increases, or at least can increase, delightfully. But in the new society, man, through his individual goals and their extension, is at once creator of historical possibilities and progenitor of social tendencies.

Moreover, this development of possibilities is not a matter of achieving some goal of an 'ideal' human being, but of enabling concrete individuals to gain self-realization. Nor should extending the sphere of possibilities be limited to a concept of 'humanizing' in which one seeks to approach an established human nature that is taken for granted. The possibilities of a society that rests upon scientific analysis also present the unforeseen, that is, the production of newness.

This applies to the development of society as much as it does to the individual, to the writing of texts as well as to the investigation of micro-electronics. Truly 'human' results always surpass predictions as a result of innovation. The capacity to enjoy, that is, the consciousness of personal development, probably is or can become one of the most effective impetuses of socialist society. Could Marx's *Grundrisse* not provide a new beginning for our preoccupation with Brecht and his theatre, or the theatre in general?

4. REASON

It has been asked whether, in the light of our growing knowledge of history, Brecht's plays have been superseded as a response to the events of his era, and must therefore be improved with the help of our present-day perception.

Apart from the fact that it is nonsensical to adapt plays to the most current stage of historical understanding, the basic assumption here is diametrically opposed to Brecht's concept of reason. Brecht understood and practised the basic dialectic within which increasing knowledge takes the unknown into account as well – a concept most recently formulated by the GDR physicist Hans Jürgen Treder[13] and also contained in Lenin's assertion of the inexhaustibility of matter.

To trivialize Brecht's concept of reason by attributing to it the primitive duality 'knowledge/ignorance' is itself a demonstration of unreasonableness: that is, ignorance. Brecht's concept of reason, granting of course the need to know things, is above all a question of attitude – the attitude towards history, towards the passing of history, towards events, towards people and their actions: because the point of departure is their recognition of being active, with the origin of their activity a contradiction within themselves. Brecht's stories, which embody his reason, are model cases that do not have to be constantly supplemented by 'correct knowledge'; but rather in their historical and poetical concreteness they can be transferred by the audience to other times and situations. And here a tenet of elementary dialectics fits neatly: the more concrete they are, the more they can be universalized. Brecht called this process 'historicizing'.[14]

The concrete process of differentiation, an expression of dialectical reason, draws a discriminating treatment from the viewer too: Is that really so? Isn't that unlikely? Is that conceivable? That's friendly! That's absurd! Why so and not otherwise? That's nice! That's good! Nice and good, but – and so on.

Reducing Brecht's reason to 'knowledge and ignorance' is like reducing Eugen Dühring's lean rationalism to the formulation 'yes, yes – no, no', which Engels already ridiculed in *Anti-Dühring*. Differentiating people's activities and attitudes is not only the philosophical starting point of Brecht's theatre, it is at the same time the source of its pleasure.

But, even where knowledge is conveyed, it is a matter of conveying not only information but also an attitude – what Brecht himself called the 'critical attitude':

> As we cannot invite the audience to fling itself into the story as if it were a river and let itself be carried vaguely hither and thither, the individual episodes have to be knotted together in such a way that the knots are easily noticed. The episodes must not succeed one another indistinguishably but must give us a chance to interpose our judgement.[15]

To that end, Brecht made suggestions which he gathered under the term 'alienation' (*Verfremdung*). But here the discussion should deal with one basic attitude which both is called for and best presents itself in terms of the subject 'reason': the view that it is within the ability of people to defend their interests. Knowledge of social and natural (and theatrical) laws is pertinent here; but just as pertinent is the strong feeling of wanting to realize one's own wishes and hopes. So this reason carries within itself as well an 'unreason', in which the future proclaims itself without already having become knowledge. When Galileo was conducting his experiments at the leaning tower of Pisa he was actually working with gravity, though the term 'gravity' would be 'unreasonable' to him since, according to the knowledge of the time, bodies were not given weight by the earth's pull but were drawn by an inner power at the centre of the earth. Again, Kafka never knew the Fascist death camps, and his surrealistic presentation of the horror of the death-machine in 'The Penal Colony' was viewed in his time as an outsider's nightmare, not as an expression of reason. History made it, through hindsight, an understandable warning. Of course, mythology is the utmost alienation or irrationality. Yet in Greek mythology Marx saw not only mistaken apperception but also anticipation of reason: 'Greek art assumes Greek mythology', he wrote. 'In other words, nature and social forms [which are the subjects of art] are themselves already worked out in an unconsciously artistic manner through the folk imagination.'[16] And so we have the safeguarding of historical man's interests through the creation of gods who, in a 'real' sense, don't exist.

Nicolai Hartmann speaks of an 'irrational remainder' that is contained in all knowledge, and which in many cases, although not all, anticipates the development of reason.[17] Similarly, Brecht's concept of reason is in total opposition to a rationalism that seeks the completion of formulae, that is, of inflexible categories and solutions, which are precisely what is so often attributed to Brecht. Nor is this reason a denial of human feelings or passions in favour of rational perception: a concept also attributed to Brecht. People's capacity to pursue their interests, that is, to go about their dealings with reason, makes a priority out of the will to achieve reason – in other words, passion. The existence of reason is the struggle against ignorance. In the search for truth, as Marx says, 90 per cent of it is the struggle against prejudice. Galileo's line, 'Yes, I believe in the gentle power of reason over people', which appears so readily as a precept in school-books, is a false statement. In terms of its *Gestus*, rather than its 'verbal' content, Galileo's situation defines his words as re-assurances against the ignorance he fears. Already in the next scene, at the court of Florence, what he anticipates has materialized: the court scholars decline to be seduced in any way by proof of the moons of Jupiter; they simply refuse to look through the telescope.

Nor does Brecht's concept of reason contain any irreconcilable contradiction between consciousness and spontaneity, for the true opposite of spontaneity is not consciousness but regularization. I can consciously make myself completely spontaneous, for instance in rehearsal, as I search for solutions. At the same time, it is necessary to dismantle a prejudice against the subconscious, which was probably stirred up by prejudices against (and judgements upon) Sigmund Freud's couch, whence the unconscious id, ego, and super-ego were supposed to be called forth from the depths of repression. But the subconscious – or habits that are no longer reflected upon – steers the largest portion of human perception.

Brecht's 'alienation' is still regarded as a destruction of habits, and related to Lenin's observation that habit can be a terrifying power. This is only half the truth, since Lenin also says that in culture only what has been integrated into the habits of daily life can be regarded as achieved. Precisely in its practical, intellectual and artistic assimilation of the world, mankind maintains its sensible impulses and patterns (concerning value judgements, aesthetics, norms, duties, and preferences) from ruling habits – not from moment-to-moment, conscious procedures of activity. And so Brecht's concept of reason contains the demand not only that habits be destroyed by alienation, but also that new habits be created through alienation. Also related to this concept is the connection with Utopia – of course only so long as this is understood as projecting the present into the future and not as a substitute for science. Utopia *presupposes* the existence of science, yet it also sets science in motion. Utopia, in the sense of realizable hopes and suspected possibilities, can be an extraordinary driving force, even when erroneous or inadequate. Can there be reason without it?

> Certain experiences could have brought you to a totally false view about what we always called the future of reason. But one man cannot alone corroborate them nor condemn them; it's too large an issue. Reason is something in which people share a stake. It is, that is to say, the egoism of humanity as a whole. This egoism is too weak, but even someone like me can tell that reason is not at an end but at the beginning.[18]

This passage, from the 1938 version of *The Life of Galileo*, may indeed help Brecht's theatre, and that of others, towards a cheerful reason which, even in the most difficult of times (and precisely then), keeps awake the human will to live. May the very generality of this concept of reason not be exactly suitable for discovering its universal concreteness – as the fundamental wish of a great many people to choose to keep on living? Isn't the dialectical breadth of this reason a useful opportunity for the theatre to counter the menacing devastation of Positivism ('what is, is'), and the no less successful menace in the barrenness of Post-Structuralism ('what's not said is the statement')? It may also counter the all-embracing 'Modern' with the true modernity of realism. Above all, this concept of reason would not merely have a part in 'the search of the entire human race for egoism' but would boldly and playfully awaken it.

5. *NAÏVETÉ*

In the last years of his life, Brecht demanded that his plays and poems be looked at naïvely – that we not, that is, stop at analysis and discovery of the societal relationships among people (the causal nexus), but instead turn these discoveries and recognitions into impulses relevant to mankind as a whole. The audience must learn not only how the bound Prometheus gets freed; they must also school themselves in the desire to free him. He called this the new *naïveté*.

Many have used *naïveté* as an insult. 'Naïve' was applied to someone who knew nothing and reacted without thinking. No distinction was made between simple-minded and näive. *Naïveté* was disconnected from knowledge; it even hindered it.

As Brecht developed the 'theatre of the scientific age', many presumed that he wanted to replace art with science. In truth, Brecht developed a theatre *for* the scientific age. Since in this age knowledge and science have become direct productive forces, it was necessary – for a theatre that wanted to present and alter this reality – to make them a subject for performance. Moreover, Brecht wished to make use of the science and knowledge of his time not to diminish art in favour of knowledge but rather, by *means* of science and knowledge, to produce once more the great, profound, and enjoyable art that the middle classes, who live on substitutes, have lost. Shortly before his death, Brecht began to be fearful, as he came closer to the conclusion that his theatre was not being viewed naïvely – as a trigger of desire, curiosity, astonishment, pleasure, anger, and so on – but as a knowledge brokerage, since knowledge and *naïveté* were deemed irreconcilable opposites. And so he came to this new concept of a *naïveté* that does not take precedence over recognizing and knowing but follows from them – something that absorbs knowledge and becomes a strengthened *naïveté*. Of course, in times of increasing complexity in human interactivity, increased knowledge and recognition of connections are needed in order to portray such activity on the stage. Though this step is still only a preparation for art, not the art itself, it is through it that theatre becomes able to work increasing knowledge into ever stronger impulses, making it possible for complexity to be experienced naïvely. Just how this occurs in individual cases is as rarely investigated scientifically as how, in science itself, new theories come into being through human creativity – in other words, after the amassing of the known, the leap into the unknown. Certainly the audience, as far as its social experience and responsibility are concerned, should be wiser after seeing *The Life of Galileo*. But this wisdom would be feeble if it were not joined with a more naïve impulse – being frightened. Why have the theatre and theatre scholars made a detour around the discovery of the new *naïveté*? Did it seem to those that are busy composing and interpreting to be too naïve? Or does it seem too complicated to want *naïveté* for complex times when one hardly understands them oneself? And so the non-understandableness of the non-understood is the easier way on the stage, and, leaving your audience perplexed, you raise perplexity to an aesthetic category.

Success, failure; desire; curiosity; delight, fear; becoming keen of hearing; being astonished; protesting, agreeing; anger; happiness, sadness; reflection; aversion; bad temper; despair; doubt; love, distrust; and so on: to release these remains the noblest function of art, and above all of the theatre, so that these naïve impulses strive to become the entertainment and delight of its audience. In 'simpler' times, in more 'naïvely' surveyable times, these impulses would be easier to attain, but by no means more necessary than in a time like ours, when it is much harder for the individual to comprehend concretely the processes of production, and of life itself, which have come about through the division of labour and sophistication. For the individual today, 'life is more difficult to get through'. But unless the individual lives his *own* life, there is no human life as a whole – nor any life for society, for 'the free development of each [is the condition for] the free development of all'. It would nevertheless be deadly nonsense to put a brake on economic and scientific development with a call of 'back to nature'. The nature called for doesn't exist, for human nature is very much part of it, and that part has changed itself enormously. And it is only through this enormous development of the economy that it can get the chance to free itself from coercive economic pressures in order to be able to motivate itself.

But isn't it precisely the huge reification of technology and science which asks that a person contemplate and savour them naïvely – as his own doing? Aren't the feeling of desire, the raising of curiosity, the awakening of passion, of anger, of protest, of agreement – in short, all subjective emotions, all individual feelings today – *a particularly urgent form of alienation*, a reworking of what Brecht calls the 'social causal nexus' into an individual driving force? Isn't that driving force today decidedly the causal nexus? Isn't the new *naïveté* that Brecht demands of the theatre a concrete demand for that 'philosophical folk-theatre' which draws its life from philosophy *and* entertainment – that is, from pleasure as the beginning and end of all knowledge? Surely here that 'end-in-itself' is realized which Marx sees as the most important reason for human existence, and which is fulfilled only through an enormous effort of society?

6. DISTANCING/IDENTIFYING

While directing the Hauptmann plays *Biberpelz und Roter Hahn* (*The Beaver Coat* and *The Red Cock* to be performed together in one evening), Brecht tried out a method which – without describing it more closely – he called 'letting the audience fall for it'. This experiment has barely been noticed, although in my opinion it was at that point that the practice of theatre changed from the theatre of social opposition to the capitalist system and its consequences, and was ushered into that phase which Lenin calls the 'positive-creative'. The term 'positive-creative' should not distract us from the fact that this is the much more difficult and extended phase: it is the transition from the 'difficulties in the mountains' to the 'difficulties on the plains'. Brecht himself hoped for the full effectiveness of his theatre only with the advent of the new society. The availability of those people who make new relations possible also makes more flexible means possible. A theatre that shows the world as changeable must commit itself to changeableness.

At the time of the first *Courage* production, the conflicts still lay, so to speak, in the streets, and were carried, still alive, into the theatre by the audience. Brecht's assertion, 'War is nothing but business, and instead of with cheese it's with lead', must have astonished even those Germans who saw Hitler as a criminal: an assertion even calling for protest, for they wanted at least to have followed a 'great criminal' and not merely the 'perpetrator of great crimes'. Even an empty stage would have been crowded with the experience of the ruins outside, which were present within the spectators.

In the *Courage* production of 1948–9, critical distance towards what was being shown was provided from the very first scene. And this clashed passionately with the audience's false emotions: even with the collapse of German imperialism in the Second World War, they were still searching for something honourable, even if it were the subjectively justified pain over a fallen relative. The soberness of the stage and of the story mobilized passions in the true sense: suffering ought to turn into learning. Such a procedure of distancing from the outset (which requires unusual acting skill) assumed that a large portion of the audience had brought a broadly similar (or similarly false) attitude with them into the theatre. The theatre began, so to speak, in front of the entrance door, with opinions, ruins, and empty stomachs. Conflict accompanied the audience into the theatre. Reality had set them up for tragedy. It was an exceptional situation which the theatre could use, in that the theatre made itself of use to overcome it.

In 'normal' times the establishing of conflict is the task of the theatre itself. In the first part of *Biberpelz und Roter Hahn*, Brecht tried to have the audience so taken in by the main character and her social battle that they would be in full solidarity with her. They identified with her, at least to the extent that they were convinced of the irresistible success of Mother Wolfen in her fight against the Kaiser and his Prussia, represented by Wehrhahn the bureaucrat. In the second part, when the celebrated heroine, now turned insurance speculator, becomes part of the corruption herself, the disillusionment is all the greater since the previous expectations for the 'self-helper' were so high. The audience should fall for it not just in their heads, but with their heart and soul. They must feel for themselves how the self-help ethic turns so easily into class betrayal that the person involved usually does not notice until it is too late.

Of course, on close examination this conflict was already established in the first part, but was hidden by the audience's enthusiasm at Mother Wolfen's victory (albeit by thievery) over the Prussians.

The audience had to see Mother Wolfen and her ways anew, once they had lived through the corresponding ups and downs with her. Therese Giehse accomplished this as Wolfen.

While directing *Richard III* in 1973, I tried to make use of the method of 'letting them fall for it' by eschewing the usual repulsion for a disfigured creature who revenges himself upon mankind, and going back to Shakespeare's original. There the hunched back and club foot are not symbols of disadvantaged impotence but provocative signs of the Iniquity or Vice. And so this figure fills the role of the Harlequin, Sganarelle, or Hanswurst, who sets the play on course, commenting upon and criticizing the action. The figure of Richard is really made up of two figures – the murderous king and his opponent, the Vice. And, as Vice, Richard mobilizes all his charm and humour against a society for which murder is a way of life: he does only what everyone else is doing. But he does it with unusual flair, using a human grasp to change the divinely ordained line of succession based on divine right – a grasp for the throat and a grasp for the crown. Up to this point the audience should go along with him, for Richard sustains his superiority over his surroundings not only through charm, jocularity, and shrewdness, but also through this 'materialism'. In the fourth act, however, Shakespeare ends this dialogue with his audience. Richard abandons the role of Vice and withdraws himself from everything that helped him achieve the crown. He destroys his surroundings; he ignores the audience. A brilliant message from Shakespeare: having achieved the crown with a human hand, he now insists on what he had himself destroyed – the divine right of kings. The awakening of the audience that feels itself ignored by Richard will be the greater the more committed it was to the Vice of the first part.

Can this method of 'letting the audience fall for it' be aesthetically extended? Can it be achieved, for instance, in times in which social achievements, processes and contradictions withdraw from daily consciousness because they are a part of daily life? The audience would then first discover and live through the conflict before it gets to the solution.

Is Brecht's statement that a monument first has to be erected before it can be up-ended relevant to this method? 'The contradiction between empathy and detachment is made stronger and becomes an element of the performance.'[19]

Do we not have here a development of a way of performing that works with alienation, artistically incorporating the alteration between distancing and identifying within a dialectic? And does this not mark the entrance of a new 'split' in the audience, one that occurs within every individual?

7. BREADTH AND DIVERSITY OF REALISM

Brecht spoke of the 'breadth and diversity of realism'. Perhaps it was not simply a poetical metaphor, as so many regard it today, but a working proposal? For the theatre in the German Democratic Republic too?

Translated by David Blostein

3

The origins, aims, and objectives of the Berliner Ensemble

JOACHIM TENSCHERT

In a public address in 1955 the eminent Swiss dramatist, Friedrich Dürrenmatt, first formulated the crucial question concerning the function and potential of contemporary theatre. That question has been at the centre of national and international theatre debate ever since. Equally popular, widely quoted and discussed, and of patently undiminished relevance was Brecht's reply. To Dürrenmatt's question whether the present-day world could be reproduced by means of the theatre, Brecht responded,

> . . . the present-day world can only be described to present-day people if it is described as capable of transformation.
>
> People of the present-day value questions on account of their answers. They are interested in events and situations in face of which they can do something.[1]

With the clarity and bluntness appropriate to this crucial question, Brecht moved his answer beyond what might possibly be interpreted as the sphere of 'purely artistic concern', placing it firmly in a social context. 'It will hardly surprise you', he continued, 'to hear me say that the question of describing the world is a social one . . . And you may perhaps agree with me that the present-day world can do with transforming.'[2]

Here Brecht's artistic and political endeavours find common ground. His artistic programme and political point of view are those of a realist and a dialectician. His answer to Dürrenmatt's question, given just one year before his death, sums up his whole theatrical activity up to that point, and at the same time constitutes a programme for future development. Taking as his point of view the thesis that it is not a matter of merely interpreting the world but of changing it, Brecht, in his declaration of 1955, refers to the chain of literary and theatrical 'experiments' (as he always called them) as attempts to bring 'the present-day world, present-day men's life together, within the theatre's range of vision'.[3] It was Brecht more than any other who, from the early twenties on, gave aim and direction to these experiments in creating a theatre of a new type with a new basic standpoint and new effectiveness.

Brecht's theatre began to take shape in the early twenties in the context of the polemic against the theatrical theory and practice of the late bourgeoisie, as embodied in its most characteristic forms of expression – the theatres of Naturalism and Expressionism. Brecht's main objection to Naturalism was that it regarded society simply as a natural phenomenon and attempted to do no more than merely copy nature. Above all, it showed human beings as totally determined by their environment, a fate from which there seemed to be no escape.

Brecht was equally critical of Expressionism, which he saw as a response to the social crisis of the years following the First World War. His objection to Expressionism was that it depicted the world from a subjective position, as 'Will and Idea', and as a vision was strangely disjointed. Expressionistic theatre was, he argued, 'quite incapable of shedding light on the world as an object of human activity'.[4]

As opposed to these forms of late bourgeois theatre, Brecht advanced a theatre that showed human beings organizing the processes to which they were subjected. His theatre sought to approach society historically, to explain things, situations, and individuals in the process of becoming, and to depict a type of human being who has recognized that the fate of man is man.

Through the class struggles of the twenties, thirties, forties, through the critique of capitalism and the struggle against the rise of Fascism, Brecht's theatre took artistic and political form. Brecht's theory and practice are the outcome of his active and committed participation in these struggles. In the end it was Fascism that called an abrupt end to the development of a Brechtian theatre in Germany. In choking the life out of the first German Republic, Fascism destroyed the political, intellectual, and social conditions necessary for the existence and effectiveness of Brechtian theatre. For this epic theatre, as Brecht called it, this story-telling theatre, telling stories, as it does, about social processes,

> demands not only a certain technological level but a powerful movement in society which is interested to see vital questions freely aired with a view to their solution, and can defend this interest against every contrary trend.[5]

When efforts were set in motion after the collapse of Fascism to reconstruct the German theatre, ruined as it was both materially and intellectually, Brecht had his plans ready. After his return from exile in 1948, he was at last in a position to put into practice his suggestions for the theatre: for new ways of thinking, of looking at things, and of playing. He could at last try out the whole amassed arsenal of experience, insights, plans, and, above all, his great plays written in exile and for the most part never as yet staged. Now all this could be systematically tested out under new social conditions. Brecht's 'experiments', those great drafts for a new theatre in the form of plays and theories, could prove their effectiveness only in a theatre established according to his plans. They had to be tested anew, confirmed and enriched through the most important of all criteria – artistic and social practice. With the Berliner Ensemble, founded in 1949, Brecht created a model for his kind of theatre. Here he could test his plays, his theories, and the fund of experience gained as a result of his experiments, under social conditions for which he had fought in all his works. In a society dedicated to constantly transforming reality, a theatre that proclaimed such efforts to be the fountainhead of all that is productive and thus a source of pleasure must of necessity find wide scope for its activities.

At the end of a talk given in exile in Sweden in that fateful year of 1939, which saw the outbreak of the Second World War, Brecht posed the programmatic question: 'How can the unfree, ignorant man of our century, with his thirst for freedom and his hunger for knowledge; how can the tortured and heroic, abused and ingenious, changeable and world-changing man of this great and ghastly century obtain his own theatre which will help him to master the world and himself?'[6]

The programme that Brecht was to draft ten years later provides the answer. It is an answer produced by a specific analysis of a specific situation. 'When Hitler's war was over', he wrote, and we once more started in to make theatre – theatre in a spirit of progress and experiment, directed towards that transformation of society which had become so urgent – those artistic methods which take the theatre so long to develop had been virtually destroyed by the spirit of reaction and shady adventure . . . How were we to organize new productions for a new audience in a theatre that had been debauched in this way – spiritually and technically ruined? . . . The question implies its own answer. Our tottering theatre could be helped to its feet not by setting it specially easy tasks, but by giving it the toughest jobs possible. Though practically incapable of even the most trivial entertainment it still stood a chance if it tackled problems it had never been set before; inadequate in itself, *qua* theatre, it must strive to alter its surroundings. From now on it could only hope to form its images of the world if it lent a hand in forming the world itself . . . [7]

At the end of October 1948, immediately after his return from exile, Brecht took part in a major peace conference in Berlin. He wrote about it in a letter:

Just one day after my return to Berlin, the city from which one of the most terrible of wars had started, I had the pleasure of being able to take part in a meeting of intellectuals for peace. The sight of that appalling devastation filled me with one wish – to contribute in my particular way to making certain the world gets peace at long last. Without peace it will be uninhabitable.[8]

The legendary production of Brecht's *Mother Courage and her Children* premièred in the midst of Berlin's ruins in January 1949, and achieved its truly epoch-making impact very much in this spirit; wherever it played, in Berlin and a host of other European cities besides, it was well received and understood as Brecht's contribution to the great task facing humanity in the second half of our century; everywhere it went people showed their solidarity with Brecht's message. Helene Weigel's creation of the title role became one of the great paradigms of the actor's art of our time.

In the wake of the production, Helene Weigel was commissioned to set up an ensemble by the then German Education Authority on the basis of a decision taken by the Socialist Unity Party. Brecht and Weigel named this company the Berliner Ensemble at the beginning of the 1949 season, that is, in the year in which the German Democratic Republic was founded. Fascism had left the German theatre in ruins. Now Brecht and Weigel set about creating a theatre that would foster a spirit of progress and an ever more daring humanity. With this in mind, the Berliner Ensemble chose as its emblem Pablo Picasso's combative peace dove. Speaking of his theatre, Brecht himself said 'knowledge of human nature, stimulus to social action, and entertainment are at home in it'.[9]

Brecht's plan was to bring together young theatre workers, who were inexperienced or had been trained along the wrong lines, and the great theatrical figures from among the German anti-Fascists who had recently returned from exile, with the aim of moulding them, through a process of collective learning, into a well-knit ensemble. It was a theatre with a frankly Brechtian standpoint on society, one guided in its theatrical work by binding aesthetic and methodological premises. As writer and chief director, Brecht supervised the work of the actors, directors, dramaturges, stage designers, and technicians in the ensemble. Above all, he instructed them in what, since the twenties, he had, with his collaborators, so successfully practised himself: the collective method of work. It was not a matter of merely proclaiming the principle; he lived it for all to see in the way he encouraged others to work with him. Two heads are better than one became an established maxim in Brecht's theatre. In the collective process was born a productive conflict of opinions; challenging, critical standpoints evolved which tested and complemented each other. The younger members learned from those with more experience, the pupils from the masters. The collective approach in the practical day-to-day work of the theatre provided opportunities for getting acquainted with the methods of Brechtian theatre, studying them, trying them out, and finally adopting them as one's own. It will be clear that this approach also fostered new artists: budding young directors, dramaturges, playwrights and stage designers, in a word, a new generation of artists. From the start it was in the collective, in working as an ensemble, that the productivity vital to Brecht's creative method was achieved.

It was characteristic of the Berliner Ensemble that its policies were put into practice as quickly as possible. Its objectives were to develop a repertoire which in its basic principles would reveal the dialectics of historical themes and their topical relevance. It aimed to develop a new art of acting that would convey to the audience insights into human and social processes in an enjoyable way, and to develop a new art of audience response which would derive pleasure from taking up a critical attitude towards the stories being enacted.

Three main emphases became apparent in the repertoire: the presentation of Brecht's own plays, mostly written in exile; works depicting revolutions and moments of social upheaval, set both in the past and in the immediate present; and finally plays from world literature which reveal social contradictions: contradictions that had been either covered up or trivialized in bourgeois productions. The main interest here was focussed on the great realist comedies.

Three emphases, too, can be detected in productions of these plays which were designed to serve as models. The productions were to demonstrate how the theatre must help to cultivate a new consciousness in the population in an entertaining and enjoyable way. Moreover, by pressing into service all the means of the theatre – dramaturgy, the actor's art, stage design, music, etc. – the productions could develop a mode of presentation which deprives the presented actions and persons of their self-evident, 'natural' familiar character, endowing them instead with features which are remarkable, not self-evident, demanding explanation, so that curiosity, wonderment, questions, insights, and understanding are provoked in the audience. Only through this 'alienated' mode of presentation, accounting for things in specific historical and social terms rather than in general human terms, could a critical approach to the things presented be cultivated in the audience. Working in this manner to create a theatre that would appeal to human rationality was Brecht's way of contributing towards a renewal of a national art of theatre.

Finally, an important aim pursued in the productions was to spread Brecht's working methods to other theatres. The progress and results of every production were fixed in the form of notations (descriptions) and photographs (modelbooks). These were made available to other theatres so that they could draw lessons from them, but also so that they could modify, enrich, and further develop the proposals. The modelbooks of the Berliner Ensemble were meant as proposals, not as directives. A partnership between theatres was what was aimed at. The principle was to be that one theatre should take up work on a play at the point at which another theatre had left off. In this way a consistent, methodical mode of production would replace an arbitrary, quasi-original approach. Essentially, this was what Brecht meant by a 'theatre of the scientific age'.

It would be a mistake to think that Brecht's theatre, as embodied in the Berliner Ensemble, established itself without opposition, that it was a kind of triumphal progress to the accompaniment of thunderous applause. Ingrained ways of thought in the field of the arts do not disappear from one day to the next, even under new and favourable conditions. And, as with everything that is new, unfamiliar, and forward looking, the Berliner Ensemble too had to force a passage with every new production. For, as Brecht says, 'Nothing is more difficult than the advance back to reason.' It was the stature of the artistic achievement, the impact of the epic theatre as living theatre, that proved irresistible in the long run. Significantly, it was in comparison with leading theatre companies from other countries at the Paris Théâtre des Nations in the fifties and sixties that the artistic impact of the Berliner Ensemble was recognized and the company was seen to possess new and special qualities.

On the occasion of the guest performance in Paris in 1955, *Les Lettres françaises* wrote,

> Living and working in Berlin is one of the most powerful personalities in the contemporary theatre: Bertolt Brecht. Like Shakespeare and Molière he has his own company, a man who does his playwriting in the midst of the players and the gales of laughter of the audience. This is theatre as theatre should be, where the smallest word, the slightest gesture is in tune with the essence of theatre, where complete command of technique allows a freedom and daring that no dramatist writing in the study could ever permit himself. The illuminated ring twinkling over the Berliner Ensemble in East Berlin is very possibly the answer, sent across the intervening three and a half centuries, to the globe of the world at Shakespeare's Globe Theatre.[10]

Brecht was to die in the summer of 1956, snatched away far too soon from his work and from the rehearsals for his *Life of Galileo*. He had scarcely seven years to test and develop his theatre for the new scientific age. Beginnings were made and foundations laid. There were some interim results, and here and there even a solution found; but, basically, in those few years full of urgent jobs to be done in the midst of pressing social developments, it was not possible to do more than demonstrate tendencies, indicate lines of advance, peg out the vast terrain awaiting artistic cultivation. The breadth and complexity of the Brechtian programme, of his plans, suggestions, and expectations, were a long way from being fully mapped.

By the year 1956 the situation in Germany had changed. Two states had emerged with two different social systems. A theatre committed to reality could hardly hold aloof from the intellectual and ideological conflicts arising from this. The theatre had to make use of its particular resources to make clear to its audience the compelling historical logic of progressive social development and the prospects this opened up.

The Berliner Ensemble retained the basic lines of its programme policy, but, taking account of the specific social situation, systematically sought out plays or possible interpretations of plays ('ways of reading') which highlighted the relationship between the individual and society. This was done with the aim of sharpening the historical sense of the audience and encouraging them to take a stand for historical progress.

The guidelines for a theatre intended to function as a model for others were also retained. Unaided, these would not have sufficed, however, to cope with the needs of the new situation or with the task of guaranteeing the continued development and creativity of the Berliner Ensemble. And so a new and decisive point was added to the programme laid down in Brecht's day: Brecht's method of working had to be shown to be scientific and dialectical, in other words it had to be shown to be applicable independently of Brecht's personality, and to be appropriate and amenable to further development by others. After Brecht's death, what the theatre had to do in the process of mounting productions was to develop new personnel: new directors, dramaturges, actors, stage designers, who, in the course of time, would themselves be capable of working according to Brecht's method. At the same time attention had to be devoted to applying these methods when working on and producing plays by other authors.

Brecht died in the middle of rehearsing his *Life of Galileo* with Ernst Busch in the title role. His friend and collaborator Erich Engel took over the direction of the piece. Engel was the man who had staged the world première of *The Threepenny Opera* at the Theater am Schiffbauerdamm (now the home of the Berliner Ensemble) in 1928; in 1949 he had assisted Brecht in the productions of *Mother Courage* and *Mr Puntila and his Man Matti*. Now he steered *The Life of Galileo* to its successful première in January 1957. This was evidence of the productiveness of the collective method, and a first indication that the theatre would continue to exist. Three years later, in the summer of 1960, when the Berliner Ensemble again played in front of an international audience at the Théâtre des Nations in Paris, it put its capacity for continued development beyond all doubt. The production of Brecht's *Arturo Ui*, under the direction of Manfred Wekwerth and Peter Palitzsch, with Ekkehard Schall in the title role, was awarded the first prize of the international theatre critics.

It was now beyond doubt that Brecht had left behind a method that was not exclusively bound up with what was unique and individual in his personality as an artist. It is in the productivity of the method that the continuity of his theatre must be sought. Of prime importance, particularly during this period, was the circumspect leadership given by Helene Weigel. After the dramatist's death she showed admirable courage in entrusting young pupils of Brecht's, who were by no means established, with positions of responsibility within the theatre. In so doing she built on Brecht's own educational practice. It was, finally, Manfred Wekwerth, Chief Director of the ensemble until 1969, who trained a team of young directors who made their mark with their own productions in the course of the sixties.

The experiments carried out during this second phase in the short history of the Berliner Ensemble followed several directions. They brought with them an enrichment of Brecht's theatre, in themes dealt with, means of expression, artistic tools, and techniques. Using Brecht's methodology we worked hand in hand with young playwrights from our own country in evolving plays dealing with our present-day socialist life. We expanded our repertoire with works by contemporary writers, fellow-activists, and allies of Brecht and his theatre: writers of the stature of Heinar Kipphardt and Peter Weiss; the same applies to classic twentieth-century dramatists like Vsevolod Vishnevsky and Sean O'Casey. With the production of Brecht's adaptation of *Coriolanus*, there took place on the stage of the Berliner Ensemble the long-awaited meeting of the two colossi of world drama, a meeting prepared for in the work preceding it. We put on Brecht's plays that had not been staged up to this point, and in doing so demonstrated our ability to approach his work creatively in applying his own methodology: these included *The Resistible Ascension of Arturo Ui*, *The Days of the Commune*, *Schweyk in the Second World*

War, *The Little Mahagonny*, *Man Equals Man*, and *Saint Joan of the Stockyards*.

During the Ensemble's second guest appearance in England at the National Theatre in London in 1965, five productions were presented. These were *The Resistible Ascension of Arturo Ui* (directed Wekwerth and Palitzsch), *The Days of the Commune* (directed Wekwerth and Tenschert), *The Little Mahagonny* (directed Manfred Karge and Matthias Langhoff), *The Threepenny Opera* (directed Erich Engel), and *Coriolanus* (directed Wekwerth and Tenschert) with Ekkehard Schall in the title role and Helene Weigel as Volumnia. These productions made it absolutely clear that here was a theatre which in theme and approach could take a stand on the great issues of our time, and which had at its command a range of artistic means of expression, impressive in its breadth, variety, and precision. Brecht's theatre, after its founder's death, is alive, well, and progressing.

In the last years of his life Brecht is reported to have increasingly emphasized the term 'philosophical theatre' when discussing his ideas on a new theatre for a new audience. The term 'epic theatre', which he had introduced in the period from the twenties to the forties, or 'dialectical theatre', as applied in the light of his practical experience with the Berliner Ensemble in the fifties, now seemed to have become too narrow, as definitions, to encompass the function, tasks, and intended effect of a theatre made for the latter part of the twentieth century. In speaking of 'philosophical theatre' Brecht calls to mind the popular theatre of the Elizabethans, and more particularly of Shakespeare. He praises 'William the great' for having understood how to recount epoch-making events in a way so entertaining that they were turned into an experience enjoyed by a wide audience, and for being able to create exciting theatre by presenting problems in their totality. He drew attention, too, to Diderot and Lessing as men who had made their name both as philosophers and dramatists.

We think of the Philosopher that Brecht introduced as a character in his dialogues on theatre and society known as *The Messingkauf Dialogues*. The Philosopher explains what is meant by philosophy and philosophizing: they are a practical, use-oriented interest in the behaviour of human beings, with the intention of exerting a positive influence on their undertakings: their achievements, hopes, expectations, and claims to happiness. 'The art of living' is what Brecht called this, and he declared that all the arts should contribute to the art of living, the greatest of all arts. The prime aim of the theatre, then, is to convey pleasure in the vitality of human beings in an entertaining way. The intention is to increase people's joy in living and to strengthen their will to live. The mentally and socially emancipated audience should derive pleasure not only from the theatrical artistry with which images from life are presented, and from the intellectual penetration of the themes, problems, and narratives presented. They should above all get pleasure from the strengthening of their will to live.

At the end of the seventies the Berliner Ensemble saw in these ideas the germs of potential growth. In 1977 Manfred Wekwerth succeeded Helene Weigel as head of the theatre. Together with his co-workers he set about developing a philosophical theatre in the Brechtian sense.

The great issues facing society and humanity in the last third of the century were to be the basis of the repertoire. These were identified as peace or war, social progress and human emancipation, or relapse into barbarism and a rejection of history. Finally, it was to encompass the idea of 'world-friendliness' as a striving for an ever more profound humanization and sensitivization of the way people live together. What, then, would constitute the dramatic reservoir for the practical realization of these basic lines of orientation?

At the centre of our work, as before, are the plays of Brecht: the task would be to rediscover them for a new audience, and to re-explore them to find messages for the world of today and of the days to come. Secondly, we would turn to writers who were akin to Brecht in their world view and way of writing: the scope ranging from the classical writers, to precursors of Brecht, to his allies and contemporaries. We would include contemporary socialist and progressive playwrights and new plays devised in collaboration with writers in the German Democratic Republic.

The names of the authors currently in our repertoire will serve to demonstrate the central tendencies in our work: Brecht, of course, Shakespeare and Goethe, and also Carl Sternheim and Carl Zuckmayer as writers working along the same lines as Brecht in the first third of this century. García Lorca and Saint-Exupéry are there too, and Dario Fo, together with the outstanding Soviet playwright Michael Shatrov. We have included contemporary playwrights from the German Democratic Republic, one of the most important of whom is Volker Braun.

A philosophical popular theatre is, of course, inconceivable without the approval of an ever-widening audience with highly diversified requirements and expectations. It follows, then, that not only must the repertoire display both breadth and variety in presenting the themes central to the theatre's basic approach and programme; the methods of performing, too, must encompass the whole breadth and variety of possible means of expression. A wide range of forms and genres is essential in order to reach an audience which is itself highly diversified. There is an interplay, a reciprocity between the artistic-experimental and the social aspects of our theatre work. Philosophical popular theatre also means, then, knowing that you are always on the way towards transforming the small circle of connoisseurs into the larger appreciative audience.

Translated by John Mitchell

4

Two generations of post-Brechtian playwrights in the German Democratic Republic

ROLF ROHMER

Bertolt Brecht's sudden and premature death in 1956 was particularly distressing because he was even then in the process of adapting his dramatic theory and practice to the requirements of a new social order. At that particular point in its history the theatre in the German Democratic Republic needed him badly.

After Brecht's return to Berlin in 1949, there was serious disagreement over the alternatives open to the theatre. Particularly at issue were questions concerning playwriting, performance methods, and the relationship of the actor to the audience. The history of post-eighteenth-century German theatre has shown that only a theatre that conforms to bourgeois interests has been universally accepted. Brecht fought against this exclusivity. From the very beginning he had disagreed with the late bourgeois concept of theatre, and he persisted in his attempt to develop an alternative to it. An alternative theatre had emerged from the revolutionary class struggles after 1918, and Brecht was, of course, not the only one to pursue new, very different forms of theatre. Piscator and his 'political theatre' and the various forms of revolutionary workers' theatre belonged to this movement as well. It was proletarian and directly connected with the working-class movement. This movement determined production methods, aesthetic images, and modes of communication. The theatre, in turn, addressed itself to the interests and struggles that attended the formation of the working class.

However, this was not the only theatre to serve the cultural interests of the workers. In the German working-class movement a cultural-political tradition was already established which was in some measure directed towards the appropriation of bourgeois theatre. A strong working-class education movement, a product of the cultural criticism and theory of the Socialist Democratic Party, organized and took mental possession of the literary tradition on behalf of the proletariat. In theatrical practice, and especially in dramatic literature, this tradition involved the continuation of accepted methods of production and reception. These were not abolished or changed, but rather re-interpreted. They gained a new historical-political perspective through the change in subject matter, through the new political perspective that was brought to bear on older plays, and through the changed spiritual and ideological assumptions of the spectators.

In the twenties new forms of theatre dominated the proletarian theatre movement. This changed, however, after the Fascists took power in Germany. An anti-Fascist democratic United Front, made up of the most diverse socio-political groupings, came into existence. The first priority of this Front was to develop common policies to deal with the immediate political situation. Since this was its primary aim, the specific interests of particular classes and social groups were of secondary importance, although this resulted in painful conflicts between theory and practice for various individuals and collectives. This situation also obtained in the theatre. Here, socialist theoreticians and artists discussed the relationship of new to traditional art forms, and the current character and possible continuation of specific socialist artistic practices. In many instances, including that of Brecht, we notice a specific attempt to conform to the requirements of the new political and cultural situation.

The development of the German theatre after 1945, and more particularly the re-establishment of the theatre in the German Democratic Republic, started from democratic and anti-Fascist precepts. In the theatre, the traditional proletarian cultural policy, which depended upon the appropriation and remodelling of extant theatrical traditions, predominated. It was strengthened by the beneficial influence of the Soviet theatre, where similar tendencies were apparent under the influence of the Stanislavsky tradition.

Brecht got into difficulties when he returned to the German Democratic Republic after the war because, in spite of his willingness to conform to changed conditions, he persisted in showing a lively interest in new forms of proletarian theatre, different from those which were then commonly accepted. The conflicts at that time centred on personalities and terminology: for example, Stanislavsky, Friedrich Wolf, and Wolfgang Langhoff versus Brecht, and non-epic versus epic theatre. These were the subject of intense theoretical debate. In fact there were fundamental differences in conceptual and methodological approaches. The antagonists often appeared to be in mutually exclusive positions, and their opposition was aggravated by the fact that they had to come to terms with a country recently liberated from Fascism. Gradually, however, because of mutual respect for each other's work, and because of their shared political and ideological assumptions, the individuals involved began to make an effort to find out what they had in common, and to put their theories to some kind of practical use.

But here an even longer process was initiated: on the one hand the possibility of disagreements in theatre practice was admitted, and differing modes in the appropriation of social reality were even seen to be socially beneficial; on the other hand, differences were reconciled and an integration of opinions took place, which gave them a more general validity and applicability.

This process of integration, for instance, is well demonstrated in Brecht's concept of *Gestus*, which can take both verbal and physical forms. These gestic forms are now commonly accepted in the German Democratic Republic, at least in theory if not in practice, and they are the most important criteria in the critical evaluation of performances. It is less recognized just how much character construction, character motivation, and the translation of character into stage action has depended on Stanislavsky's methods and on related traditions in the German theatre. This relationship is clearly in evidence in the training of actors in the German Democratic Republic. Brecht himself – comparing his theatre to Stanislavsky's – pointed out the dialectical relationship that existed between them.

From the mid 1950s onwards there were important social changes in the German Democratic Republic: the building of a socialist society had begun. This is a long-term process in which, especially at the beginning, there are phases of fast radical change in certain areas, and then phases of long-term gradual development. At the beginning of this period the collectivization of agriculture was initiated; in industry, which had already been nationalized, the problem was one of a huge increase in productivity, and of trying to instil a responsible and creative relationship to the means of production in the workers. For a long time these were the important themes in literature, especially in drama. Brecht took this into account in his own creative work. In the Berliner Ensemble he produced the play of a younger author which portrayed developments in agriculture: this play was Erwin Strittmatter's *Katzgraben*. Brecht himself was attempting to dramatize a true story which dealt with the work of oven-builders in an industrial plant. The result of this attempt was the *Büsching-Fragment*. For us, it is not just all these artistic works which are significant, but also the theoretical statements and ideas which Brecht produced in this period, for instance, his notes on *Katzgraben*.

The transformation of social conditions again raised the question, but in a fundamental and novel way, of the relevance of theatrical traditions to the new social order. Until then the theatre had operated under the influence of social forces which, however different in their individual phases, had belonged to the general transition from imperialism to socialism; the formulations and functional strategies of the theatre were all based firmly on them. Brecht had always tried to make the fundamental social mechanisms of human behaviour quite clear, and also to put across one basic fact: that social conditions must be changed if the human situation is to change. Brecht wanted to use this knowledge as a stimulus for social activities. Is such a closely designed and strategically orientated theatre still needed nowadays since society has in fact evolved into a further stage of development?

Brecht attempted to delineate the new social reality with the dramatic means and methods at his disposal. The insight into the mechanisms of social relationships and processes and the impetus for changing them had to be maintained. But now the immediate practical problems, and the fact that a real possibility existed for social change, provoked new theatrical solutions. Brecht tried to modify his playwriting and change his theatrical methods. The changeover from the 'epic' to the 'dialectic' theatre shows this clearly. Death, however, forcibly removed him from this exciting endeavour. He was no longer there to provide the answers to the new questions that had been raised. The task therefore fell to the younger generation to provide solutions.

Belonging to this generation are the playwrights we could call

Brecht's disciples: Heiner Müller, Peter Hacks, and Helmut Baierl, although the international fame which the first two of them enjoy is the result rather of their departures from Brecht. All three wrote plays that dealt with topical problems: in fact in his *The Wage Slaver* (*Der Lohndrücker*) Heiner Müller even dramatized the same story that Brecht had dealt with in his *Büsching-Fragment*. Their style and method of playwriting were – however individual and different – unmistakably Brechtian. They were particularly adept at *Verfremdung* ('alienation', or 'distancing'), which went beyond the external sequence of dramatic events and the activities of the characters to discover their relationship to the social and historical background. Indeed, they developed these methods further and in many different ways. Hacks, for example, even developed a language which because of its stylistic peculiarities revealed his subject matter through alienating it. In Heiner Müller's and Helmut Baierl's plays, the characters argue and discuss, and in this way their differing positions are made clear, and the various ways of behaving in contradictory social situations are demonstrated and tested and the correct mode of behaviour finally shown. The intention was to propagandize. These plays show clearly the dialectical relationship between epic theatre and its subsequent modifications, and therefore the evolution necessary under changing social conditions.

Through distancing us from character and concentrating on overt argument and discussion, the analysis of social background and a sensitivity to social conditions is made possible. The plays remind us of Brecht's didactic pieces of the twenties rather than of the plays he had written during his years of exile. This has also been recognized by the critics, who have referred to the works of Müller and Baierl as a didactic theatre of instruction. However, unlike Brecht's earlier didactic plays, social alternatives are now presented and characters are confronted with real choices. The playwrights' analyses are presented in terms of the immediate situation and the choices confronting the characters. This is why arguments and discussions are so important in the plays. Formerly, the attitudes of the characters in the didactic plays were seen as socially representative; characters were made to confront each other and to become conscious of social and class relationships and problems. Now what has become important is the discovery and assertion of appropriate behaviour in a period of social change. Rarely are changes in social conditions so directly presented as changes in artistic practice as they are in these plays.

But 'didactic theatre' is not to be defined entirely in terms of its formal characteristics, however important these might be. Essentially it is a continuation of a characteristic form of the proletarian theatre of the twenties. It was hoped that this type of theatre, which was securely based on the interests of the working class, could be reintroduced into a socialist society. The political agitation of this form of theatre had appealed directly to the proletariat. Brecht's plays attempted a dialogue with the audience, an audience that was, in effect, taking part in the cultural and political activities of the theatre. This intention is quite clear in Brecht's didactic plays. He attempts to create premises that would lead the audience to discover connections and establish trains of thought that would encourage them to react and join in. If Brecht attached less importance to the dialogue as a theatrical event in itself, this was not the fault of this theories, but rather of the social and cultural limitations of the German theatre itself. In bourgeois-capitalist culture, popular theatre forms that were too close to the common discourse of the people were ignored. The few remaining elements of communication in bourgeois literary theatre had withered away and were subjected to manipulation by the imperatives of mass entertainment. Brecht could not rely on an effective, commonly accepted theatrical tradition. The tradition of social communication that was still valid in the cultural lives of the proletariat faded into the agitatory and propagandistic tendencies of the proletarian theatre that was supplanted by the class struggles of the twenties. A rapid transition to a rich and communicative theatre could not be taken for granted, and was in fact stopped abruptly by the events of 1933. But the young playwrights once again took up the challenge.

These playwrights at first concentrated on intensive communication with the audience in the form of 'didactic theatre', the aim being a dramatic dialogue with the audience. But this type of theatre did not prove popular. After a short but significant appearance it lapsed, and the playwrights chose to follow other directions. There are many reasons for this. For a theatre of this kind to function it is necessary to have a variety of elements besides the play itself. What is particularly necessary is an audience and playwrights versed in the practice of theatrical communication. We know from theatre practice in other cultures that such theatrical codes can be realized only after long practice. It is not surprising, then, that these skills were not in place; after all, these traditions had been banished from the German theatre. The proletarian theatre of the twenties was too short lived to be effective. It was also so completely tied to the class struggles of the period between 1918 and 1933 that it could not have been reproduced without great changes. Nevertheless, the impetus of the new concept of the relationship between the theatre and its audience was not entirely lost. It resulted in the marked and persistent efforts of the theatre in the German Democratic Republic in the 1960s to develop contact with its audience, and every so often one finds concepts and programmes in individual theatres all over the German Democratic Republic that are founded on the tenets of the proletarian didactic theatre.

The Landestheater in Halle at the end of the sixties and beginning of the seventies produced examples of new theatre–audience relationships. It was followed by the Volksbühne in Berlin and even more recently by the Mecklenburg State Theatre in Schwerin. All attempted consistently and intensively to develop untraditional and untried methods of communication. This long process has been affected by international cultural and theatrical practices, and also by changing conditions in the German Democratic Republic itself. These attempts are, therefore, not a direct continuation of the theatrical experiments of the fifties, but aim at new solutions.

In order to understand better this dialectic of continuity and innovation in the development of the theatre in the German Democratic Republic, it is useful to compare it with that of other socialist countries. There we also find two different kinds of theatre which, although different in many ways, we recognize from the history of the German theatre. These two types are even more opposed, and are obviously seen as alternatives. In the Soviet theatre the latest research has established the following historical groupings: plays for the masses; the *Proletkult*; the work of Meyerhold, Tairov, Mayakovsky, and others; then the 'late' Stanislavsky, the 'late' Gorky, the so-called drama of revolution, and the theatre of the thirties. These are followed by a new departure: the development of the Sowremmenik, Moscow Taganka, Ochlopow, Towstonogow, and other 'studio theatres'. More recently there has been rivalry between the two types of theatre in socialist countries, and especially in the most recent Soviet theatre. We might ignore for a moment the connections with international cultural and theatrical movements and concentrate on the fact that this change is closely tied to the various stages of development of socialist society, that is to social, cultural, and political factors. Unfortunately this topic cannot be dealt with in any detail here. In any case, the disappearance of this other type of theatre in the German Democratic Republic is due not only to the lack of theatrical communication but above all to the priority of other cultural requirements.

Under these conditions was Brecht still needed? The results of his work are undisputed, but they are used in many very differing and contradictory ways. The Berliner Ensemble, for instance, initially staged all of Brecht's works, even including those he wrote in the 1920s. Then more works by other authors were chosen and included in the programme. Because of the dictates of social developments in the German Democratic Republic, a further development of Brecht's theatrical and aesthetic principles was required and applied. Manfred Wekwerth, a collaborator of Brecht and the present Artistic Director of the Berliner Ensemble, called this long-term strategy 'the theatre of change – the changing theatre' ('Theater der Veränderung – Theater in Veränderung'). Brecht's influence is to be felt on far more than the Berliner Ensemble – his works may be found in the repertoires of all the theatres in the German Democratic Republic, and its aesthetic principles have influenced, although in differing degrees, the artistic practice of many producers, actors, and companies. In this way Brecht is still alive and relevant to the day-to-day theatre of the German Democratic Republic.

At the same time, however, there are problems in accepting his work. Many of the younger generation find Brecht's plays, especially those written after 1933, too long, too obvious, and too insistent. However, these young people are concerned with present-day problems, with the complicated issues of contemporary socialist reality, and demonstrate a constant hope and desire for change. The younger generation is interested in plays that deal with specific issues, with intense situations and conflicts, and which deal with these openly.

The authors of the 'third generation' have to take this into account. A renewed interest in the proletarian theatre of the twenties has appeared and has been promoted by many different theatre companies. The presence of Brecht can once again be felt, although unrecognized by the younger generation of playwrights. This may be seen, for instance, in the growing interest in the early plays of Brecht. Much in contemporary theatrical method and practice would be unthinkable without the influence of Brecht.

Something similar happened in dramatic literature. Here, however, the differences from Brecht are more marked than the similarities to him. In Hack's early historical plays his closeness to Brecht is quite clearly seen. However, he soon demonstrated that what he had learned from Brecht's style could be used to show a different view of social processes, a view he had gained from his involvement in the concrete developing conditions of socialist society. The plots of his plays and their effective strategic impetus were no longer aimed at immediate long- or short-term social changes. Ironically, he dismisses Brecht's attempts to achieve social change as 'union plays' (*Gewerkschaftsstücke*). He perceives his characters rather in terms of basic human ideals, and humorously but critically he allows us to become conscious of the extent to which they fall short of them and of their aspiration to achieve these ideals later. In *Frau Flinz* and *Johanna von Döbeln* Helmut Baierl adapted two of Brecht's plays, placing them in a socialist society, and showed how the same situations and same characters could – under different social conditions – lead to different results. However, finding these methods inadequate, Baierl later developed his own original dramatic ideas. Heiner Müller probed deep into historical processes and contradictory historical situations, which entailed serious and often passionate human decisions. He portrayed these decisions using his poetic and highly individual language and allegorical style. He used his language and style to expose social clichés and to deconstruct a view of history that was far too self-assured. Spurred on by the concern that people might fail when faced with history, and that they might not be able to cope as they should, Heiner Müller's plays take on a dimension of alienation which can provoke an unexpected response from the audience.

The younger author Volker Braun, who was also brought up on

Brecht's methods, presents us with quite clearly contradictory fables and richly conflicting human dilemmas in socialist everyday life. He himself calls them 'stories'. In his works the strict causality and objectivity of the sequence of events, which Brecht emphasized in his dramatic plots, is often forced into the background by the behaviour of his protagonists, producing surprising and strange yet socially significant results, to which the protagonists are often less equal than the other characters. Braun puts the increasing individual productivity of the people – free, as they are in a socialist society, from exploitation – firmly into the picture. At the same time he makes it quite clear that their unrestrained activity needs objective public criticism. All these were not merely up-to-date modifications of Brecht's playwriting techniques, but were in fact new solutions.

These few examples show only the decisive changes in Brecht's heritage. An overview of the development of drama in the German Democratic Republic since the mid 1960s would reveal a huge variety of materials, themes, forms, styles, dramaturgical peculiarities, and poetical characteristics which are difficult to categorize, and which can in no way be fitted into the dramaturgical and theatrical polarities which were so prominent in the controversies immediately after 1945. Most artists very understandably refuse to be put into categories because they believe that their creative subjectivity is thereby misinterpreted and their artistic development belittled. Categorizing is all the more invidious when a society aims to liberate all artistic endeavour and to give artists the chance to work in their own creative surroundings. We are inclined – and personally I think that we are historically right to do so – to understand this as a valuable addition to and enrichment of our art. It is not out of disrespect for the artistic generation of the sixties and seventies that their achievements are not described here, but it is impossible to attempt to do them justice in such a brief survey. Nevertheless, critical voices, complaining about the unsatisfactory nature of the new drama, have been making themselves heard recently. They do not complain merely about a lack of quality in the individual plays, but above all about a deficiency in the treatment of socio-historically significant subjects and problems. Critics condemn the lack of aesthetic profile which, if it existed, would provoke theatre companies to develop and project aesthetic qualities of their own. A wider artistic range is already sought after and the demand for it gets more and more persistent. Research establishes that there is an increasingly obvious tendency towards grouping and ordering the huge variety of creative works, and that there is even a tendency to categorize works in terms of epochs.

Besides those authors who follow immediately on Brecht, there are also those, for instance Helmut Sakowski, Armin Stolper, Claus Hammel, and Rainer Kerndl, who stem from other literary traditions, but whose work nevertheless shows traces of Brecht's influence. A measure of Brechtian dramatic technique has, however, become a common attribute of plays written in the German Democratic Republic. Many young authors no longer trace it back to its source, so it has become what we might call interiorized. At the same time research has made it evident that, as opposed to the strategy of alienation derived from the epic theatre, the cartharsis stemming from the Aristotelian theatre has regained significance, without, however, continuing the typology of this dramaturgy and theatre in its purely historical form. Authors such as Jürgen Gross, Christoph Hein, Heinz Drewniok, and Albert Wendt, who began to write in the seventies, and even more recent writers differ, for instance, from Volker Braun in that they discuss the dialectic of subjective demand and social productivity, by questioning critically the subject or the possibilities of its realization in society.

This transition makes the division into epochs quite clear. In the criticism of the most recent generation of writers there is scepticism as well as anger in the face of the worsening of the world situation since the end of the seventies. The question goes something like this: what on earth have we been able to achieve up to this point? At the same time there is an insistence on forming a more effective socialist society and way of life. Brecht is no longer so integral a part of the formulation of these and related questions in drama, although without doubt it is he who first posed the questions that we now have to answer. In order to understand this fully we must remember the period after 1933 when the alternative proletarian theatre had to be pushed into the background. Brecht had, moreover, to accommodate the various points of view held by that anti-Fascist United Front to which I have already referred. He was deprived, too, of the possibility of producing his plays, and therefore of developing them in relationship to his audience. These factors made Brecht literalize his theatre both in theory and in practice. He was able nevertheless to preserve the instructive and didactic aspect of his work. But he did so at a price – he had to increase the importance of fable to his concept of the epic theatre, and fable would, of course, become of central importance in his work.

In Brecht's writings the fable has become the nexus on which all aspects of the play converge, and in terms of which reality must be interpreted. He achieved it so well in his own work that his methodology has been adopted, at least in part, by non-epic playwrights. On the other hand, because he subsequently concentrated so much on fable, Brecht was prevented from reworking his early plays. It is understandable that he should not have attempted to do so in 1949; the conditions were not favourable. When attempts were made to do so after Brecht's death, the instigators had to contend with the predominance of the tradition of the fable, which had been confirmed by the influential productions of his plays and by the effectiveness of their literary structure. So it is understandable that the following generations of dramatists turned away from Brecht's example in their search for their own up-to-date model of communicative theatre, although they, and others involved in the theatre, continued to value his ideas, as they still do today.

What characterizes the plays of Müller and Braun, of Gross and the most recent playwrights, is 'open-endedness' ('Dramaturgie der offenen Enden'), as Braun expressed it. This does not mean that the stories have no ending, although this can be the case. The 'open endings' are serious and deliberate alternatives to the characters' decisions in the plays, serious considerations of the social and historical implications of the subject, and provocations leading to discussion of the play in question. The works of these playwrights demand the means of intense communication, they demand dialogue. This kind of theatre has still to achieve maturity – and so once again we think of Brecht. Heiner Müller, for instance, uses the power of his eloquent poetry to fight against clichés of thought and behaviour which an extemely powerful media-culture which derives from the West attempts to impose on us. At the same time, in the extremely imagistic language that is characteristic of his plays, he uses the conventions of the media to speak to his audience and he provokes criticism through his excesses. In this creation of extreme tension one of the specific demands is the use of dialogue, and the question arises of how it can be made more effective. Spurred on by this question we can discover in Brecht's notebooks and other writings just how much the development of media-culture and the changing social behaviour and means of communication occupied him. One can see how this stimulated his thoughts on creating theatre. This is why it is worth following through on Brecht.

In various theoretical essays and comments, Volker Braun has sketched the outlines of a future socialist theatre. He starts from the assumption that in a socialist society conflicts will be tougher because, when all people are completely equal and when free citizens constantly search for real alternatives, decisions will have to be taken which will have momentous social consequences. The theatre would be the place where these conflicts could be enacted with less risk – in the presence of the general public, who could even take part in the dialogue. The theatre would be delightful, and it would not sacrifice any of its principles. His plays take into account the growing readiness of the public and of the theatre to make use of these ideas. Brecht's thoughts on the relationship between work and pleasure, between acting and reality, between the art of watching and the joy of active change, establish a viewpoint from which his successors, more confident and secure, look into the future.

5

Productions of Brecht's plays on the West German stage, 1945–1986

KLAUS VÖLKER

Bertolt Brecht's rise to fame began in the 1920s with *Drums in the Night* and with pieces that he called *Versuche*, or essays. As the director of these 'essays', he experimented with an open form of theatre, which was intended to bring out the evolving character of history, and to show the world as changeable. He was only partially able to realize his notions of epic theatre by the time he went into exile in 1933. His sole public success remained *The Threepenny Opera*, the adaptation of *The Beggar's Opera* by John Gay, with music by Kurt Weill; indeed, immediately after the Second World War this work was all he was remembered for.

1948 saw the world première of *Mr Puntila and his Man Matti* in Zürich, then *Mother Courage and her Children* in Berlin. Shortly after this came the partition of Germany into the Federal Republic of Germany and the German Democratic Republic. Brecht chose the GDR, where he could develop the Berliner Ensemble theatre. Although the Berliner Ensemble was producing some of the most significant German theatre after 1945, Brecht's theatre aesthetic was highly controversial, and the first few years he worked in considerable isolation, steering his way around doctrinaire socialist realism, residual Nazi notions of theatre, and the missionary zeal of Stanislavsky followers.

Brecht's choice of the GDR effectively produced a boycott of his works in the FRG during the Cold War mentality of the 1950s: people shied away from the political ramifications of the works of this Communist poet, who lived in that other Germany. Consequently, there were few Brecht productions. The dates 17 June 1953 (GDR), October 1956 (Hungary), and 13 August 1961 (the Berlin Wall) were sufficient admonitions to keep the boycott alive. The only theatre not to observe this boycott was in Frankfurt, where Harry Buckwitz mounted excellent productions of Brecht almost every year from 1952 until the mid sixties.

From the mid 1960s on, things began to change. The Berliner Ensemble gradually became a theatrical Mecca; here young directors from the West found fresh impetus for their own work. West German theatres began inviting students of Brecht as guests. Soon there was actually a bull-market in Brecht; he was quickly elevated to the rank of a classic: he was art, not politics. Most productions correspondingly removed any prickly agit-prop elements from his plays. Every action has a reaction; soon people had their fill of Brecht. Max Frisch could say scathingly of Brecht that his work was characterized by 'the penetrating ineffectiveness of a classic'. Before long critics and audiences alike were afflicted with Brecht-fatigue (*Brecht-Müdigkeit*). Resistance to Brecht continued during the 1970s; or rather it was not so much a resistance as a lack of demand, as artists and intellectuals, with the general failure of political hopes and ambitions, retreated into more private and aesthetic domains. The political Brecht was now out of tune with the mood of the times, and the poetic Brecht was consigned to schoolbooks. He was now as much a classic as Goethe and Schiller, but not a classic of the kind that he himself wished to be: a classic in the vein of Marx, Engels, and Lenin – a playwright with ideas that could be applied.

Much the same thing happened in the GDR. Brecht became the official poet whose example could be invoked against younger and more rebellious writers. He was the Stanislavsky of the seventies. The experimental, exploratory period of the Berliner Ensemble effectively ended with the 1964 production of *Coriolanus*, to be replaced by a museum-like conservation of the 'classic' Brecht. Only Ruth Berghaus was predisposed to re-evaluate Brecht and to modify him. She was dismissed from her position. From the mid seventies to the mid eighties there was only one innovative Brecht production in East Berlin, and this was not a product of the Berliner Ensemble. In the Deutsches Theater, Alexander Lang directed *Round Heads and Pointed Heads* in a lively comic-strip style. It consisted of a brilliant combination of political cabaret, slapstick, and music-hall elements.

The leading directors in the FRG after 1945 were Gustaf Gründgens, Karl Heinz Stroux, Boleslaw Barlog, Oskar Fritz Schuh, Harry Buckwitz, and Hans Schweikart: these men also ran the municipal and state theatres. The 1970s ushered in a new group of directors: Hans Hollmann, Peter Zadek, Hans Neuenfels, Claus Peymann, and Peter Stein. From the start these new directors had nothing to do with the traditional theatres. They did not begin as assistants to the older generation of directors. They admired the theatre of Brecht: their Mecca was the Berliner Ensemble. They were enthusiastic about the final productions of Fritz Kortner and, like Peter Zadek, they looked to the theatre in London for inspiration, or, like Klaus Michael Grüber, to Giorgio Strehler in Milan. Both Brecht, through his systematic analysis of theatre in *Theaterarbeit*, and Kortner imparted a great intellectual energy to the West German theatre. The new directors had learned their trade by involvement with Brecht's plays, but for them it was actually his theories that were influential; their directorial method was strongly shaped not by the texts of the plays themselves but by the way he had worked with the actors through debate and consensus. Stein and Zadek, among others, began to question the routines of the municipal theatres and to change their structural organization.

Early in his career Peter Stein staged *In the Jungle of Cities* in the workshop of the Munich Kammerspiele (1968), but he incorporated into his production of this early work the political self-awareness of the mature Brecht, and he even included songs and texts from later works. It was a riveting, high-quality production, but also rather myopic, and one from which Stein later distanced himself.

In 1970 Stein founded the Schaubühne in West Berlin, and opened it with a production of *The Mother*. The intent here was less on making a public political statement than on stressing the ensemble-politics of the theatre: the production was the result of a series of debates, decisions, and compromises among the artists. It also paid homage to Therese Giehse, who was cast as the Mother. She was a friend of Brecht, a veteran performer under his direction, and a revered role-model for the actors of the Schaubühne.

After the production of *Mother Courage* at the Deutsches Theater in 1949, Friedrich Wolf, himself a playwright, described Brecht's methods as too painful. 'I prefer the opposite way', he wrote, 'where the spectator swallows the medicine and does not even realize that he is being treated.'[1] Brecht disliked being 'betrayed' in this way. He did not see art as the sugar to coat the pill of socialism; rather, it should sway the audience while it reproduces reality. In 1955 he declared to the actors at the Berliner Ensemble: 'True art is not pleasing.'[2]

It now seems commonplace that Brecht's plays should be performed in the way that Wolf recommended; they are sugar-coated pills that can be swallowed with no difficulty. Brecht's exhortation, 'Change the world, it needs it', has degenerated into an empty slogan. It commands our assent without any difficulty. Everything is performed smoothly, there are no rough edges, the poetry is harmonious, and at the conclusion there are no questions left unanswered. Brecht today seems to be an author of no consequence. He had wanted to achieve an operative, effective classicism, but his parables are now perceived as harmless and sophisticated. They arouse in neither the performers nor the audience the productive pain that their author so desired. Brecht commands universal assent because his plays seem to confirm what everyone already thinks.

During the 1970s, Brecht's influence on West German theatre was as a director rather than as a playwright; directors worked with his methods in realizing plays and projects. He was still respected as an author in those plays where he remained open, that is, where his attitudes were not based on a simplistically materialist concept of nature. Accordingly, his early plays – *Baal, In the Jungle of Cities, Mahagonny* – were more frequently performed, since they expressed feelings and ideas that contemporary generations could relate to. In addition, they discovered his incomplete fragment, *The Fall of the Egoist, Johann Fatzer*.

In 1926 Brecht planned a series of plays dealing with man's experience of big cities. *Fatzer* was meant as the second in the series, after a revised version of *In the Jungle of Cities*. The play described the alienation of men and women in a society dominated entirely by capital. The disintegration of the Garga family in Chicago was meant to typify the fate of the masses who had left the villages in the wake of advancing industrialization in order to find work and better living conditions in the towns. Brecht conceived the egoist Fatzer as typical of the little man who tries to grow rich by cunningly adapting himself and buying promotion into the ranks of the privileged, at the expense of members of his own class, but he comes to grief in the process.

Modern society needs the Gargas, the single fighters with a dream of getting rich one day. Garga is followed by Galy Gay, a human fighting machine, in *Man Equals Man*. Fatzer deserts the army with three others, but unlike them he cannot enjoy life, and refuses simply to be a wheel that is turned by the stream of history. When they foil his suicide attempt, he says, 'I cannot accept your mechanical way of life; a human being is not just a push-button.'[3] *Fatzer* is an unfinished play, a play without solutions, a play that asks painful questions and is open to question. In it Brecht tries to link the asocial Baal with the young comrade in *The Measures Taken*. Because Fatzer refuses to accept the social role his comrades assign him, they execute him. His execution, however, solves nothing; they, in turn, are shot as deserters. Brecht wrote of *Fatzer*: 'The whole play, it is impossible, destroy it as an experiment lacking reality!'[4]

This lack of reality constitutes the fascination of producing *Fatzer* today, as long as the production can concentrate on the contradictory tensions within Fatzer, not on being a seminar on Brecht's failed intentions. This was the problem with the production of *Fatzer* that Frank-Patrick Steckel directed at the Schaubühne in 1976. He accentuated its fragmentary nature, but only to demonstrate the miscarried genesis of the play: the audience became mere participants in a Brecht training-college. What the play really needs is a visionary interpretation, such as Klaus Michael Grüber conceived for his production of Hölderlin's *Empedokles* (1975).

The Austrian poet Ingeborg Bachmann has suggested that Brecht's 'ineffectiveness' could be attributed to his ability to find 'great words at the right moment' in a play. 'But these great words and these great gestures', she added, 'were either not popular enough or too sublime to touch the heart of the public. I believe he has no public. To them, he is as foreign as Hölderlin, and there is no one who understands his pathos, his elevated tone, which I admire so greatly.'[5] Bachmann rues the fact that though Brecht is performed all over, is found in every schoolbook, yet his work falls on deaf ears. She proposes that his work be understood as an attempt at salvation; ironic, catastrophic, lacerated, yet grandiose. A work like *Fatzer* is witness to a language that we only dimly sense, but that we can never fully possess: 'We realize it in a fragmented fashion',

Bachmann writes, 'in his poetry, concretized in a line or in a scene, and suddenly grasp that here we are experiencing this language.'[6]

In their 1978 *Fatzer* production in Hamburg, Manfred Karge and Matthias Langhoff came to the realization that the play could not find an audience. They presented it as an addendum to *The Prince of Homburg*, presented in a strongly anti-Prussian interpretation. Karge and Langhoff made no attempt to eliminate or moderate the disparate, contradictory, irreconcilable elements in *Fatzer*. They exposed the fear and terror that lay at the heart of the play, and they demonstrated that the work was still open to our questions. The public did not accept such visionary art; they saved their applause for the production of *The Good Person of Szechwan* that Giorgio Strehler was mounting at the same time in the same theatre. This brilliant Cinemascope soap opera, showing the poor in unbelievably opulent settings, was in effect a bright, festive socio-romantic musical, unwittingly giving by example the answer to a central concern of Brecht: 'How can a parable become luxurious?'

Today most West German productions of Brecht's works are given a humanized treatment – but they lack any attempt at an understanding of the innately paradoxical nature of the characters. Where Brecht sought to gain insight through distancing, now the subscription audience is treated to comforting intimacies. Consequently, these productions, however brilliantly staged, are often stillborn, presented without passion and without desire for insight.

The situation is not dissimilar in the GDR. Manfred Wekwerth's 1978 production of *The Life of Galileo* for the Berliner Ensemble radiates the same attitude. Wekwerth has declared it to be objective and scientific – neatly avoiding any similarity to, or association with controversial figures, alive or dead, and current or past conflicts. *Galileo* displays Wekwerth's mastery of a style that is in reality no style at all, but rather a kind of jerry-built entertainment for octogenarians, pedantically eliminating every risk and contradiction. Clearly there is an audience for such entertainments, an audience that regards them as genuine masterpieces. Brecht would not have liked such masterpieces, which require no effort. For him, there was no art without risk or effort, or drain; as he wrote in the mid fifties:

Going down early to the void
Up from the void I am filled anew.
When with nothingness I've stayed
I again know what to do.

When I love, or when I feel
Then it's just a further drain.
But I plunge into the cool
And am hot again.[7]

The times are not favourable for Brecht; our well-known directors avoid his plays. But should we not be making use of his glory and reputation? The exception proves the rule: there are performances of his plays which have an experimental character, or in any case a vital energy, as, for instance, in the productions of Claus Peymann and his Bochumer Ensemble, before he moved to the Burgtheater in Vienna.

Also in Bochum, Alfred Kirchner staged a fresh, unconventional *Saint Joan of the Stockyards* in 1979, in a huge abandoned factory. The audience was kept in constant motion during the play, moving from one stage-area to another, and parting to let the police charge the strikers. The central impulse of the production was not the play's parable, but its individual situations, which could forge for the audience a direct link with the reality outside the factory: the crisis in the steel and coal industries in the Ruhr region, the strikes, the high number of unemployed, the massive police response to student demonstrations. St Joan, wonderfully played by Therese Affolter, was portrayed as an idealistic leftist student, strengthened through an inner fire and the force of her arguments. As a spectator one was confronted with the omnipresence of TV and video cameras; the atmosphere was one of total control.

Kirchner also produced a similarly unconventional *Mother Courage and her Children* in 1981. The play was set in the present, shortly before the outbreak of the Third World War. The production gave the impression of a reality created by television and newspapers. On a screen onstage the audience sees references to contemporary events – visions of atom bomb blasts, animal experiments, and disarmament discussions. Kirsten Dene as Mother Courage was a very young Mother, full of energy, a modern Widow Begbick as supermarket cashier. At the end of the play she was as bright as at the beginning –

unbroken, unchanged, practical. She didn't pull the cart, she shoved it, and shouted her song with an insolent courage. Another detail stays in the mind: when Kattrin began her drumming on the roof of the hut a military jet swooped down overhead, drowning out her warning. Then the pilot brutally strafed her, to the sound of John Lennon's 'Imagine'.

Kirchner's techniques resemble those of Piscator in the twenties, techniques that Brecht rejected in his own plays. As long as Brecht was alive, Piscator did not direct a single one of his plays; their conceptions of political theatre differed too greatly. Piscator wanted to dramatize the struggle of daily life directly; Brecht wanted translations of reality. Brecht recognized the dangers of keeping his works open to the currents of the moment; he required artistic distance, and so he invented parables, paraphrases, and translations. Nevertheless, he intended his plays to be topical. Kirchner was perhaps overly simplistic, but he managed to achieve good political cabaret, and his actors were able to present Brecht in a modern and credible manner.

Jürgen Flimm also prefers to give the plays a contemporary setting, with modern sets and costumes, but he does not change the text itself. His methods are certainly debatable, but there is no debate about the fact that his adaptation of *Baal* at Cologne in 1981 was highly successful and convincing.

It is well known that Brecht remained fascinated by the character of Baal his entire life. The alterations he made to the first version of the play reflect his own changing outlook; he continued to be attracted to Baal's positive sentiments and modes of behaviour, to his enormous appetite for pleasure and longing for happiness. He also created other characters in whom something of Baal is found. Galileo comes immediately to mind, sublimating his insatiable hunger for the world in the constant acquisition of knowledge, to whom thinking is sensual pleasure, and all sensual pleasures stimuli to thought. Baal wants only pleasure; Brecht demonstrates that his downfall is due to the fact that in the final analysis he is incapable of enjoyment. Contemporary young people seem to be able to identify with the egoistic Baal figure, even though they may express themselves in a more guarded and inhibited way. In this outcast they see an embodiment of the impossibility of achieving happiness within a saturated, totally neurotic society. Baal causes his own destruction, but he never gives up reaching for the stars right until his death.

Flimm set *Baal* in a big modern city, in which there are no trees, no landscape, no river – nothing but concrete; nothing is happening. Baal, played by Hans-Christian Rudolph, is a modern outcast; he belongs to the drop-out generation, and refuses to be a compliant member of society. At the outset he closely resembled the young, bespectacled Brecht. Gradually he became a drop-out student, then a wandering bum, smoking a joint in some desolate subway station with his buddy Ekart. This Baal is bent on self-destruction: he destroys his poems, and refuses all well-intended advice. The set is a bare red box, serving as Baal's garret, café, and bar. Stage right was a huge spool of cable. When Baal goes out into the forest the back of the set opens to reveal not natural woods, but a soulless underground pedestrian mall. The foresters are construction workers wearing plastic hardhats. This is the jungle of the city in which Baal dies.

In a radio interview Flimm indicated what he was conveying with this production:

> The play shows how a man withdraws from all social connections, how he leaves, takes off, tries to evade his society, how he tries to begin a new life as a new person. How he tries to start afresh and to take up again with his friend Ekart. But he fails miserably and dies like a cornered rat, his claim to lead his own life, to realize himself, unfulfilled. This play describes, moreover, how the artist behaves in society, and how that society rejects artists who do not find its favour. Day-dreams of a violet sky do not guarantee success; in our present society there is no longer the freedom to realize great individual abilities.[8]

Flimm's production captured the mood of that young generation, who saw no future for themselves, who idolized popstars like David Bowie (who played Baal in an English television production of Brecht's play). In his songs they saw a reflection of their own anti-social attitudes: the only important thing is the heroic gesture when confronting the abyss, struggle is useless, there are no attainable goals, all that counts is that last moment of defiant self-fulfilment: 'Though nothing will / Drive them away / We can beat / Them / Just for one day / We can be heroes / Just for one day' ('Heroes').

Flimm's production also managed to convey an elegiac mood, awakening in the spectator a yearning for the lost landscape that informed and energized Baal. The urban jungle he dies in is reminiscent of Klaus Michael Grüber's staging of *In the Jungle of Cities* (Frankfurt, 1973). In this production the fight between Shlink and Garga is not even staged, but is only a haunting memory; the performers stumble wearily around onstage in a sea of old worn-out shoes. Through such innovations Grüber captured the nightmarish quality of memory and the wish-dreams for the future.

Most of Brecht's plays are not as involved in the conflicts, emotions and contradictions of the time as are, for instance, the plays of Kleist, Schiller, Büchner, or, indeed, Shakespeare. Perhaps these classics are sufficiently removed in time for us to be able to adapt them. Brecht is so foreign because he is still too close to the problems and miseries of our time, and so only seems to be antiquated. There are also quite persuasive contemporary productions of Strindberg, O'Neill, or Tennessee Williams: playwrights that Brecht despised for their preoccupation with psychology, their themes of sexual and familial conflicts, and the exploitation of private feelings.

Recently, of Brecht's major plays only *Mother Courage* has been performed with any frequency – in Bochum, as we have seen, and most recently in Vienna and Hamburg. The Burgtheater production in Vienna in 1986 was directed by the East German, Christoph Schroth, who also worked with the Berliner Ensemble. Mother Courage was played by Elisabeth Orth, the daughter of Paula Wessely. She was portrayed as quick and jolly, practical in a motherly way, a pleasantly bourgeois business woman. Schroth delivered a good, safe production, dialectically and politically Brechtian, i.e. school-marmish, with a little wit, a little finger-pointing, as if to say that war and peace exist in the world, but that war isn't really necessary. Brechtian lessons are taught in a gentle, friendly way – contemporary emphasis is occasionally given to props or costumes (a white police coat or a steel helmet, for example), there are projections on the scrims – everything is as it should be, yet it doesn't work.

The Hamburg production, directed by Wilfried Minks in 1986, was more courageous, smoother, zestier. Appearing as a resolute young Mother Courage was Eva Matthes, a wonderful actress, a veteran of Fassbinder and Kroetz, who had performed the whole gallery of young girl roles, from Desdemona to Joan of Arc, to Büchner's Marie. The Brechtian curtain fluttered, the band struck up and invited a sing-along, the whole thing was a half-hearted, carefree excursion into exaggerated cabaret: one must simply keep a stiff upper lip, whistle a happy tune, and not be intimidated by all these grousers and gloom-and-doomers around one.

You simply cannot approach Brecht by observing the scruples of Heiner Müller, Minks seemed to be saying. He sets his sights on mass audience appeal, and reaps the applause accordingly. Only fitting, then, that in this production a grand old lady of the popular theatre narrated the scene titles and the surtitles. This is a Brecht love-in, a cosy intimacy with Brecht, precisely where – especially with this anti-war theme – alienation, distance, shock are necessary to generate insights into the play.

Current productions of Brecht, then, seem to display only two approaches; well-meant school broadcasts – the pedagogical pointing finger – or simple delight in the fun of theatre. After all, Brecht the comic playwright cuts a good figure, and generates box-office. Many *Puntila* productions, the recent versions of *Arturo Ui* in Recklinghausen in 1986 and *Man Equals Man* in Frankfurt in the same year, and always *The Threepenny Opera* – these are not bad, but they are in the final analysis inadequate: the work of disillusioned survivors of 1968, who have overcompensated for their earlier humourless political theatre by producing vacuous comedy.

Man Equals Man in Frankfurt is an empty farce, only attesting to critic Alfred Kerr's scathing comment in 1928 that the characters playing the elephant were the highpoint of the performance. It lacks the provocative dialectic that Brecht learned from Karl Valentin or Chaplin; the audience seems happy to learn that soldiers drink a lot of beer, but the farcical tone blunts the comic edge, and turns it into actual beer-hall humour.

Mr Puntila and his Man Matti is the most popular hit today. Perhaps Brecht should not have even tried to adapt the original, since the plot itself suffices, in the hands of good actors: sharp, hair-splitting, love–hate dialogues between master and servant, brilliantly realized in, for instance, the Hamburg production of Frank-Patrick Steckel in 1983, or the Bochum production in 1985 with Traugott Buhre and Branko Samarowski.

In West Berlin the Freie Volksbühne managed to mount a successful production of *Puntila* in 1985, even with the otherwise wonderful comedian Otto Sander miscast as a sad, weary Puntila. The focus of the production was Katharina Thalbach as Eva Puntila, who self-confidently sets her hook for Matti against all logic of the original fable, but quite understandably in this context: the father is just a drunk, and the servant is a very sympathetic young man. But the production tries to create a kind of chummy intimacy with the audience, which simply destroys Brecht's intent.

Brecht never intended to affirm the public's opinions; in Brechtian terms, he wanted to provide insights in pleasurable form, or, put another way, he wanted to open their eyes and ears. Like all great poets he was no optimist. In Germany today, however, he is performed by disillusioned optimists who have lost their faith in life, who want to offset their own bad conscience by Brecht's good conscience. It was Heiner Müller who said that Brecht was a pessimist of the intellect and an optimist of the will. Müller always worked on his traumatic experiences and expected his public to learn through being shocked. He learned much from Brecht, not by imitating him but by changing him. As he said, 'There is much that is no longer possible after Brecht – or only possible in a different fashion'.[9]

Heiner Müller is the most important contemporary German playwright. His plays are inconceivable without Brecht, in that they developed through a dialectical discussion with him. Müller never imitated Brecht, but he learned from his method. Thus he translated or adapted for the German stage the plays of other famous playwrights – Shakespeare, Sophocles, Chekhov, and of course Brecht himself. And like Brecht he began to direct some of these adaptations – *Macbeth*, for instance – as well as some of his own plays. He is a very clever author, but his cleverness is not merely a gimmick to sell his own plays; it arises rather from pure curiosity. He asks the question, 'How can I assimilate other material, other ideas, without losing my integrity?' In collaboration with Robert Wilson, he seems to be exploring his own text to discover whether there are aspects to it that he never imagined, aspects that could be fruitful for some forthcoming project; this, of course, adds another dimension to Wilson's productions.

Heiner Müller has found a very convincing way of working both with and in opposition to Brecht. In his work Brecht is both preserved and challenged in a thoroughly convincing manner. He has said of Brecht, in a statement that is still valid:

> Brecht, an author without a present, a work between past and future. I hesitate to put this forward in a critical sense: the present is the age of the industrialized nations; our coming history, I hope, will not be determined by them. Whether it is to be feared depends on their politics. The categories of right and wrong do not apply to the work of art. The Statue of Liberty, in Kafka's version, holds aloft a sword, not a torch: to make use of Brecht without being critical of him is to betray him.[10]

Translated by Peter Harris

6

Ups and downs of British Brecht

JOHN WILLETT

1986 marked the thirtieth anniversary of Bertolt Brecht's death, and also the thirtieth anniversary of the first visit of the Berliner Ensemble to London, an event that changed the face of the English theatre. They came only a fortnight after the playwright had been buried in East Berlin, and his shrewd instructions to them about the special demands of an English audience are among his last writings. Moreover, in 1986 it was thirty years since my wife and I went to Berlin at his suggestion, to meet him, his family and collaborators, and the members of his company: the result of an article which I had written about him for *The Times Literary Supplement* the previous winter and of a meeting in London with Elisabeth Hauptmann, his long-standing collaborator and adviser on English life and literature. That was the time of the founding of the English Stage Company and the start of George Devine's direction of the Royal Court Theatre. Their production of John Osborne's *Look Back in Anger* would soon introduce a spate of new, outspoken, ungentlemanly authors, who had never been to Oxford or Cambridge, and would call for actors of a kind then alien to the West End stage.

The year 1956, then, seems to provide a clear starting point for the story of Brecht's reception and influence in Britain, as also for my own rather fluctuating observation of it. But before embarking on that we must not forget that a small but significant core of British interest in his work had been building up since the early 1930s, encouraged first by the Communist (and primarily anti-Nazi) cultural front in music, theatre and such magazines as John Lehmann's *New Writing*, and then by reports from America following Brecht's arrival in California in mid 1941. Auden and Christopher Isherwood had known and been impressed by his writings even before Hitler came to power; Stephen Spender translated one of his poems. But it was the pioneers in and around the old Unity Theatre and the Workers' Music Association – notably Herbert Marshall, André van Gyseghem, and the composer Alan Bush – who did most to familiarize left-wing audiences with his name, and to a very limited extent with his theatrical approach. Such politically grounded organizations were essentially amateur, even though some well-known actors came up through Unity's ranks; and their heyday coincided with the Popular Front movement and the years of Roosevelt's New Deal.

Then, after 1945, Brecht's ideas began coming to us again, this time from across the Atlantic and through the enthusiasm of Eric Bentley and Hoffman Hays, whose articles and translations became our main source of information about what Brecht had been up to since the outbreak of the Second World War. So we could read Hays's translations of *Mother Courage*, *Lucullus*, and some of the new poems, along with Bentley's critical writings and translations of the *Two Parables*, a few of the theoretical writings, and *The Private Life of the Master Race*. All these appeared before the original German texts, for which the world had to wait until the resumption of the *Versuche* in 1949, followed as late as 1955 by the first volumes of Suhrkamp's collected edition.

Finally, in the 1950s, there was Kenneth Tynan, who became theatre critic of the *Observer* in 1954, then more briefly of the *New Yorker*. By his reactions to the Paris productions of *Mother Courage*, first by the Théâtre National Populaire under Jean Vilar with Germaine Montéro as Courage, then by the Berliner Ensemble with Helene Weigel at the 1954 International Festival, he for the first time put Brecht on the British theatrical map – a map that in those days was effectively confined to about a square mile of London between Kingsway and Sloane Square. He also went to bat for Brecht against some of his leading detractors, such as Ionesco and the actor Richard Burton; and the Berliner Ensemble regarded him as an important friend. I never knew him well myself, but he was a strange and interesting man, capable of writing very brilliantly, and he had great theatrical flair, which gave him an infectious enthusiasm for Brecht as an author (if only in translation) and above all as a director. The immediacy of his judgements makes a startling and impressive contrast to the much slower acceptance of Brecht by the literary critics, who were (and in many cases still are) hesitant to acknowledge the writer's stature, and all the more so if German literature was their subject.

For until then the Germanists of the United Kingdom had shown remarkably little interest in Brecht, if indeed they knew of him at all. Admittedly a lot of his work was as yet unpublished, and the rest of it was not all that easy of access. But I cannot forget the reaction of one well-known university professor around 1950 when I asked him how he was going to handle Brecht in the book which he was writing on the German theatre. He had not read him, he replied, and clearly saw nothing odd in the fact. And this was part of a general British academic indifference to anti-Nazi writing throughout the period of the Third Reich, which not only forced so important an authority on Expressionism as the late Richard Samuel to move to Australia but also led to the exclusion of major exile periodicals (like Brecht's own *Das Wort*) from our libraries. Now, of course, there is a special branch of Germanistik devoted to 'Exil-Literatur', but the fact that it is hived off as such suggests that it has been put in a ghetto and is not yet accepted as an integral part of literature proper.

It was Kenneth Tynan, therefore, who broke through this awful indifference by vividly communicating Brecht's particular quality direct to our theatre two years before the Ensemble arrived in the West End to back up what he had said with their productions of *Mother Courage, The Caucasian Chalk Circle* and the Farquhar adaption *Trumpets and Drums*. The order of events at that time was as follows:

July 1954. The Berlin *Mother Courage* directed by Brecht and Engel in Paris, is reviewed by Tynan in the *Observer*.

June 1955. *Mother Courage* (in a patchwork English translation) is directed and played by Joan Littlewood with Theatre Workshop at the Barnstaple Festival. Carl Weber is sent from the Berliner Ensemble to advise, but is excluded from rehearsals.

February 1956. Blitzstein's adaptation of *The Threepenny Opera* is produced by Oscar Lewenstein at the Royal Court Theatre, with Sam Wanamaker as director. Brecht is consulted. Unlike the

New York production with Lenya two years earlier, it is not a box-office success. The newly formed English Stage Company takes over the Royal Court, under the artistic directorship of George Devine.

May 1956. The ESC performs John Osborne's *Look Back in Anger*, which sets the media talking about Angry Young Men, provincial accents, changing values, the new universities, and Colin Wilson's book *The Outsider*, all of which is seen as part of an English 'new wave'.

July 1956. The British- and French-owned Suez Canal is nationalized by a radical Egyptian government.

August 1956. Brecht dies in East Berlin. A fortnight later his company opens a three-week season at the Palace Theatre, London.

October 1956. Britain and France attack Egypt (the 'Suez War'). At the Royal Court Theatre George Devine directs *The Good Woman of Setzuan* in Bentley's translation, with Peggy Ashcroft in the lead.

November 1956. The USSR attacks Budapest and deposes the Nagy government. Cease-fire in Egypt and breakdown of the British prime minister.

Apart from the Berlin *Mother Courage*, which I had already seen in 1949, and Joan Littlewood's Barnstaple performance, I saw all the productions mentioned. In those electric days I was a freelance writer, living mainly in France.

From that point on, Brecht's plays and ideas have been part of our theatre – prickly, challenging, widely misunderstood and often contested. The impact of the poetry came only later, but over the years virtually all the plays have been performed one way and another: from *Baal* to *Turandot*, by amateur groups, drama schools, student theatres, fringe producers, travelling and provincial companies, followed in due course by the major London subsidized theatres and opera houses (all except Covent Garden). And some of our best actors and actresses have performed in them. Only the commercial theatre has held back, for obvious box-office reasons, much as it has in New York: big casts, difficult musical scores, low returns, high risk of boredom, the implied Communism whether of the play's message or of Brecht's own life in exile and later in East Germany. Since most Anglophones have the luck to live in free and reasonably stable societies I would guess that this last was not a major factor. But it certainly plays a part, whether for Brecht (among left-wing theatre people) or (among backers, right-wing critics and some outstandingly successful actors) against.

I did not like the English productions which I saw in 1956. Blitzstein's adaptation of *The Threepenny Opera* was too cute by half, with a lightweight Macheath and an amiable Peachum; I wrote an analysis of the text for Elisabeth Hauptmann. Peggy Ashcroft was much too sweet a *Good Woman* and an instantly forgettable bad man; part of the fault there, I felt, lay in the softness of Bentley's translation, which led me for the first time to make one of my own that would shun the slightly soppy implications of his inaccurate title. From then on I became convinced (as the current edition of *The Oxford Companion to the Theatre* now puts it) 'that the uncomplicated approach of amateurs under a good director can often do greater justice to Brecht than that of professionals with strong prejudices for or against'; and for many years I went to professional British Brecht productions with reluctance, if at all. For there was every chance that they would be positively embarrassing to anyone who had seen the plays done in German, by Brecht's own company or by others, and/or who knew the original texts.

This makes me a patchy witness to the process by which Brecht's theatrical influence gradually became evident in Britain during the 1960s: on the musical (*The Lily-White Boys* by Christopher Logue, a poet who had sat in on the work of the Berliner Ensemble before Brecht's death), on the biographical play (Osborne's *Luther* and Robert Bolt's *A Man for All Seasons*) and, above all, perhaps, on the production of Shakespeare with less conventional actresses, drabber costumes and a new emphasis on clear narrative and political substance. None the less there are professional Brecht productions which I remember with pleasure and admiration, such as the *Arturo Ui* which Michael Blakemore staged (originally for the Glasgow Citizens, then in 1969 in London) with the late Leonard Rossiter in the title part; I saw this after having seen Ekkehard Schall in the

Wekwerth/Palitzsch production, and still thought it brilliant. Likewise the Sadler's Wells *Mahagonny* directed by Michael Geliot, and the Half-Moon Theatre's productions of *The Mother* and *In the Jungle of Cities*, directed respectively by Jonathan Chadwick and Robert Walker. At the Royal Court, meanwhile, Brecht's own plays were taking a back place, though his example surely affected such emerging playwrights there as John Arden and Edward Bond.

In 1971, while the National Theatre was at the Old Vic, there was an interesting experiment when Manfred Wekwerth and Joachim Tenschert were brought in to adapt their Berlin production of the Brecht *Coriolanus* for performance by English actors using Shakespeare's original text. I saw this at a dress rehearsal, with Anthony Hopkins and Denis Quilley in the Schall and Thate parts, and thought it first rate: less thoroughly rehearsed than the marvellous Berliner Ensemble battle scenes perhaps, but with a much stronger group of Plebeians and, of course, a better play. It fell quite flat when it opened, for reasons which I have never understood. Then there was David Thompson's production of *The Good Person of Szechwan* at Greenwich, which broke new ground in two ways: for first of all it used Brecht's much shortened so-called Santa Monica version of 1943, which has Shui Ta trading in opium instead of tobacco; and it also had the dual role played by a man instead of a woman: two measures which knocked much of the easily exploited sweetness out of the play. The Santa Monica version, for some reason which again escapes me, has still never been published in German, though doubtless it will be in the new East/West collected edition. It can be reconstituted from the Methuen and Vintage Books English-language editions, which also include Brecht's outline of its story from the Suhrkamp *Materialienband*.

Since then there has been no falling off in the volume of productions, which have meantime so improved, on the whole, as to persuade even the sceptic that our theatre is now able to make something of Brecht: in other words that it is not just the exceptional performance which is likely to be worth seeing. Thus it is no longer quite so modishly 'Brechtian' to use Brecht's more superficial mannerisms (the projected titles, for instance, and the half-curtain); nor do you so often feel that he is being staged primarily because he is an irresistible challenge to the director and the leading actors, a kind of

Himalaya waiting to be climbed; but rather because of his tone of voice, his meaning. It feels to me now as if he were being seen as a direct riposte to the each-man-for-himself, weakest-goes-to-the-wall ethic of Mrs Thatcher's sub-Reagan government; he is being played with a greater sense of purpose, even if that purpose sometimes goes with an unduly simple and optimistic view of political theatre.

I may be getting naturally less critical, but I do nowadays find myself going to Brecht productions at the National, the RSC, the Almeida and other London theatres in a much less gloomy spirit than before. These may be flawed, like the National's *Galileo* and *Threepenny Opera* and the RSC *Courage*, but often the people involved are the first to realize the fact; in other words the *aim* is better. And during the 1980s I have seen some really good things, like Roland Rees's travelling Foco Novo production of *Edward the Second* at the Roundhouse, Di Trevis's *The Mother* with the Eisler songs at the Cottesloe (National), David Leveaux's *Trumpets and Drums* at the Guildhall School and Ian Giles's clean and direct *Fear and Misery of the Third Reich* at the little Croydon Warehouse. (Perhaps the most memorable of them all was the revival of *The Decision* at the Almeida Festival in June 1987, directed by Stephen Unwin and conducted by Robert Ziegler: seemingly the first proper performance of this stunning masterpiece anywhere for over fifty years.)

To round out all this growing theatrical experience of Brecht some brief reference should be made to the role played by broadcasting, and particularly by the BBC. The story really deserves separate treatment, starting with the first performance to a British audience of *The Threepenny Opera* (and indeed of any Brecht work) by BBC radio in 1935. But it is a matter of record that, from the 1950s on, much of the spade-work involved in introducing us to the plays was done by such Third Programme drama and features producers as H. B. Fortuin, John Gibson, R. D. Smith, and, most particularly, Martin Esslin, who eventually headed the drama department. In television, moreover, not only the semi-official BBC but also our commercial channels have followed suit. Here I recall a *Mahagonny* directed by Philip Savile, an *Arturo Ui* with Nicol Williamson in the title part and a *Caucasian Chalk Circle* with Sarah Kestelman (one of the rare English actresses who can sing the Brecht songs). Above all, in 1982 we had the BBC *Baal*, with David Bowie as the poet, in a production directed by Alan Clark. Bowie is a very strange actor, in that rehearsal to him is not so much a way of developing his part and his interpretation as a chance to try out a number of fresh and interesting approaches. I greatly admired his singing of Brecht's own tunes with their loose speech rhythms, though the hybrid sets and the routine competence of the BBC Television Centre rather dampened the effect. In the end the production lost its way between naturalism and artificiality, and I was involved enough to share some of the blame.

Brecht's plays and their production are of course only the most public and conspicuous aspect of something bigger; a coherent if often contradictory body of work which adds up to an aesthetic, a philosophy rooted in the history of his time and his country: something that embraces not only his own writings (of all sorts) but also his use of close collaborators in other media. Whether our actors and directors will ever get the best out of the plays without exploring this wider area of his creativity is doubtful, and at the centre of it lies the Methuen Brecht edition which bears the general title *Plays, Poetry and Prose* and started appearing in 1970. Originally intended to appear volume by volume in parallel with its Random House equivalent (which ground to a premature halt), and edited by Ralph Manheim and myself, this aims eventually to include all the plays.

In addition we have published short stories, diaries and the bulk of the poems, and are currently preparing an edition of the letters. The songs and poems from the plays will follow, likewise a supplement to *Poems 1913–1956* (which itself came out in 1976), and in due course the *Working Journal*, a volume of dialogues and a new edition of the critical prose. One of the most interesting points here is that the *Poems* volume is now into its third or fourth edition though neither Methuen nor Random House ever reckoned that it would sell. I am convinced that this is the most important volume that we have yet published, and moreover that its chronological arrangement gives it a certain advantage over the existing German editions, making it a part not only of the literature but also of the history of those forty-odd years. For the poetry has always been the real core of Brecht's plays, from *Baal* onwards, and its strength justifies and informs those aspects of his theatre which in themselves are open to criticism, and might otherwise irritate or bore an audience.

It is the poetry, not the actual situating of the plays (other than *Fear and Misery of the Third Reich* and possibly *Drums in the Night*) that deals directly and by closely concentrated observation with the events through which he lived; and so, unless we start with the poetic element, we may fail to see quite why his writing is all that passionately relevant to our own world. Even when he wrote, he had little concern with surface topicality, preferring to work by parable, intellectual analogy and emotional detachment; with the result that today it is tempting to see his plays as being about the theatre and its techniques rather than about life off stage. And yet it is just at this distance in time that the German experience as lived by his generation and conveyed in his poetry seems so tragic, moving, exciting, often heroic and creatively stimulating in a way that is all the more instructive because we have not yet been through it ourselves. It has slipped into history, lurking below the surface of the present-day two German states. Yet, because it remains controversial and capable of giving pain, the evidence of such eyewitnesses of the first half of this century in central Europe has come to have a special value, and never more so than when it is so beautifully and condensedly expressed.

Perhaps this combination of pain and remoteness comes across most sharply when the witness is a communist like Brecht, just because the ideals of that movement were once so high and so optimistic. Their memory, as conveyed by him, makes a bitter contrast both with recent accounts of the German anti-Nazi emigration in Stalin's Russia (by David Pike and others) and with the demolition of some of the old bases of communism by today's consumer ethos. The changes which these have brought in the outlook of a country like ours are not so much a sign that Brecht's world has disappeared into the past, as some younger playwrights evidently believe, but rather a charge against our own less hopeful age – not least against those left-wing parties who fail to give any focus and discipline to the visions which for many people express socialism's aim. There are poems of Brecht's which encapsulate so much, and move so economically from the small specific object to the great human issues, that they are almost unbearable to read aloud. This is where the study of his deeper relevance for our own time has to begin.

In other directions, more tangential to his actual writing, there is a new awareness of the wider implications of Brecht's work. Thus, for the first half of 1986, Caspar Neher's stage designs were exhibited in

England – the first such exhibition outside the German-speaking countries, and their only representative showing anywhere in the last twenty years. There could hardly have been a better corrective to the kind of design exhibitionism which has been invading our richer theatres than Neher's beautiful concentration on the movements of the play; and the show's 160 drawings from Austrian, German and British sources, reinforced by photographs, tapes, dummies and projections, were stimulating both for those concerned with the visual arts and the visual aspect of the theatre and for the creative exploitation of Brecht's ideas.

There has also been a great increase in our understanding of the musical element of Brecht's work. To some extent this is an international phenomenon, owing much to such bodies as the Viennese group 'Die Reihe', the New York Kurt Weill Foundation and the Berlin Hanns Eisler-Chor; and musicians can view it as part of the shift away from pure hermeticism to more intelligible and socially purposeful musical forms. But it also affects our theatre musicians – notably those engaged by the Almeida, and by the National Theatre under the composer Dominic Muldowney – and whereas in the 1960s it was rare to hear Weill's Brecht settings played authentically, or Eisler's and Dessau's played at all, the situation has now changed radically. This has brought a new concern with the problem of how to sing such works, and the difficulty found by conventionally trained singers (with their vibratos and their preference for vowel sounds) in communicating the texts set by the composers of this whole non-purist school. Here we have a remarkable model in those performances by Eisler himself which are interspersed among his conversations with Hans Bunge recorded between 1958 and 1962: an unbelievable mixture of wheezing, grunting and croaking delivered with great musicality and dramatic and literary sense by a small round man short of breath, in such a way that you hear every syllable, every consonant, every semicolon.

Now available on a set of East German records, these are what inspired the virtuoso singing of the Austrian composer-chansonnier H. K. Gruber, who recently performed at the Almeida and on BBC television with his colleagues of 'Die Reihe'; and they also influenced the two Brecht records which Robyn Archer made for EMI with Muldowney, John Harle and the London Sinfonietta, starting in

1981. Together with David Bowie's 1982 RCA record of five *Baal* songs, using Muldowney's arrangements of the Brecht tunes, this lugs the most vivid and attractive part of Brecht's theatre out of the special realm of Berlin exotica, making it relevant to our own musical and poetic concerns.

Ever since Max Frisch made his often-quoted remark about Brecht's being reduced in Germany to the 'penetrating ineffectiveness of a classic' we have heard complaints from other countries that Brecht is no longer interesting to the Western theatre, that his ideas are old hat, the premises of his thinking no longer valid; in short, that rigor mortis has set in and cannot be broken until the Brecht heirs start allowing go-ahead directors to reinterpret and rewrite his works in their own up-to-date ways. This is, of course, patent rubbish; but it does seem nevertheless that the West German theatres have gone off Brecht during the last decade or more; the East Germans (including the Berliner Ensemble itself) no longer have anything infectiously new to say about him; the Slavs associate him, wrongly but understandably, with a discredited Socialist Realism; while, as Bernard Dort says, the French too often dismiss him as a relic of the 1960s. Is the English theatre then all that different? So far as I can see, it is. For here the ups and downs of Brecht's local fortunes are not so much changes in his reputation and theatrical status – seminal today, boring tomorrow – as changes in our grasp of his achievement. In Britain he has always been both seminal and boring, depending on how he is presented and understood; and what goes up and down (but on the whole more up) is our ability to understand and present him.

The picture of those thirty years as I have sketched it, from an admittedly subjective point of view, is of a nagging obsession with Brecht's work: work that has throughout intrigued and challenged the theatre, while increasingly attracting those in the other arts and media and eventually making its way (via people like Bowie and Sting and Jim Morrison and some of the pop critics) into the awareness of a younger and wider audience. Only the grumpiest objectors, basing themselves partly on the old cold war accusations and partly on a new, not entirely convincing shock-horror reaction to Brecht's sex-life, are still trying to pull him down; but in spite of recent feminist support they have lost a certain amount of credibility in the last thirty years, and carry little weight in our generally left-inclined theatre.

Why, then, should we see Brecht so differently from our opposite numbers in other countries? What distinguishes us from the United States, to start with, is our important sector of subsidized theatre, not only in London but throughout the country: without this the production of the plays would seldom be feasible outside schools and colleges. But many European countries have a firmer structure of subsidy than Britain, and yet it is they who have been turning their backs on Brecht. I cannot help wondering, therefore, if it is not the sheer gradualness of our assimilation of his work that has made it deeper and more durable than theirs. We are slow learners when it comes to foreign works and ideas; but we have been steadily learning about Brecht since 1956, and what we do learn tends to stick.

There are, however, persistent snags and faults in our understanding which it will still take time to overcome, and perhaps the most constructive conclusion which I can provide to the Anglo-Brecht story is to set out some of the main obstacles as I now see them. They are, in no particular order:

(1) Self-importance. Our theatre has become a temple of (almost Thatcherite) individualism, in whose upper levels of acting, direction and design Ego Rules OK. The trouble is that Brecht himself had a weakness for stars, particularly outside Germany: he wanted big names for his plays even where they were not all that suitable – Gielgud for Galileo, he told me for instance – whereas the unorthodox and unestablished are more likely to have the straightforwardness and fresh spirit needed to put his work across.

(2) Love of spectacle. Alas, none of the directors who understand Brecht seem truly expert at spectacle in the Lloyd-Webber mode, and even *The Threepenny Opera* demands a smaller and simpler stage than the National gave it last year in the Olivier Theatre.

(3) Strained topicality. Those directors who are frightened that Brecht's political message isn't topical enough for today often try to work in 'contemporary' references in the form of slide

projections or video material or even changes of text and setting. In our country, where the German experience between 1919 and 1945 has uncomfortable lessons for us, this blurs Brecht's point. As with Shakespeare, either the man has something to say to us or he doesn't; and you can't improve matters by dressing the play up differently.

(4) Anglicization. Making Brecht's soldiers act like the British army; his clergy like the Church of England; his workers or peasants speak Cockney or yokelese. Cosy for the actors, but disastrous for the play.

(5) Adding 'earthiness' and a 'plebeian' touch by a liberal sprinkling of words like 'fuck'. Brecht was the reverse of snobbish, but he was not very informal and he was sparing with his obscenities, which were never pointlessly used.

(6) Mangling the verse. There are two common ways of doing this in our theatre: (a) by ignoring the punctuation and the line breaks and speaking Brecht's irregular free verse as if it were prose; (b) by putting too much performance and self-expression into the words, as though the actor must somehow be betraying his profession if he does nothing more than communicate them clearly.

(7) Ditto for singers. Obscuring the sense by vibrato and treating the text as secondary, a mere pretext for the emotions of the music.

(8) Dropping the standard Brecht settings in favour of inferior ones by the director's friends and colleagues.

(9) Having the translation done by well-known writers unaccustomed to Brecht's original language. This is not a question of errors (easily correctable) but of false rhythms and, above all, mistakes of *tone* such as lead straight to misinterpretations of character by the actors. Not that it takes a particularly best-selling writer to create these, but the practice of going by names rather than linguistic competence in the choice of translators is a sure recipe for trouble.

Such are some of the more glaring handicaps to the proper understanding of Brecht in the United Kingdom as they have emerged since our theatre first got to know him in 1956. They are still being met with, and they leave us with a lot more to do. He cannot be immobilized yet; the ups and downs must go on. Nobody can sit back and say, 'Now we know it all.'

7

Crossing the desert: Brecht in France in the eighties

BERNARD DORT

In the 1980s Brecht is no longer a force to be reckoned with in the French theatre. He is indeed still performed, but mechanically, as if his work belonged to the conventional repertoire. Moreover, he is generally thought to be dull, that is, when he is not dismissed as old hat.

Although it is difficult, if not impossible, to obtain precise figures,[1] generally speaking about eight plays by Brecht are performed each year – although for 1985 I could find a reference to only three. The number is nevertheless considerable, although it is paltry in comparison with the statistics for the Federal Republic of Germany, which averages about eighteen plays and forty-three productions each year. However, it is certainly fewer than there were in the sixties and seventies.

Generally speaking, these productions are mounted by small theatre companies. Brecht is no longer performed by the National Theatres: he is not acted at the Comédie-Française – although its former director, Jean-Pierre Vincent, made his reputation working on Brecht – or at the Odéon, Chaillot, or at the Théâtre National de Strasbourg. *Round Heads and Pointed Heads* was presented at the Théâtre National de L'Est Parisien in 1981, but the production was brought from Belgium, performed by the Studio Sainte-Anne, and directed by Philippe van Kessel. Brecht is better served by the Regional Centres for Drama: *The Life of Galileo* by Marcel Marechal at Marseilles; *Man Equals Man* by Phillipe Adrien, then at Ivry; *The Threepenny Opera* by Martin-Barbaz at the Centre du Nord-Pas de Calais. So much, then, for the subsidized theatre. The commercial private sector continues to ignore Brecht. All that remain are the small companies, who perform Brecht fairly regularly. Brecht has returned to his starting point.

Which plays are still performed? The great works of his maturity – *Mother Courage* or *The Good Person of Szechwan* – are no longer at the top of the list. Preference is given to his early works, the plays of the 1920s: *In the Jungle of Cities*, *Man Equals Man*, *The Threepenny Opera* have recently each been performed at least three times, as opposed to one performance each for *Mother Courage*, *The Caucasian Chalk Circle*, and *The Life of Galileo*.

Who performs Brecht nowadays? The old guard of the period after decentralization, who fortified themselves on Brecht during the sixties, now refrain from performing him. Years have passed without a production by Roger Planchon or Guy Retoré. Marechal has directed *The Life of Galileo*, and Bernard Sobel has returned to Brecht only through the intermediation of Heiner Müller, and his adaptation of Brecht's *Fatzer* fragment. The situation of the third generation after decentralization is even more striking. They have all, at one time or another, flirted with Brecht. They now keep themselves at a distance. One thinks, for instance, of Jean-Pierre Vincent and of Antoine Vitez. Oddly enough, Georges Lavaudant is the only exception. His starting point was not Brecht but rather Robert Wilson or Carmelo Bene. He has now turned to Brecht, and his production of *Puntila* in 1978 was certainly the last of the great Brechtian productions to follow decentralization. The second production, which he added to the repertoire of the Théâtre National Populaire, where he joined Planchon, was the diptych *Baal* and *In the Jungle of Cities*, which was presented at the end of the 1986/7 season. Finally Brecht has been deliberately avoided by the so-called New Mannerists (or neo-Romantics?) – one thinks of Alfredo Arias, Claude Regy, and Daniel Mesguich. Only Ariane Mnouchkine remains. The influence of Brecht is to be found in all her work. However, the Théâtre du Soleil has never directly attempted a play by Brecht. In 1968 the Théâtre du Soleil projected a production of *Baal*; they worked on it, but it never materialized. Didactic pieces have always been part of the training of the actors at the Théâtre du Soleil. Without the example of Brecht's epic theatre, *1793*, if not *1789*, would have been inconceivable. Mnouchkine's most recent production, *L'Histoire terrible mais inachevée de Norodom Sihanouk roi du Cambodge*, is rooted as much in Brecht as it is in Shakespeare.

The publication in France of works by Brecht has also declined. L'Arche has published a major part of his writings and has proposed new translations or revised and corrected editions of the plays, but since the appearance of Brecht's *Working Journal* (1976), which appeared less than three years after it was first published in Germany, and his early *Journals* (1978), L'Arche has not brought out any important work by Brecht. The *Letters* have still not been translated, neither have the *Materialien*; editions of variant versions of the plays have yet to appear in print. The only recent Brecht publication of any consequence was the fine complete edition of *The ABC of War*, published by the University Press of Grenoble (1985); but that had little impact. The Bibliothèque de la Pleiade has announced the addition of Brecht's plays and poetry to its lists: it is a consecration of sorts, but we might have to wait a while for its appearance.

The end of the seventies saw the appearance of several summings-up of Brecht's achievement: the two volumes of *L'Herne*, the *Obliques* collection and also the pamphlet by Guy Scarpetta: *Brecht ou le soldat mort* (1979).[2] Today the time for syntheses, like that for polemic, seems to have passed. Studies are narrower in scope and less ambitious: for instance, *Bertolt Brecht penseur intervenant* by Jean-François Chiantaretto,[3] or *Celui qui dit oui, celui qui dit non, ou la réception de Brecht en France (1945–1956)* by Daniel Mortier.[4]

Even the thirtieth anniversary of the death of Brecht in 1986 provided no occasion for celebrations or for reappraisals. If one spoke of Brecht at all, it was because Strehler was directing *The Threepenny Opera* at the Châtelet. And then he was mentioned with some reservations. Brecht was ignored in discussions about the theatre. I remember a round-table discussion about the German theatre that was held at the Centre Pompidou at the beginning of 1986: with the sole exception of Bernard Sobel, all the theatre practitioners present were, whether intentionally or not, silent on the subject of the author of *A Short Organum*. Concern with Brecht is viewed as a regression, a return to the early 1950s and the heyday of the Cold War. No further proof is needed than an article that recently appeared in the music section of the newspaper, *Libération*, which suggested that Kurt Weill be rescued from Brecht's clutches:

> Let's face it: it is really a good thing that rock music today has taken over the music of Kurt Weill, and in particular the songs on which he collaborated

with Brecht. It restores them to their aspect of threadbare and mocking refrains, bruised banterings, streetsingers' complaints, finally rid of their shitty Marxist implications. Let Bertold [*sic*] go and stuff himself. Dirty bastard! For if there is something worth saving in Brecht and Weill, it is above all that poetic realism, that '*fantastique social*' so dear to Mac Orlan. We are fed up with Bolshevik propaganda and with Brechtian 'distanciation'. We now know the exact extent of that distance: 24 cm, the length of a Nagant revolver; 7.62 mm, the standard handgun of the NKVD.[5]

Have we parted company with Brecht? Will he continue to exist as a survivor of and witness to the 1950s? Obviously not. Although he may, at the moment, be going through an arid period, Brecht is not entirely absent from the French theatre. His influence is still felt there, although in a less impressive and striking way than it was two or three decades ago. To perceive this we must first retrace our steps.

The first appearance of Brecht in the French theatre coincided with the overwhelming movement towards decentralization. He was absorbed into the ideology of the 'Popular Theatre'. Jean Vilar opened his first season at the Théâtre National Populaire at the end of 1951 with *Mother Courage*. The Berliner Ensemble productions at the Théâtre des Nations of *Mother Courage* (1954), *The Caucasian Chalk Circle* (1955), *The Life of Galileo* (1957), *The Resistible Ascension of Arturo Ui* (1960), and *The Mother* (1960) nourished a whole generation of new directors. At the forefront of these were Roger Planchon, Guy Retoré, and Gabriel Garran. Brecht appeared at that time to be the touchstone of the popular political theatre to which the proponents of decentralization aspired. He was also something of a bugbear: in the view of the established commercial theatre and of right-wing or centrist local authorities he was synonymous with indoctrination and subversion. He was not, therefore, acted in the old subsidized theatres, with the exception of *Mr Puntila and his Man Matti*, directed by Retoré for the Comédie-Française but presented at the Théâtre Marigny (1976), and of the adaptation of *Antigone*, presented by Jean-Pierre Miquel at the Odéon (1972). Nor was Brecht acted by the established independent theatres, for instance the Company Renaud-Barrault. On the other hand, he was one of the most popular playwrights on the stages of the decentralized theatres. According to statistics established by the Association Technique pour L'Action Culturelle (ATAC), in 1972 he was the third most performed playwright, with 48 productions, far fewer to be sure than Molière, who was represented by 136 productions, or Shakespeare (84), but more than Chekhov (38), and Marivaux (34).

These Brecht productions were the fruit of a compromise between French stylization, inherited from Copeau and the Cartel, and a sometimes servile imitation of the Berliner Ensemble. Some of them seemed, from the Brechtian perspective of the periodical *Théâtre populaire*, with which I was associated, cursory and tainted with populism (one thinks particularly of Jean Dasté's *The Caucasian Chalk Circle* of 1956). Nevertheless, perhaps for that very reason, they appealed to their own public. They were, moreover, the occasion of triumphs of acting, of Jean Vilar as Ui, Georges Wilson as Puntila, and Jean Bouise as Schweyk in Planchon's production of Brecht's play. Some of them, especially the memorable *Arturo Ui* of Vilar, had a particular impact because of the contemporary political situation: for *Ui* it was the Algerian war and the ambiguous circumstances of de Gaulle's return to power. Nevertheless, in spite of their numbers and their success, these productions were not sufficient to establish a French Brechtian tradition. That was, perhaps, because they remained hybrids, and therefore vulnerable. The majority of theatre professionals, among them most of the young actors, were not particularly interested in Brecht: he was not immediately established as a truly popular playwright.

Another aspect of Brecht came to attention in the 1960s; a Brecht not of the major plays but of the didactic pieces, of the youthful works and of the fragments. Two productions served as models: *The Bourgeois Wedding*, directed by Jean-Pierre Vincent and Jean Jourdheuil in 1968 (subsequently revived several times), and *The Business of Bread* by Manfred Karge and Matthias Langhoff, presented by the Théâtre de la Commune d'Aubervilliers in 1972, which was the French version of their *Brotladen*, presented by the Berliner Ensemble the previous season. These marked a departure from the models established by the Berliner Ensemble in the 1950s. They were distinguished by their humour, by a high-spirited, even ferocious style of acting, and by what one might call a new scenic materialism, which borrowed from developments in painting, particularly the new representationalism, and broke with Brechtian orthodoxy. This was the context for productions such as *In the Jungle of Cities* (1972), also directed by Vincent and Jourdheuil; *Baal* (1976), directed by André Engel at the Théâtre National de Strasbourg; *The Caucasian Chalk Circle* (1975) at the Théâtre de Liberté under the direction of Mehmet Ulusoy; *Mother Courage* (1973), directed by Antoine Vitez in a version which appears polemical when compared with the famous model conceived by Brecht himself; and, finally, *Mr Puntila and his Man Matti*, directed by Georges Lavaudant for the Centre Dramatique National des Alpes at Grenoble in 1978.

What all of these productions shared, despite wide differences in style, was a similar stance of rejection. Gabriel Monnet, who played Puntila in Lavaudant's production, justified it: 'We no longer acted Brecht as past Brechtians had done, that is to say from within. We picked him up, we looked at him as if he were an externalized object. There seemed to be no reason why we should not treat Brecht as we treated Shakespeare and Musset.'[6] This rejection went far beyond the rejection merely of Brechtian models, it included the whole of the Brechtian *vulgate*. André Engel's production of *Baal* was performed not in the main stage of the Théâtre National but in the horse-breeding establishment at Strasbourg. The public was invited to follow the journey of Baal from the riding school to the courtyard of this establishment, passing through the stables, which took on the appearance of departure platforms: the distancing did not depend on the separation of the stage from the auditorium, it was inscribed rather in an itinerary undertaken by both the actors and spectators. Lavaudant employed the main stage of the House of Culture at Grenoble, but he did not create a reproduction of Finland, exotic as that might have been. Rather his *Puntila* is set on a highway, at the very spot where it runs out, poised over the sea or mere vacancy. At the end of the play the back of the stage is opened up, and Grenoble itself appears as part of the stage picture. Matti sets out for this very town, abandoning once and for all the theatre of his master, Puntila, and attempting on his own behalf the conquest of society and of reality. Moreover, Lavaudant rejected the farcical elements, the 'popular' comic aspects of *Puntila*:

> Personally I don't like farce. It doesn't appeal to me unless it is very abrasive, very violent . . . in fact one would like to get rid of the whole hearty aspect of the play: cigars, rakes, buddies, but also the open air, crayfish, and sunsets. One should undermine and erase this whole dimension of good living: this

façade conceals a state of crisis. The setting contributes in a way to this effect since the stage is covered with tarmac, and for most of the time it is raining on this highway.[7]

The response to Brecht in the 1970s was divided. On the one hand his work was seen as suited to the theatre of intervention or agit-prop: the small theatre groups which, after having gravitated around the Théâtre du Soleil, sustained themselves on Dario Fo and then on 'The Theatre of the Oppressed' of Augusto Boal. Moreover, Boal was himself impressed by *The Jewish Wife* and *Fear and Misery of the Third Reich*: he incorporated them into his 'theatre forum'. For all these groups the Brechtian text served only as a means of approaching reality and of activating the spectator-participant, yet the intent is recognizably closely related to that of the didactic pieces. On the other hand, Brecht was scoured for answers to questions concerning the theatre and the nature of representation itself. Lavaudant, indeed, set this up as a sort of agenda: 'I want the audience, when it leaves *Puntila* to say not only "There are lousy bosses", but also to ask "What is the scenic space? Why do we have theatre? How do you act this scene?" These are also questions that interest me.'[8] Brecht's dramatic technique is used either to undercut the scenic fiction or it becomes a means of theatrical self-questioning itself. Its central preoccupation, the relationship between the analysis of reality and the analysis of dramatic illusion, remains unaddressed.

One sees here the inability of recent French theatre to convey the full impact of Brecht's work. In some measure this inability is the result of Brecht's very success. His techniques have been used and abused, and have frequently been applied in a very mechanical way, servilely imitating the normative productions of the Berliner Ensemble. No doubt the proliferation of misunderstandings about distanciation has also contributed to this failure. Possibly the French word *distantiation*, which is a poor equivalent for *Verfremdung*, has something to do with it: it implies a measure of remoteness of the actor from his role and from his character. We have sought for and greatly overvalued the concept of the cold and distant actor. We have chosen facility and attenuation. At times actors have opted for detachment: and in doing so have condemned themselves to sterility. The result has been a predictable Brecht, a Brecht without surprises; and astonishment is an essential part of *Verfremdung* and is possibly even its driving force. In short we have rejected process in favour of procedures. We have behaved like the coachman in Brecht's remarks on *The Life of Galileo* who, coming into contact with the automobile when it was first invented, and 'mistrusting the practical instructions accompanying it . . . would have harnessed horses in front – more horses, of course, than to a carriage, since the new car was heavier – and then, his attention being drawn to the engine, he would have said, "Won't work here."'[9]

However, it is not only Brecht's theatre practice that is at issue. That the French theatre has distanced itself from Brecht is also the result of the cultural climate and of changes in ideology. One can speak of the return of repression, the repression that has occurred since this theatre first put to the fore its civic, political, and even revolutionary mission. I am not so much concerned with the choice of repertoire (although in terms of 'modern classics' Chekhov now seems to have the edge over Brecht), as with the conception that the actors have of their profession and of the role this type of theatre assigns to the audience. As far as the actors are concerned, the result is obvious: narcissism once more holds sway. A new wave of Stanislavskyism, heavily tinged with Actors' Studio methodology, has swept over our theatre schools and the products now occupy our stages. The stage, far from being thought of as a platform or podium, is conceived of rather as an intimate or private space where the actor can discover and fulfil himself. Listen, for example, to what Claude Régy has to say about teaching at the Conservatoire: what he requires from his students, and, indeed, from the actors he directs as well, is to plunge 'into the depths of their being, and to show without fear the most violent, the most horrible, and the most secret things that had previously always been concealed', finally 'to lead them out of themselves'.[10]

The proliferation of one-man or one-woman shows, or the presentations of purely literary texts by one or two actors has the same effect. No doubt there are economic reasons for this: it is the result of having to mount productions on a small budget. It is also the result of complacency on the part of the actor. The actor is his own subject. What he expects from the audience is not a political commitment or a judgement, but complicity. The desire for identification once more haunts the theatre. And this identification is aimed not at the role or the character but at the spectator himself in the same quest, the same alchemy. One realizes that the objectives of this theatre – which are not those of the French theatre as a whole but of what is for the moment a not inconsiderable part of it – imply a rejection of Brecht. It considers him crude and obtuse.

It is the entire French intellectual climate that is to blame. There is no doubt that it is characterized at the moment by a rejection of the idea that thought is capable of changing the world. We have moved from a period of criticism (that is to say of 'negative thought') to one of assertion. It is not just that Marxism is in crisis. Certain intellectuals have made it their major aversion: often those very intellectuals who around 1968 had hailed it as the ultimate science and philosophy. They exalted Brecht as a precursor of what they took to be the thought of Mao Tse-Tung. This connection is not of my own making; they wrote at the time in *Tel quel* of the Brecht of 'la scène rouge'.[11] Today they reject him precisely because of the way in which they had caricatured him then. As we are told on the cover of Guy Scarpetta's *Brecht ou le soldat mort*, 'Acted everywhere, read and commented upon, Brecht seems to be the ultimate and incontestable example of that monstrosity: militant art.' Guy Scarpetta has had enough of this idolatry, of the unanimity which it provokes, and of the antiquated mythologies that accompany it; hence his book, the first major attempt to demystify the Brechtian imposture. Having shattered the stereotype, Scarpetta reveals a new image of Brecht, one that is infinitely more narrow, dogmatic, and totalitarian than that of the generally accepted legend. He reveals a Brecht characterized by reductive theatrical conceptions, blind to modern art, and in fundamental agreement with the logic of Stalin; a Brecht unable finally to carry the fight against Fascism to its conclusion, to pull it up by its roots, and sympathetic, however obscurely, to tendencies such as anti-semitism. But this book is more than a simple attempt at demystification: through the figure of Brecht, Scarpetta poses questions about the relationship between the cultural avant-garde in the twentieth century and totalitarianism. He reveals the connections that paradoxically can link a revolutionary writer to the most abject regressions of modern barbarism.

No doubt *Brecht ou le soldat mort* has already fallen into oblivion, like the work of the 'new philosophers' of the end of the 1970s with which it is associated. But, going beyond the affectations of fashion, a question nevertheless presents itself: what do we do with Brecht when we have, I will not say rejected Marxism, but renounced all concept of what Brecht termed 'an intervening thought', when we no longer think that it is possible or necessary to change society and the world, when thought no longer assigns itself the task of establishing the possibilities? In one of his last pronouncements, a piece written for the Fifth Darmstadt Colloquium on the Theatre in 1955, Brecht stated that in order to be reconstituted by the theatre, 'the present-day world can only be described to present-day people if it is described as capable of transformation'.[12] This is a point on which he did not waver: his objective was always 'to bring the present-day world, present-day men's life together, within the theatre's range of vision'.[13] He never ceased to believe that this vision of the transformability of the world alone gave drama a conceptual basis. Yet, in contrast to preceding decades, the present dominant ideology is sceptical of this transformability, even when it does not reject it out of hand. What good, then, is Brecht?

No doubt it is impossible today to accept Brecht's work as a whole without reservations. It belongs to history, to our history. Perhaps it is afflicted by what Max Frisch called 'the penetrating ineffectiveness of a classic'. The question remains open. Perhaps Brecht is merely a classic: the witness of a past age. If so, one must distinguish the theoretical and practical disposition from the dramatic texts, and treat the latter as one does all classical texts – that is to say, with a sense of their difference. But, divorced from their context are they still of any great interest? For Brecht's texts have, perhaps, only a limited autonomy; they are tied to a certain vision of the theatre and of the world. Or does Brecht nevertheless remain, at least in part, our contemporary, in which case his projects still concern us. If so, it is possible, even essential, to come to terms if not with the totality of his works then at least with fragments or selected moments from them. I mean by this not simply one play or another, chosen from his various works, but rather his concept and practice of the theatre, and a general idea of its function.

This second hypothesis is obviously the one that I share. It is also corroborated by the facts. Such an approach to Brecht persists and bears fruit, as in the 1986 production by the Théâtre du Soleil: *L'Histoire terrible mais inachevée de Norodom Sihanouk roi du Cambodge*, with a text by Hélène Cixous. Although it was successful and filled the Cartoucherie for almost an entire season, the press was curiously reticent about it; although they praised it, they scarcely discussed it, and passed in silence over its implications. As a result it has not been sufficiently noticed that this was in every way an epic production in the Brechtian sense. And the Brechtian inspiration cannot merely be attributed to an imitation of Shakespeare; indeed it is questionable whether one is entirely compatible with the other.

It is certainly true that the failure of Strehler's *The Threepenny Opera* at the Châtelet offers evidence for the first hypothesis. The production was far from negligible. In essence it picked up from Strehler's earlier productions of the work in 1956 and 1972. These two productions, particularly the first, were memorable. But it was clear that something was no longer working. The Brechtian dramaturgical machine was no longer functional, even though the scenic machinery was almost up to scratch. Not that Strehler was unfaithful to his earlier productions, or that the new production was artistically inferior (putting to one side for the moment the distinguished but polyglot cast); rather he adhered too closely to them. He was faithful to their letter but not to their spirit. Since 1956 the world and the theatre and Strehler himself have changed. In reviving *The Threepenny Opera* he behaved as if nothing had changed. The 1986 production was presented not as if he were dealing with a classic, but as if the work were self-sufficient and had only to be true to itself. In spite of the success of certain details, the overall failure was the result of this larger cause. *The Threepenny Opera* is not yet a classic. Perhaps it will never be one. It is a work written to be presented in the context of a specific dramatic method and of a particular point of view. It does not survive self-congratulation; and the work of a director, of an epic director like Strehler, survives it even less.

But let us return to the Mnouchkine production to formulate some aspects of what I shall call the Brechtian paradigm, that is, to define in more detail the positive lessons that the contemporary theatre may draw from Brecht. Without doubt, among the most important of these acquisitions is the art of the parable. The productions of the Théâtre du Soleil confirm this: in order to speak of that which is close to us we should travel by a roundabout route. In fact we should take a double detour: we should travel via Cambodia and Sihanouk in order to confront the problems of our own national independence and of a government dominated by a single individual, be he de Gaulle or Mitterand; we should travel via Shakespeare, and via the Shakespearean Chronicle Play, to dramatize materials that are painfully contemporary. To this art of the parable we should add, in the case of *Sihanouk*, the use of epic narrative: what the spectacle of the Théâtre du Soleil tells us is not merely what happens, a series of events, but rather an occurrence and how it occurs. Action, here, is converted into fable: it is made intelligible by virtue of the fact that it is presented as a succession of events and as a process, and that it articulates a point of view from which the events are narrated. It is the Théâtre du Soleil which recounts this 'terrible and unfinished history'; no one else; neither historian or witness; without a sense of being present, of having taken part in the events. And those who present it are committed actors, who are well informed, but who do not pretend to know everything. They do it to engage the audience. They do not make a distinction between the audience and those who act and speak. Brecht's language does not pretend to be universal. It is impossible to take a short cut by asking who is speaking, and on whose behalf.

Another acquisition is the idea of the *Gestus* – or, more precisely, the social *Gestus*. What was extraordinary in the Théâtre du Soleil production was not the way in which some of the actors presented their characters, which were not particularly complex, but rather the way in which they showed how they comported themselves, carrying each *Gestus* to its conclusion, without allowing one to contaminate the next. The actors did not construct a character. What they presented rather was a series of comportments, which might be contradictory. Sihanouk (Georges Bigot) could at one moment be as playful and light-hearted as a comedian in the silent cinema, and at the next he could be as contorted and self-absorbed as a product of the Actors' Studio: he played one *and* the other. He would be at one moment a fully realized imp and then a Buddhist priest. It is the spectator who is astonished, and who is compelled to understand and contemplate it. Character is a result of this; something shared between the actor and the audience; not a given. It has been remarked upon, notably in

Walter Benjamin's comments on the epic theatre, although it has not been sufficiently realized in practice, that Brechtian acting is a series of comportments. It is both concrete and discontinuous; and this style of acting is not limited to Brecht. How else would one act Shakespeare?

One should also consider the role that Mnouchkine assigns to music, beginning with her Shakespeare productions. Indisputably she is inspired by Far Eastern models. But these are not incompatible with Brecht. One can too easily overlook Brecht's close working relationship with composers, from Weill to Dessau and including Hanns Eisler, who influenced him profoundly, and the importance that Brecht attributed in the development of his epic theatre to what he called gestic music. Here too, without precisely imitating Brecht, the Théâtre du Soleil conforms very closely to his practice.

However, it is in its concept of theatricality that the Théâtre du Soleil is most Brechtian. In fact, a production like *Sihanouk* presents us with a twofold critique: that of the theatre as an illusion that is taken for a reality, and of life imbued with a certain theatricality in the ferment of totalitarianism. This extends to Sihanouk himself, in demonstrating the exceptional character of the individual, while also revealing his blindness and impotence, and his inability to seize his historical destiny. Nothing could be more like Brecht. Does not his theatre, after all, propose a twofold analysis of life and of the theatre simultaneously – of a theatre that purports to imitate life, and of a life that takes on the dimensions of theatre? In the contemporary theatre the same thing is to be found, perhaps, in the work of Robert Wilson.

Brecht is not as absent as a superficial analysis of his role within the contemporary French theatre might suggest. He may not be as prominent and as influential as he was twenty years ago. Yet, while he might not be contemporary, he is not situated outside of time either. Towards the end of the 1960s Bernard Sobel and Antoine Vitez spoke of him in much the same terms: one wished to put 'Brecht and his heritage in disequilibrium'.[14] The other declared that he did not feel the need 'either to rescue or not rescue him', but rather 'to deal with him'.[15] Though they hardly achieved their aims, nevertheless they at least suggested a way in which Brecht might be put to good use. It is not a question of returning to an unqualified adoption of Brecht, nor of totally rejecting him with the exception of a few texts. Rather, one should start by acknowledging his lack of relevance (which does not exclude the possibility that one might from time to time underline his contemporaneity). Brecht's work has become historical. To present him is to relativize him or to 'distance' him. It is to take account of the distance that separates us from him. It is to recognize how tangential he is to the history of the last thirty years. Nevertheless, taken on its own, such an approach would send us back to the concept of Brecht as a classical playwright, which I have already said appears to me to be utterly sterile. If we have to relativize him it is because in this way we will be able to preserve him. In this way we will be true to his objectives and to his dreams: the vision of a theatre and of a world united in its contradictions, which is constantly changing and transforming itself.

Rereading the last section of *A Short Organum*, one comes once again across the following quotation:

> That is to say, our representations must take second place to what is represented, men's life together in society; and the pleasure felt in their perfection must be converted into the higher pleasure felt when the rules emerging from this life in society are treated as imperfect and provisional. In this way the theatre leaves its spectators productively disposed even after the spectacle is over. Let us hope that their theatre may allow them to enjoy as entertainment that terrible and never-ending labour which should ensure their maintenance, together with the terror of their unceasing transformation. Let them here produce their own lives in the simplest way; for the simplest way of living is in art.[16]

Brecht in our time can only be fragmented, historical, and Utopian. As Heiner Müller declares, he is 'awaiting history'.[17] But, while we too await it, we can discover the traces of a tragic history that he lived to the full, and distinguish the traits of a fortunate history which he never ceased to dream about. Nothing is more relevant, or more fertile. For Brecht presents us precisely with the means of conceptualizing and representing the bonds that unite history and Utopia: that is indeed the subject of some of his plays, for instance, *The Life of Galileo* and *The Caucasian Chalk Circle*. I spoke at the outset of 'crossing the desert'. I will not retract that phrase. Do not forget, however, that crossing the desert is also a stage on the road to the Promised Land, although it entails heavy losses, and lacerating reappraisals.

Translated by Colin Visser

8

'His liberty is full of threats to all': Benno Besson's Helsinki *Hamlet* and Brecht's dialectical appropriation of classic texts

PAUL WALSH

Estimates of Bertolt Brecht's legacy to modern theatre are often based on notions of a Brechtian style, pieced together from his plays, his theoretical writings, and the modelbooks that document his directorial work. By concentrating on Brecht's own plays and the staging innovations he introduced in them, we have neglected his radical rethinking of the relations of theatrical production that link dramatic texts, producers (directors, actors, dramaturges, designers), audiences, and society. In this we have ignored that aspect of his work which points beyond the particular Brechtian corpus to challenge theatrical tradition itself and the means by which it is transmitted and sustained. Ironically, this oversight has facilitated the accommodating absorption of Brecht's plays and theories into the very repertory they set out to challenge. By reducing Brecht's theory and theatrical practice to a question of style, the organic tradition of which T. S. Eliot wrote has accommodated and defused even this most contrary impulse.[1]

One way this absorption is achieved in the theatre is by promulgating the sovereignty of the text as an immutable object rather than as the product of a particular matrix of productive relations. A text is reread in terms of a prescribed performance style reconstructed from 'legitimate' past readings and renderings. To be 'true to the text', one must play its 'style'. Thus, for example, when Brecht's plays are produced – but only then – theatre practitioners are held to the letter of 'Brechtian law' (which is how his theories are reconstituted). The repertory as a whole is spared from subversive examination of the structures of power and authority that sustain it. The power exercised over the repertory by tradition is particularly evident in the disposition of authority over classic texts. Who, ultimately, speaks for the classics? The answer is simple if not quite obvious: 'tradition' does. The classic text is subsumed under the authority of tradition and tradition adjudicates over appropriate readings and acceptable renderings.

This simple delineation of logocentric spheres of influence tames potentially discordant works by reducing the terms of discourse to legal or quasi-legal issues of text and style. This allows such works to be assimilated into the eclectic corpus of the contemporary repertory and re-interpreted in terms of dominant and often inappropriate productive relations.[2] Within the domain of modern Western eclecticism, for example, a lack of personal commitment is called versatility, while acquiescence to authority is masked as a sincere respect for the intention of the text. Brecht sought to free actors and directors, and their audiences, from such hierarchies of power embedded in tradition by replacing acquiescence to authority with personal commitment to exploring and elucidating in production the relationship between past culture and present function. This was among the major thrusts of Brecht's theatre work at the Berliner Ensemble and motivated his theoretical practice during the last decade of his life.

From his 1946 production of *Antigone* in Switzerland to his death, Brecht wrestled with issues of accommodation and tradition. Turning from the generalized parables of his wartime exile in America, he sought to uncover the historical specificity and concrete reality of plays from the classical repertory. In his effort to bring the classics of Western culture to bear on the task of building a new Germany on socialist principles, he tried to establish a repertory and a standard of acting that incorporated the old in a new way: a repertory that included Lenz, Goethe, Kleist, Hauptmann, and of course Shakespeare ('without whom a national theatre is almost impossible').[3] Of the twenty-one plays performed by the Berliner Ensemble during his lifetime, just under half were by contemporary playwrights. Five of these were by Brecht.[4] The greater part of the repertory was made up of critical adaptations and interpretations of old plays.[5]

With the number of pressing problems facing the German Democratic Republic at the time, it seems curious that Brecht should have turned to plays from what he called 'the dawn of classicism'[6] – plays by Lenz, Goethe, Farquhar, and Molière. Yet, as Heiner Müller observes, Brecht's 'adaptations of classical theatre do not represent an attempt to circumvent the demands of the day but rather a revision of the revisionism of classicism and its tradition'.[7] In this, Brecht's approach to the classics was informed by the productive exchange of what Robert Weimann calls 'past culture turned present function'.[8] The classic text and its historical context were reread from the perspective of present concerns and issues. Exploring the relationship that links a particular production with a larger tradition and examining that tradition in terms of the real and present needs of society, Brecht and the other members of his Ensemble sought to uncover the historical specificity of the text in rehearsal by playing it back from the present into what Brecht called 'the historical situation prevailing when it was written'. This includes, but is not limited by, 'the author's attitude and special peculiarities'.[9]

By resiting the text in the context of ongoing history (made new by the accumulated knowledge and experience of the intervening years), a production aims first to clarify and elucidate the socio-historical, political, and economic realities that conditioned the text's production and original reception. This brings out contradictions displaced, or silenced in the text. Revealed by the Ensemble through exploratory rehearsals, these contradictions are then analysed and elucidated in terms of the concrete physicality of performance and the *mise en scène*: design, gesture, characterization, blocking.[10]

The approach is that suggested by the Philosopher in *The Messingkauf Dialogues*. By 'treat[ing] the text as a report which is authentic but has several meanings', textual authority is superseded. 'I'd say the writer's intentions were only of public interest when they provoked the public's interest', the Philosopher of *The Messingkauf Dialogues* expostulates:

> His words can be treated as sacred if they are the right answer to the people's questions . . . If he respects these interests and respects the truth, then you should follow him; if not, then amend him.[11]

An adaptation of a classic text must help to articulate the interests and needs of the public for whom it is intended; this public, as always for Brecht, 'earns real contemporary money and eats real contemporary beef'.[12]

Brecht's adaptations often involved considerable mending of the original to emphasize what had emerged through historical recontexting. His unfinished adaptation of *Coriolanus*, for example, is only about 60 per cent as long as Shakespeare's original, and of this about 17 per cent is wholly new. In his adaptation of Farquhar's *The Recruiting Officer*, Brecht retained only about one-third of the original and rewrote two-thirds, advancing the action to the 1770s to incorporate sentiments and documents from the American revolution that elucidate issues of imperialist expansion intimated in the original. Still, as Arrigo Subiotto points out, the effect of the adaptation is very close to that of the original: 'qualitative differences are a result of Brecht's travelling further along the path tentatively indicated by Farquhar'.[13] In this Brecht held fast to his purpose: to recoup for future, politically progressive generations what he called the 'original freshness, the element of surprise . . . of newness, of productive stimulus' that are the hallmarks of classic plays.[14]

The productive vitality of this dialectical method of critical appropriation is evident today in the work of contemporary directors such as Peter Stein, Giorgio Strehler, and Benno Besson.[15] Of these, Besson is the least known in North America. Called Brecht's 'most brilliant student' and a major figure in the Brecht school, Besson worked at the Berliner Ensemble from its founding to Brecht's death, collaborating on adaptations of plays by Lenz, Molière, and Farquhar.[16] He directed Brecht's *The Good Person of Szechwan* at the Berliner Ensemble in 1957, and the world premières of Brecht's *Days of the Commune* with Manfred Wekwerth in 1956, and *Turandot* in 1965. At Brecht's death, Besson left the Berliner Ensemble for Berlin's Deutsches Theater and later the Berlin Volksbühne, where he worked with some of the finest playwrights in the German Democratic Republic (including Heiner Müller, Peter Hacks, and Hartmut Lange) on adaptations of Aristophanes, Sophocles, Shakespeare, Molière, and Lenz.

Besson has spent much of his career pursuing Brecht's 'revision of the revisionism of classicism' and the results have been stunning. His 1979 production of Shakespeare's *The Tragicall Historie of Hamlet, Prince of Denmarke*, mounted in Helsinki at the Swedish-language Lilla Teatern,[17] employed the processes developed at the Berliner Ensemble to elucidate a text that had drawn considerable attention and commentary from Brecht during his lifetime and comment upon its position within the contemporary repertory. Besson's analysis of the play's fable and his resiting of it in the dialectics of history recall Brecht's own reading of the play and its title character. Through Besson's production, the full complexity of this reading becomes clear.

When Brecht adapted *Hamlet* for broadcast on Radio Berlin in 1931, he began with a deft transposition of Horatio's lines to Fortinbras from the end of the play to a narrative prologue that promised the audience a 'brilliant example of medieval drama' telling 'Of carnal, bloody, and unnatural acts/Of accidental judgments, casual slaughters . . .' (V.ii.370ff).[18] Brecht refocussed attention from the personal fate of the title character to the social relations of feudal war-lord society and historicized Hamlet's acquiescence in the barbarity of the society in which he lived. 'Hamlet is quite simply an idealist who collides with the real world and gets knocked off course,' he wrote some years later, 'an idealist who becomes a cynic. To act or not to act is not the question, but whether to be silent or not be silent, to condone or not condone.'[19]

For Brecht, Hamlet's fourth-act vision of 'Fortinbras and all the fools he's found/March[ing] off to battle for that patch of ground', as he wrote in his 1938 sonnet, 'Shakespeare's Play *Hamlet*', is the turning point of the play: 'At that his too, too solid flesh sees red./He feels he's hesitated long enough. It's time to turn to (bloody) deeds instead.'[20] In Brecht's reading, Hamlet betrays his new-found humanist approach to reason because he lacks a socially viable praxis: 'Faced with irrational practices, his reason is utterly unpractical. He falls a tragic victim to the discrepancy between such reasoning and such action.'[21] He sets aside his 'so human and reasonable inhibitions' against slaughter to embrace the old feudal hierarchies that inscribe violent retribution in an acquisitive desire for power. Forgetting the natural nobility he had attributed earlier in the play to all men, Hamlet re-iterates the unnatural hierarchy of social violence and proves in the end to be 'most royal' (V.ii.387).[22]

Shakespeare ended his play in a compromise with theatrical convention and an earlier version of the story. Formal compromise mirrors Hamlet's own tragic embrace of the role of avenging barbarian. Brecht commented on this in his *Working Journal* after seeing a production of the play in Helsinki in 1940: 'All this thinking and planning, all this agony of conscience ends uncertainly, haphazardly, in a chaos of intrigue and accident.'[23] A few years later he re-iterated his view of Shakespeare's recidivistic characters and called for an end to such 'Barbaric delights!': 'We know that the barbarians have their art. Let us create another.'[24]

Benno Besson's production of *The Tragicall Historie of Hamlet, Prince of Denmarke* speaks to this challenge by re-examining Shakespeare's text in the light of Brecht's reading. Besson sought not to disguise the barbarity of represented events but, through a use of popular stagecraft, to break the mesmeric hold traditionally enjoyed by the title character over the audience's perception of the world of the play. Like Brecht, Besson focussed on the historical nature of this historical tragedy to separate the play from its most famous character and open the way through critical distance to a fuller exploration of the social relations depicted in the action. This he achieved through an accelerated pace, physical and gestural exaggeration, and defamiliarizing masks which drew attention away from Hamlet's psychologizing soliloquies and soaring poetry to the sociology of power at court. Besson brought the events of the play to bear on the character of Hamlet rather than allowing the play's most famous and persuasive character to dominate the audience's response.

The most striking innovation of the production was Besson's use of masks. This served several functions. It restored the legendary stature of characters who are often viewed in individual and personal terms, emphasizing function and social status over psychological nuance. It freed actors from a tendency to play themselves by theatricalizing roles and their interrelatedness. No longer able to rely to the same degree on personal or daily habits of interpretation and communication, actors had to explore new relations with the text and the audience. Designer Ezio Toffolutti spoke of this in his programme note when he suggested that the use of masks 'forces the actor to express his role . . . with the whole body, attaining a more concrete representational mode'.[25] Similarly, the audience had to break with habits learned from film and television of reading individuals entirely through facial expressions rather than through interactions and relationships. Audience attention was directed to the presentation of the role rather than to the presenter. The masked actor becomes less an individual than a part of history and of the overall structure of the play.

Behind the mask of Hamlet, Besson cast the talented comic actor Asko Sarkola. Capitalizing on Hamlet's childish impertinence and his egocentric need to dictate the terms of discourse in each of his verbal encounters in the play, Sarkola used exaggerated gestures to elucidate both the historical sources and the social consequences of Hamlet's dilemma. Here the attempt to resolve contradictions between a historically new thought and the haunting demands of past and present experience was acted out at a rakish pace. Hamlet entered for the 'To be or not to be' soliloquy at a dead run, exhibiting the mad countenance that earlier had so affrighted Ophelia. Spinning like a child's toy around the dagger in his hand, Sarkola bellowed through the opening of the play's most famous speech then slackened to a deadly serious and threatening halt at the sight of fair Ophelia. Though a departure from tradition, this is not out of keeping with the antically disposed character of Shakespeare's text.[26] During the Mousetrap scene, Sarkola played Hamlet's intention to 'tent' the King 'to the quick' quite literally (II.ii.583), probing the King with the point of his dagger and threatening to open a wound if none could be found. The old violence haunted the new order in Hamlet's every gesture. At Claudius' hasty departure from the evening's entertainment, Sarkola draped his character in a tattered mantle and raved like a 'very-peacock' (III.ii.274) in possessive superiority.

At times exaggerating, at times playing counter to the 'memorable scenes' of the play or ignoring them completely, Sarkola tore the text from the incidental iconography that accompanies traditional renderings. He avoided, for example, the visual poses associated with Hamlet's mordant fifth-act reveries over 'poor Yorick' and instead impaled the skull on a nearby spade to make a grotesque, impromptu puppet that he led giddily around the stage mimicking the way his father's ghost had led him around in Act I. The 'fine revolution', which Hamlet has the trick to see and fear (V.i.84), was re-inscribed in the traditional hierarchy of social power: of rulers and ruled, of revengers and victims. The gravediggers and Horatio – the calmly rational and deeply saddened counsellor – registered the audience's dismay at the mad decadence of this royal court rotting in its own contradictions.

The original vitality and power of the text, negated by enervating tradition and sensational eclecticism, was revived by the disruption of expectations in a rich application of the dialectics of *Verfremdung*.[27] While nuances were lost, much was gained; above all, as Bengt Jahnsson notes in his review of the production: 'that one comes to ponder over *Hamlet* in a new way'.[28]

Unlike his mentor, Besson left Shakespeare's text virtually intact. The only major cuts were Claudius' confession speeches (III.i.49–54; III.iii.35–73). This redoubled the audience's suspicions about Hamlet. While not tampering drastically with Shakespeare's text, however, Besson emphasized story over poetry, pacing the play at a breakneck speed that served to 'make the connection of events credible' as Brecht had instructed in *A Short Organum*.[29] What was lost of the savorous beauty of Shakespearean language was compensated for in the renewed clarity of the story, the rich design, articulate groupings and gestures, and the tragi-comic tone that refocussed audience attention on the flow of the action and the social relations mapped out in it.

Toffolutti enclosed the proscenium stage in a net of coarse rope hung with panels of billowing parachute silk that were raised or lowered to suggest various locales. Bengt Jahnsson described the effect: 'Hamlet, the court and the world are imprisoned in this net. The gaps are large, however. Anyone can come and go. But they all believe they are prisoners.'[30] A clearly defined pattern, masked by shifting appearances, defines the society of the play; existing structures can be escaped from or broken through but the characters internalize them and are imprisoned in repetitions. Hamlet's dawning self-consciousness – what Besson calls 'his insight into his concrete identity'[31] – intimates a possible dismantling of old hierarchies. In his mortal terror and morbid fascination, however, he fails to realize this potential and escapes instead into an adversarial madness that replicates the uncomprehended structures that govern this society.

Predominant here is the feudal hierarchy of paternal authority which Besson sees as the source of both 'Hamlet's illness' and the worship of masculine violence and acquisitive retribution that marks our own century. 'The bourgeois enlightenment of the eighteenth century', Besson wrote in his programme note, enthusiastically set out to uproot the feudal past. In the name of progress it believed it could quite simply suppress this past in the depths of the unconscious, in the metaphysical night of the 'Dark Ages'. The ghosts of that night haunt us all the more. Knightly honour and courtly ideals, the unconquerable revenger, the ghost, all return from the dead. And it is precisely this spirit of knighthood and knightly honour which dresses up that cruellest form of human violence: paternalism . . . In our century, the spirit of knighthood walks again in the heroes of westerns and thrillers who, with their fingers on the trigger . . . poison our children of 'the scientific age' with splendidly agreeable images.[32]

From his modern perspective, Besson examined the apparent contradiction between the barbarity of Old Hamlet's war-lord ethos and the more subtle barbarity that governs the rationalized court of the brother-slayer Claudius to uncover a more striking contradiction. The rationalized society ordered by domestic control and international law merely replicates in displaced form the power structure it sought to escape.

The socio-political determinants of this structure and its consequences for social relations are clearly indicated in the opening scenes of the play. Besson gave particular prominence to Horatio's recitation of the recent history of the state of Denmark (I.i.79–107), lines often cut in modern productions. Presented as a jocular lecture on imperialism by a comic-opera buffoon, Horatio's song-and-dance recital of 'the main motive of our preparations,/The source of this our watch, and the chief head/Of this posthaste and romage in the land' (I.i.105–7) probed, in a memorably entertaining fashion, the bowels of a society bent on future wars. The naïve presentation of Horatio's sophisticated exposition underscored that which was being expounded,[33] preparing for Fortinbras' eventual triumph and emphasizing the private nature of young Hamlet's ruminations by setting them in an international perspective that emanates from outside the fictional frame of the story. Similarly, Claudius' opening address to the court (I.ii.1–66) emphasized the temporary nature of the compromise of Machiavellian statesmanship with the old order of feudal war-lords. Contradictions were smoothed into lulling similitudes as Claudius, dressed in civilly balanced pastels and lace, flitted around the court circumscribing affairs of state and family with leisured efficiency and rational dignity. Swords were out of place; Claudius' weapons were mobility and diplomacy, vigilant surveillance, and an authoritative *fiat* which sent ambassadors and informants to the ends of the earth. Movement was control. The full import of Claudius' rhetorical appropriation of the world would not become clear until the play's end when the contradictions worked their way back to the surface and the doors were opened to Fortinbras, the truly vigilant and efficient new war-lord, who combines the power of Old Hamlet with the order of Claudius to supersede them both.

Hamlet, a passive outsider at court, has shirked both the warrior ethos of his father and the rationalized order of his stepfather in favour of a new humanism based on reason. At his first appearance he is draped head to toe in a black lace shawl that Gertrude draws off at 'Good Hamlet, cast thy nighted color off' (I.ii.68). Hamlet can neither escape the court nor can he escape the haunting presence of the old order of fathers and sons. Old Hamlet returns in Act I to force his son to toe the line, wrestling him to the ground and pummelling him with his tale of retribution. Hamlet covers his ears and blubbers in terror: 'I am bound to hear' (I.v.5–6). The contradiction of speech and gesture, in this scene and throughout the production, marks the violence of what the ghost unfolds. The father's command – 'So art thou to revenge' – enters Hamlet's ears like poison. As he acts out his father's narrative of the scene in the garden, he is reduced to a writhing mass.

The source of Old Hamlet's power is clearly the oversized sword he carries in his hand. Old Hamlet bequeaths this power to his son in the form of an ironically diminutive dagger, which Hamlet carries until his fifth-act transformation on returning from England. The dagger serves as a grotesque reminder of the ghostly order Hamlet had wished to escape. It defines his every gesture and limits his actions. As Hamlet tries and fails to find a use for it, the dignified introspect of tradition becomes a gesticulating, erratic clown infected by a libertarian madness that is 'of threats to all' (IV.i.14). Eventually (on his return from England) Hamlet embraces a more threatening madness that replicates the mendacious rationality and manners of the court.

The full terror of this ultimate madness is marked for the audience by the reactions of Horatio. From the start Horatio has served as an observer of events at court and in the world, and as mediator and interpreter for the audience. While his devotion to the prince is unyielding, his silent criticism of Hamlet's misplaced energies and excesses grows more intense as the play progresses. The absolute horror that Horatio registers with his eloquently ambiguous question, 'Why, what a king is this!' (V.ii.62), after being told of the death of Rosencrantz and Guildenstern marks the cruel transformation that Hamlet has undergone in his absence from the court. Through Horatio's silence, the audience sees another possibility, a vision of a different course and a different outcome unexpressed and uncomprehended in the play.

A second contradiction emerges as the motorforce of the drama: a contradiction between the liberation of humanist reason and the repression of hierarchical violence, either in its war-lord ethos or rationalized as law. The latter is more insidious as it purports to extend reason to social interaction but serves only to mask the old patriarchal hierarchies under a new guise. By focussing on the moment of historical transition in which a consciousness conditioned by the barbarity of the past confronts the promise of renaissance humanism, Besson found in *Hamlet* new substance for a contemporary audience caught in the anguish of late capitalist class alienation and disillusioned with the failed humanist vision. Hamlet's introspection proves costly precisely because he lacks a viable praxis, which prevents him from seeing clearly beyond himself and taking action on behalf of the community. He is unable to marshal his admirable qualities to deal with the real problems of the world. Instead he is haunted by the past and entrapped in old paradigms that he chooses to call his fate. Besson's desentimentalized treatment of the fable and its legendary characters allows the audience to cut through the cult of personality and see the story from the perspective of our own present and possible future.

In such a situation, Claudius' particular guilt for the murder of Old Hamlet is hardly at issue. More to the point are the uses made in the play of the power of fathers over sons and over daughters.[34] Besson emphasized the tragi-comic implications of this society's entrapment in an Oedipal desire to replicate old hierarchies. He graphically illustrated, for example, the incestuous source of Laertes' controlling advice to Ophelia in Act I, Scene ii (where Ophelia was literally carried on stage astride her brother); similarly he demonstrated Polonius' jealous regard for family honour at the expense of his offspring in the several advice speeches and spying scenes that define his function at court. Later, Claudius recalls these paternal gestures when he persuades Laertes to avenge his father's death.

Ophelia is the most obvious victim of this patriarchal control, and her tragedy is made all the more poignant because it is played out in a madness truer and more desperate than Hamlet's. She is used, then reduced to silence by her family and by the court. Lilga Kovanko played the mad scene in a torn and bloody dress – raped and beaten by a battalion more real than Claudius' battalion of sorrows (IV.v.78–9). The urgency with which she entreated the royal couple – 'Pray let's have no words of this', pointing to the blood on her dress (IV.v.46) – underscored the violence of her situation and the extent to which she had silenced all thought of herself in acquiescence to the power of others. Like Horatio and even Gertrude, she is reduced to passive silence. And it is through the dismissed and dispossessed figures that the audience comes to judge the play.

In an interview published in 1983, Besson objected to the suggestion that, as heir to a Brechtian legacy, he was bound by an inherited style:

> Brecht pondered, felt, considered things in a remarkable manner. It was a sort of standard he gave. Each took what they wanted. But it was not an inheritance. As far as I'm concerned, I am unable to say what was given to me. In any case, this 'thing' – I can't name it – [was] perhaps a kind of attention to the world, a sensitivity, a sensuality. And also a respect for everyone on stage, a tactfulness, an enormous respect for actors . . .[35]

Denying the patrilineal implications of inheritance, Besson frees both himself and Brecht's theories from hierarchical metaphors of legal and economic paternalism to suggest new relations of production and transmission based on attention, sensitivity, sensuality, and respect. What he claims to have gained from Brecht is a heightened awareness, to which he gives expression through a theatrical practice of his own that reveals the relevance of Brecht's principles and the productive exchange between past culture and present function explored in his work at the Berliner Ensemble to the new cultural terrain that has opened up in the thirty years since Brecht's death.

Besson's production of *The Tragicall Historie of Hamlet, Prince of Denmarke* offers an example of how Brecht's experiments in adaptation and appropriation of classic texts open the way to a reassessment of not only a particular text but of the adjudicating authority ascribed to tradition, including the authority ascribed to 'Brechtian tradition'. In extending Brecht's approach to classic texts to more general issues of cultural production in the present world, Besson applies the Brechtian standards of commitment and sensitivity to the task suggested by Robert Weimann: 'to stimulate a *Praxis* by which the culture that we receive and the culture that we leave behind can be made to meet and engage in struggle through potent interaction'.[36]

9

Blocking Brecht

MAARTEN VAN DIJK

Over thirty years ago, after watching Brecht's staging of the Berliner Ensemble production of *The Caucasian Chalk Circle* in Paris, Kenneth Tynan made one of his vatic pronouncements:

> Unless we learn it soon [Brecht's method], a familiar process will take place. Thirty years from now Brecht will be introduced to the English critics, who will at once decry him for being thirty years out of date. The ideal way of staging *Henry IV*, *Tamburlaine*, *Peer Gynt*, and a hundred plays yet unwritten will have been ignored; and the future of the theatre may have been strangled in its cot.[1]

It would therefore appear legitimate to inquire at this distance in time, or at this time of 'distancing' Brecht, to what extent his ideas on the practical aesthetics of theatrical production have been absorbed by the English-speaking world, and if there is anything still to be learned from his method. To what extent was Tynan's prophecy correct? From the evidence it would appear that two things have happened. Like the other greatly influential theoretician of this century, Stanislavsky, Brecht seems to bear out what Eric Bentley said of the Russian director: 'Perhaps many are sure what they see: but others are sure they don't see straight.'[2] There seems to be a general assumption among Anglophone theatre practitioners that Brecht's theoretical writings lead to Marx, or to confusion, or to further aesthetics, or to academic hairsplitting, instead of directly to theatrical practice.

Secondly, Brecht's photographic models of his productions and his advice about how to put them on have been seen by most modern directors as placing impossible constraints on their creativity and originality. The folly of following Brecht's directions, it appears, has been demonstrated. They point to the current 'museum-like' productions of the Berliner Ensemble, and the failure of 'faithfully Brechtian' productions like William Gaskill's National Theatre *Mother Courage* of 1965. They argue that the originally fresh elements of epic staging – visible, bright lighting, half-curtain, minimal sets, 'cool' acting style and so on – have become either clichés or, as in the case of the Ensemble, fetishes. The Germans, for their part, seem to suffer from terminal Brecht burn-out. John Willett describes the English state of Brecht-play more hopefully (or dialectically) in 'Ups and Downs of British Brecht'. In North America, apart from university or experimental groups, the major theatres experience Brecht as box office, if not political, poison. The 1987 Stratford, Ontario, production of *Mother Courage*, directed by John Neville, played to 26-per-cent houses.

Thirty years after Tynan's warning, the 1983 Royal Shakespeare Company production of *Mother Courage* made his remarks seem eerily significant. And because this was touted as an important revival – the first really major production in England for twenty years in one of the national subsidized theatres – for which the RSC had long made plans (and had long held the rights), it will be treated symptomatically here, letting the one stand for the many, in order to give a sharp focus to a discussion of what has been learned about Brecht, and what there still is to learn about him as a practical theatre man, with specific reference to blocking. The RSC *Mother Courage* raised several questions that will explain this paper's punning title. What is the block so many Anglophone directors have about Brecht? Why do they seem to block his intentions in their work? Why are they so reluctant to learn from a carefully worked out practice that could be useful to any director in blocking a play? Why does the blocking of the characters in a production of a play by Brecht nearly always lack the realism and story-telling clarity of the famous photographs of the models?

As publicity previous to the opening of the RSC *Courage* stated, twenty years really was a 'long and shameful period of neglect' for an acknowledged modern masterpiece.[3] With Judi Dench, a fine comic actress, in the lead, directed by Howard Davies, who had previously mounted *The Days of the Commune* for the RSC, designed by John

Napier, responsible for the epic sets of *Nicholas Nickleby*, and with a new translation specially commissioned from the hot young playwright and screenwriter, Hanif Khureishi, the production was intended to be a major event. Instead it was a major disappointment. The critics found it difficult to agree about the reasons. Some blamed the unwieldy set, others the lack of emotion displayed by Judi Dench; but most chose, as usual, to blame Brecht, who was 'long on politics, short on humour' (*Plays and Players*); who only 'creates cartoon sketches' (*The Month*); whose 'underlying theories emerge as simplistic or too generalised' (*Plays and Players*); who in this play numbs us with a 'constant reprocessing of the same material' (*Sunday Telegraph*).[4] Michael Ratcliffe in the *Observer* seemed to sum up a prevailing view among the critics, even those who had talked of masterpieces: 'In practice an austere and over-extended chronicle whose length and episodic nature have always seemed to me repetitive rather than inevitable.'[5]

The critics also generally agreed that this production was an attempt at 'revisionist Brecht'.[6] Howard Davies, who was said to 'know his Brecht', had announced his intention not to follow the modelbook, but to catch 'the spirit of the original'. He had purposely left it very late in rehearsals to consult the model in order not to be 'dictated to by it'. Davies took this approach because of his experience directing *The Days of the Commune*, which he felt had been a failure for being 'too derivative'. In his opinion the 'Brechtian idiom is too much a part of our theatre language now for it still to shock and disturb'.[7] And Michael Billington, the *Guardian* critic, applauded 'the attempt to jettison the museum-piece approach to Brecht' which had been a problem with other English 'sub-Berliner Ensemble productions'.[8] Hanif Khureishi also said that one of the things he was hoping to do with the play was to 'make it warm and funny, instead of it being a kind of long, tedious, stodgy, anti-war play. I wanted Mother Courage's warmth to come out.'[9]

Casting Judi Dench, whom *The Times* called an 'actress of legendary warmth', was no doubt part of this revisionist intention of providing a new kind of Brecht production; for, as her director said, she 'contradicts conventional expectations of the kind of actress suited to the role'.[10] Miss Dench in an interview before the opening said, 'I didn't read *Mother Courage* until the day before rehearsals', and director, designer, and translator all gratefully acknowledged they had never seen a production of the play.[11]

In the face of such carefully nurtured protection from the dangerous ideas of the playwright, so proudly proclaimed, one might have expected a fresh, warm, original production. But, instead of demonstrating the director's assertion that the Brechtian idiom was too much part of our theatrical language to shock and disturb, his production shocked and disturbed through its complete unfamiliarity with the idiom. The traditional ignorance of the critics was as nothing compared to the ignorance of those in charge of putting the show across. John Napier's 'original' set was a major handicap. A Heath Robinsonish, neo-constructivist treadmill, with the wagon at one end and an abstract cart-tent-flag at the other, with a weathervane in the middle, it did not work on opening night and was still regularly out of order months later. Flaps refused to open or close, objects fell off, and the wagon often got stuck. As a result, the performance of Miss Dench, it was generally acknowledged, suffered 'death by scenery'.[12] The critics were unanimous, however, in commending the performance of Zoe Wanamaker as Kattrin, and she subsequently won the British Theatre Association award for Best Supporting Actress. Yet she was patently giving an exhibition of the False Pathos Brecht excoriated in *Theaterarbeit*. She had a generally sentimental view of the role, which found extreme manifestation in the variety of inarticulate noises she uttered throughout the performance. At the end of the scene in which Courage decides not to go with the Cook to Utrecht and abandon Kattrin, Miss Dench gave Kattrin a warm hug. Miss Wanamaker responded with wide-eyed wonder – a look which clearly meant, 'Why, she *hugged* me!' Having received a most theatrical wound in Scene 6, Miss Wanamaker thereafter crept Dickensianly about the stage – her version of Smike in *Nicholas Nickleby*. Miss Dench milked the final lullaby for all it was worth, ending in sobs, and then, going after the disappearing armies, pathetically called out, stressing each pause, 'Take – me – with – you!'

The so-called warmth, therefore, that the translator and director wanted to put into the play (and about which they might have been more wary had they consulted *Theaterarbeit*), amounted, as usual, to nothing more than a pandering sentimentalism which coloured most of the performances as well as the 'new' musical score by George Fenton. Again, when this music worked it was closest to the original of Paul Dessau. When it did not, which was most of the time, it drowned the words, upstaged the action, aimed for atmosphere instead of meaning (gypsy-style violins and tunes were much in evidence), and in the case of Yvette's song, accompanied by a banjo, descended to pop-song banalities. Eilif's 'Ballad of the Soldier', and the 'Solomon Song' were treated as musical-comedy turns. In the latter, the Cook (played by Trevor Peacock), required by the dramatic situation to be cold, hungry, and exhausted, executed an energetic Cossack dance. The songs were a seamless part of the action. Most significantly, from the very start of this production until the end, the fog machines worked overtime, covering the stage, literally and metaphorically, with clouds of unknowing.

The reasons why these clouds seem to blow up so frequently whenever a major production of a Brecht play is mounted in the English-speaking world were mostly foreseen by the author himself: the reluctance of directors to bother with 'foreign' theories, to learn by 'copying' the work of others, and the striving for striking effects and originality whether or not they bear any relation to the play being directed.[13] But the main reason is more fundamental – the overwhelming tendency to see Brecht's theory and practice as a style rather than as a *method*.[14] This tendency is reflected in Hanif Khureishi's assertion that he did not think 'there is anything left of the alienation concept in *Mother Courage*. I think that in a way the character goes against some of the things Brecht believed about alienation.'[15]

Typically, this remark shows that, while being continually disparaging about 'alienation' as a theatrical device, Anglophone theatre people generally have no idea what the term really means. This is unfortunate because what Brecht meant by it and how it can be implemented has significant implications for any director's basic task of traffic-control – the blocking of the play. A lack of understanding in this area generally guarantees problems with the production of a Brecht play. Theatre professionals coming into contact with Brecht's ideas tend to share Grotowski's view that, while the aesthetics are interesting, they are too abstract, too vague, and give no clear indication about 'how can this be done.'[16] In fact, Brecht gave most precise indications, but a reading of the theory and recourse to the modelbook are required, and too many directors obsessed with not being 'derivative', are most reluctant to do that. But it has been thirty years, so perhaps the time has come for a slightly tighter focus on the 'how to do it' of Brecht's blocking, which represents a significant and useful contribution to staging techniques.

Blocking in the modern sense, is a comparatively recent innovation in the theatre and really begins with the Duke of Saxe-Meiningen, although Goethe with his chalk-squared stage at Weimar also has a claim. The Duke's belief in 'dynamic' blocking, which tried to avoid regularity, too much random movement, and a geometrically central focus, and which would be contained within a cohesive compositional framework to create a 'natural' impression, has in essence remained the basis of blocking practice for most directors since.[17] The desired effect is of pleasing architectonic shapes so disposed as to look natural, but not too natural to distract the eye from a central character or event. The essential principle of modern blocking is composition.

On a much more basic level, blocking is often viewed simply as an 'organic' (one of Stanislavsky's favourite terms) device for obtaining variety: positions are changed, characters 'cross' from one part of the stage to another, cross their legs, light cigarettes, pour drinks – all the business familiar from hundreds of amateur and professional productions, trotted out when a director or actors feel the pace is slack, or 'life-like' touches are needed. In fact, as Brecht remarked, in real life people move quite infrequently, remain standing or sitting for a long time, and maintain their positions in a group until the circumstances change. In the theatre fewer, not more, changes of position are required than in life. Theatrical incidents need to be purified from anything accidental or insignificant, otherwise a 'veritable inflation of meaningless comings and goings' results.[18] Actors should resist their natural tendency to draw attention to themselves by movements, when they are not directly involved in the main action. In his notes to the *Courage* model, Brecht made further trenchant remarks about gratuitous blocking:

> Positions should be retained as long as there is no compelling reason for changing them – and a desire for variety is not a compelling reason. If one gives in to a desire for variety, the consequence is a devaluation of all movement on the stage; the spectator ceases to look for a specific meaning

behind each movement, he stops taking movement seriously. But, especially at the crucial points in the action, the full impact of a change of position must not be weakened. Legitimate variety is obtained by ascertaining the crucial points and planning the arrangement around them.[19]

Seldom have dramatic theorists given such practical advice; seldom has it been so ignored. The groupings and blocking of the Berliner Ensemble are thought in some way to be 'stylized' (hence alien), or uniquely part of the Brecht idiom, and therefore 'used-up', museum pieces, instead of painstaking experiments resulting in methods perennially useful to working theatre people. Having once witnessed any performance by the Berliner Ensemble, audiences must surely view performances by many other actors and companies as unbearably fidgety, fussy examples of theatrical inflation.

For Brecht the blocking or 'grouping' was the core of a production, the main procedure by which a director put the story of a play before the public. This process entailed 'the placing of the characters, the establishing of their relation to one another, the changing of their positions, exits and entrances'.[20] The blocking had to tell the story elegantly and clearly. He developed distinct ideas, moreover, about the kind of blocking that did *not* tell a story elegantly and clearly.

The wrong kinds of blocking in fact told *another* story, by placing leading actors in prominent positions so that everybody would look at them, obscuring or trivializing incidents through atmospherics, or working up a factitious suspense which was not that of the story. For Brecht the main culprits were Naturalism, with its apparently accidental and 'casual' positioning trying to make characters look like 'real life'; Expressionism, where reality was sacrificed to subjectivity; Symbolism, with its evocation of the underlying and ideal; and Formalism, with the emphasis on making pretty pictures for their own sake.[21] Brecht thought the essential principle of blocking was montage. Not composition but decomposition. The playwright was concerned from the start of his career with the same principles that motivated the artists of the Berlin Dada movement, and of the *Novembergruppe* – montage and photomontage replacing the traditional approaches to composition, a selection of apparently random elements placed together so as to comment on each other.[22]

This 'separating out of the various elements' was a formal factor in such works as *The Threepenny Opera*, where Brecht attempted to dissipate compositional focus through the use of projections before scenes, songs separated cleanly from the action, visible sources of light, on-stage orchestra, back-projections, and so on – in fact, all the stylistic elements that are commonly thought of as 'Brechtian'. In his notes to *The Threepenny Opera* he called this technique 'complex seeing', the equivalent of a footnote, which would enable the audience to think '*about* the flow of the play', rather than 'from *within*' the flow of the play.[23] The eye, through the act of glancing at the bottom of the page would, as it were, disrupt the suspense of the narrative. The breaking of an audience's focus would put a stop to heavy breathing or hypnosis. Sometimes, in a work like *The Seven Deadly Sins of the Petit-Bourgeoisie*, the different elements – words and political message, dance, song, mime, and quartet – so alienate each other, they might be said to cancel each other out. Still, Brecht stuck with this formally structured complex seeing throughout his life. In *A Short Organum* he continued to insist on the use of scene titles so that the different episodes would not 'succeed one another indistinguishably'. This would counteract the bourgeois theatre's tendency to play everything smoothly.[24]

Brecht's insistence on 'each scene for itself' is not difficult to understand; it is clear what he wants from the printed texts of his plays. Yet this aspect of his approach to montage, it seems, gives directors a tremendous amount of trouble. They tend to ignore it as just another 'old-fashioned' Brechtian stylistic device, no different from back-projections and political slogans. The RSC *Courage* provided a typical example. The main problem with John Napier's set was its inability to set one scene off from the next. Round and round the treadmill wagon went, in full view of the audience, blending one scene into another. There was no possibility of changing the wagon's appearance except superficially – the actors had to set the scene on stage. Props, so crucial to showing the change in Courage's circumstances, therefore got short shrift. The whole point of Scene 6 – where Kattrin gets wounded because she is taking care of her mother's goods, and Courage curses the war – derives from Courage having just laid in a large supply of wares. Judi Dench was obliged to mime most of the businesswoman's stocktaking – when she could, for it took most of the first part of the scene to set up after the change from the scene before. The significant end of the scene with the curse was fudged in the same way; Miss Dench was too busy loading up and getting ready to move off again. While the actual revolutions of the stage took as long as one imagines a change behind a curtain would take, a superficial atmosphere of hurry and effort was created without providing an opportunity for adding realism through the use of significant props. Because no set or costume changes were possible, and there were no scene titles (too derivative?), the audience got no sense of time passing, of the actual grinding length of the war – surely crucial for this play.

Running Brecht's scenes together in this way was also done by John Dexter in his 1981 mounting of *Galileo* for the English National Theatre, otherwise a much better production. Scenes were changed by stage hands in white boilersuits, and characters from one scene who were required in the next remained on stage. Without the virtuoso display of gradual ageing achieved by Michael Gambon as Galileo (who remained on stage for most of the play), the sense of passing time would have been as vague as in Howard Davies's *Mother Courage*. One suspects that this avoidance of Brecht's montage stems from a mistaken idea directors have of 'pace'. They confuse meaning with momentum. In order to generate excitement, to keep up audience interest, and to maintain suspense, you must 'get on with it'. Audiences, it is feared, see a scenic break as a slowing down of the action. Directors equate Brecht's so-called detachment with a dragging pace. Therefore, as long as something is moving in front of an audience it can feel that something is happening. Such pace is, of course, similar to the effects generated by what Brecht considered the false blocking of Expressionism.

The type of montage described so far, with the events of one scene juxtaposed abruptly with those of another, closely resembles the use of editing in film, especially by Eisenstein. The narrative is developed sequentially and in 'jumps', as Brecht put it.[25] The second type of montage he developed in his mature work has much stronger ramifications for blocking, and lies at the heart of the Brechtian 'method'. It could perhaps be described as montage within the scene, or the 'Brueghel Effect' and amounts, not to sequential, but to simultaneous story telling. The term 'vertical montage' has been coined by Franco Ruffini in the context of the semiotics of theatrical performance.[26] To use another analogy from film: it is the technique of Jean Renoir (who was asked by Brecht to join his Diderot Society) of layers of action unfolding in deep focus and long takes, rather than in a series of rhythmically edited shots.[27] Montage within the scene was very much part of the theatrical language of Berlin in the Weimar Republic. It was practised by Piscator, and the Truppe 31 with its satirical collective creation, *Die Mausefalle*, and was taken to its formal extreme with the six simultaneous scenes on several levels in Ferdinand Bruckner's *Die Verbrecher*. The essential differences between these approaches to montage and the approach of the mature Brecht lay in his combination of it with realism.[28]

In his essay on Brueghel, Brecht commented admiringly on the separation of story and compositional elements: Alpine peaks set in a Flemish landscape, the Duke of Alba's army marching through the Alps during the conversion of Saul, and, most of all, on the fact that 'though Brueghel manages to balance his contrasts, he never merges them into one another'.[29] This technique might perhaps be more accurately described as 'polyphonic lines of action' through an analogy with the other art form as closely tied to time as drama – music. These analogies were drawn by Brecht himself, and, while they point to similarities, they also reveal the differences between cinematic technique and his theatrical strategies. After a discussion with Adorno in Los Angeles about the difference between film and theatre, he noted that, like the microphone, which is monaural (at least at that time), the camera gives us only *one* eye. Brecht's 'fundamental reproach' concerning the cinema was its 'rigid fixation of the spectator's point of view'. The actors act only for this 'eye', and all incidents therefore become, in his significant word, '*einlinig*' (literally: 'unilinear', but to keep the musical parallel straight, the word 'homophonic' precisely conveys Brecht's meaning). Furthermore, because of mechanical reproduction, film reduces everything to a constraining, unchangeable, finished result. The 'audience has no chance to modify the actor's performance'. Perhaps the polyphonic lines of action of Brecht's directorial method were an attempt to combat the effects of the *Einlinigkeit* to which audiences were all too accustomed; this conclusion would certainly fit his political stance concerning the theatre.[30]

In any case, in his mature productions, Brecht developed this montage within the scene, this complex seeing, to an extraordinary degree of subtlety, especially so in *Mother Courage*. One of the delights of working as a director on a Brecht play comes from discovering the many layers of activity and subtextuality in scenes of action that at first seem innocuously uncomplicated. In *The Impossible Theatre* Herbert Blau describes his astonished discovery of Brecht's polyphonic storytelling when rehearsing *Mother Courage* with the Actors' Workshop. A play which, on the surface, had appeared to be static and lacking in familiar dramatic 'action', turned out in rehearsal to be crawling with little stories going on everywhere; and, as in Brueghel, many important events were hardly visible, had to be searched for, or were caught only in reverberation. Clarifying and embodying all the lines of action in the play's small, two-page Scene 5 (Tilly's Victory at Leipzig) in which Kattrin rescues a baby from a burning farmhouse, and Mother Courage demands a looted fur coat from a soldier as payment for a drink, took Blau's company many hours of rehearsal to work out – and a few minutes to perform.[31]

In fact every scene in this play, including the more complicated ones, has the stage divided into separate areas of significant action. For example, in the first scene the wagon defines the demarcation between the safe haven of the family and the threatening incursions of the Recruiting Sergeant. In the second, the stage is literally divided into two, with the camp kitchen on one side and the General's tent on the other. The notes to the model demonstrate the importance of every detail in such scenes. Brecht comments admiringly on how the actor Bildt prepared the capon as a virtuoso of the kitchen, but with restraint, so that the action did not distract from the scene in the tent.[32] In the RSC *Courage* the Cook simply wiped his table over and over again during Eilif's scene with the General. Ironically, such perfunctory gesturing, the equivalent of 'rhubarb and custard' in crowd scenes, drew one's attention *away* from the main event. The various voices in a fugue must not compete for attention.

A further example (among many others) of polyphony can be found in the brief interlude in the third scene when Courage talks politics with her two suitors and they all sing the hymn 'Ein feste Burg' while Kattrin tries on the hat and red boots, the whore's paraphernalia. The minute detail in which this moment is described in the model reveals the reason for the polyphonic lines of action. On one side a cynical discussion of war and the ingratiating singing of the Protestant hymn is going on; on the other, a mute girl realizes that she will get love during war only by being a prostitute. At the RSC the moment was unspecifically treated as a bit of lyrical 'atmosphere', before the *real* action of the attack. The political conversation was largely cut, then conducted inaudibly inside the wagon; the hymn was reduced to a few bars and whistled; Kattrin parodied a whore's walk – evidently she wanted to mock the profession instead of learning it. Angelika Hurwicz has remarked how Brecht's stage pictures were painted in as great a detail as those of a novelist. If the public complained about not understanding anything he was not prepared to tell the actors to speak more loudly, but would change the blocking. Apparently he found performances in which he could understand every word very tiresome; the duty of the theatre was to speak to the eyes of the audience.[33] He often rehearsed the lines of action separately, with the result that when put back in the whole action, these 'scenes' sometimes did not fit. This happened with the little scene of Azdak's investiture as judge in *The Caucasian Chalk Circle*. Instead of smoothing over the awkward 'joins', Brecht emphasized them, making a little playlet of the scene.[34]

Hurwicz describes Brecht's stage pictures as 'novelistic', but he was very reliant on the illustrations of the 'crucial points' provided by designers like Neher and von Appen. These illustrations were the starting point for his blocking, and bear a very close resemblance to the 'storyboards' used routinely in the making of movies today. Ruth Berlau's photographs show how much Brecht thought of each scene in terms of 'shots'.[35] The gests of the actors, the careful groupings, the significant, non-random movements (in his recollections Eric Bentley has described how Brecht disliked stage crosses on lines), all of these told a story, and combined to provide a connected series of 'routines', a species of montage where nothing was left to chance – something quite familiar to actors of frantic farces.[36] Every event on stage was significant for Brecht; if it was not, it was dropped. He was also capable of achieving maximum gestic effectiveness from the total *absence* of event. In Scene 10 of *Mother Courage*, the war-battered wagon stops outside a prosperous farmhouse, and mother and daughter listen to the complacent singing of an invisible resident: 'What goes on in their minds', says the model, 'should not be shown;

the audience can imagine'.[37] In the RSC production a young woman was brought on stage, singing while washing her long blonde hair in a bowl, and lit by a shaft of golden sunlight – she ignored Kattrin and Courage. In this case a decision was made *for* the audience, where Brecht felt, quite rightly, the decision was up to them. Sometimes 'complex seeing' results from not seeing anything at all, and simplistic vision is the result of seeing too much.

In Brecht's productions when one 'routine' was finished, it was cleanly 'rounded off', as in gymnastics, and replaced by another – the Berliner Ensemble principle of 'one thing after another', instead of 'one thing out of another', articulated in the *Courage* model. Instinctively understood by most actors, but not quite so easy to describe, the process involved in 'one thing after another' refers on its simplest level to comic routines like double-takes or pratfalls, where all the steps must be clearly distinguishable and carefully timed for the joke to work – rather like the *lazzi* of the *commedia dell'arte*. These functioned much like Brecht's models, could be clearly described or illustrated, and were even assembled into handbooks. Charlie Chaplin worked in the same tradition, and many of his early films, like *The Immigrant*, or *Easy Street*, also provide clear illustrations of such routines, loosely linked by a situation into a 'story' whose parts are a good deal more significant than the whole – in other words, they ignore an Aristotelian 'plot'. This comes close to the more sophisticated level on which 'one thing after another' operates, implying a sequential montage of discrete events that, linked together, form the distinctively Brechtian dialectical narrative. Whatever one may think about the ideological implications Brecht attributed to this technique, it has a simple practical advantage for the working actor and director. Routines worked out in rehearsal can serve as guides, and there is no mystical state of creativity that has somehow to be generated before real work can begin.

Another inspiration for Brecht's view of character as essentially fragmented must surely have been Diderot's famous and admiring description in *The Paradox of Acting* of David Garrick performing his party trick by placing his head between folding doors:

In the course of five or six seconds his expression will change successively from wild delight to temperate pleasure, from this to tranquillity, from tranquillity to surprise, from surprise to blank astonishment, from that to sorrow, from sorrow to the air of one overwhelmed, from that to fright, from fright to horror, from horror to despair, and thence he will go up again to the point from which he started.[38]

In *The Messingkauf Dialogues* Brecht describes how he filmed Helene Weigel making herself up, and then cut up the film so that 'each frame showed a complete facial expression, self-contained and with its own meaning'. He then showed these pictures to others, asking what the various expressions meant. Their answers were remarkably similar to the expressions Garrick managed to achieve, putting the eighteenth-century theory of the 'passions' into practice. Weigel, it was thought, managed to suggest 'such things as anger, gaiety, envy, compassion'. Brecht's advice to her was a summary of Diderot's position: 'she only needed to know her own expressions in order to be able to express the various moods without always having to feel them'.[39] Thus, while linked by narrative throughout the play as a whole, or by the simultaneous performance of 'mini-dramas' in individual scenes, each element, going in stages from facial expression of emotion, to gesture, to movement, to scene or song, to story, was in Brecht's scheme to preserve its individual and distinct character. It was a systematic, and no doubt intentional, unravelling of everything that had formed the basis of the integrative Wagnerian *Gesamtkunstwerk*, the intention of which had been to operate 'organically' and directly on the subconscious with no intervention of the conscious mind. 'The subconscious', however, as Brecht put it, 'has . . . a bad memory'.[40] His relish in exploding the nineteenth-century romantic impulse for synthesis ought to be communicated in productions of the plays.

These principles have a profound implication for the actor and director. At the heart of the Stanislavsky system of acting training and practice (and still the prevailing *modus operandi* in the Anglophone theatre) is the assumption that the actor 'improvises in public', thus creating for himself, and for the audience, the illusion that the events on stage are happening for the first time. Brecht's central position states that everything the actor does in performance has been previously thought about, chosen, rehearsed detail-by-detail, and then presented with the light, easy '*Gestus* of showing' that typifies the pleasure to be derived from a slick and well-rehearsed, carefully calculated comic or gymnastic routine. Brecht is not concerned with 'inner truth' at all, but with the correct physical expression of a story. The same applied to characterization, where no attempt was made to create a 'through-line' of action, nor to carry the full significance and weight of a role cumulatively throughout a performance. Weigel's Courage began each scene anew.[41] Such an approach must be useful to any actor performing a large part, although this planned inconsistency with an emphasis on the contradictory aspects of character, is diametrically opposed to Stanislavky's recommendations. Perhaps it is significant that on three different occasions Judi Dench was hoarse and seemed exhausted by the end of her performances as Mother Courage. There would, however, appear to be a similarity between the carefully rehearsed 'finished product' of each moment in a Brecht production, and the finality and 'finished' nature of film which he found so objectionable. The similarity is only apparent. Brecht sought to enrich an audience's point of view through 'complex seeing'; and, as his last directive to the Ensemble shows (concerning the tour to England), he was more than ready to adapt to different circumstances. This did not mean that the actor had to give the audience the impression of watching someone going through the birthpangs of creation; her job was to communicate the easy attitude of someone handing over the result of experiments made and problems overcome. The modelbook was to be an aid in this process; it was intended to be neither a template nor a corset.

The working out in detail of the separate lines of action is especially important, as Brecht pointed out, in scenes of excitement and heightened feeling where most directors still go for the jugular. The model gives theatrically effective and sensible examples for the Catholic attack in the third scene, but in the RSC production the generalized stagey 'panic' of the actors drowned most of the ironic possibilities the model suggests. Lesley Duff as Yvette missed getting the necessary laugh on her line 'Did I hear the Catholics are coming?' because she was frightened like everybody else, instead of thrilled about the arrival of new customers ignorant about her social disease. The climactic Scene 11 (approached by the RSC in a generalized tragic tone), in which Kattrin wakes up the town with her drumming, is crowded with polyphonic lines of action. The peasant couple chooses the survival of their farm over that of blood-relations in the town, their son sympathizes with Kattrin, the Young Ensign wishes to display his command-worthiness to his soldiers, the soldiers are contemptuous and uncooperative, the attempts to avoid noise create noise, ending, literally, in a polyphonic duet for drum and axe. Again, the model gives examples of how carefully the scene needs to be choreographed, down to every beat of the drum. Each 'line' needs to be played discretely so that there is no generalized feeling of suspense for the actors to catch. This 'tragic' scene, if properly played, is full of laughs, and is the more tragic for that reason.

Such irony, carefully constructed to prevent performers 'catching the tone' of a scene, is often difficult to master by actors who have, within the compositional mode of blocking, become accustomed to being either at the centre, or at the periphery of events; not both at the same time. While rehearsing John Dexter's National Theatre production of *Galileo*, Stephen Moore, the actor playing the Cardinal Inquisitor (he also played the Chaplain in the RSC *Courage*), made a highly suggestive comment. He told Jim Hiley, the author of the production's casebook, of his fear that he might not 'get the Pope dressing scene' because he thought the audience would be distracted during the delivery of his speech by the comings and goings of the dressing ritual. It would be the equivalent of asking the public to perform 'the old co-ordination exercise in which one hand describes a circle across the front of the tummy while the other pats the head'.[42] In other words, Mr Moore was afraid of being upstaged by Brecht's polyphonic lines of action. The stage directions, by the way, add 'the shuffling of many feet', so the 'seeing' is even more complex.

What concerned the actor and made him wonder if he was 'droning on and being a bore' was, of course, a particularly telling example of the alienation effect in full operation, created by the juxtapositioning of two distinct elements of action. Yet the true significance of this effect for the practitioner is that, in fact, he need never worry his head about alienation. Once a director has understood the polyphonic method, any individual performance can be alienated, even that of the most unsuspecting Method actor. For Brecht it was primarily a director's job to bring a play's incidents to life through adequate blocking. The director was to blame if something would not work, not the actor. He liked to tell the story of the bad Hollywood director who, having seen his film, turned sadly and reproachfully to his star and said, 'But you *promised* me you were an actor.'[43] In the words of *A Short Organum*: 'Elegant movement and graceful grouping, for a start, can alienate . . . '[44]

This attitude does not imply a contempt for the actor's contribution on Brecht's part; on the contrary. The major factor in alienated blocking, and its *raison d'être*, is the social *Gestus*, and its invention depends on the work of the actors. Their ability through inventive miming to show clearly a character's attitude to other characters, to the situations in the play, and to the ideas of the playwright, will generate the comedy, irony, and detachment of the true epic theatre: 'Our theatre's significant stage groupings are not just an effect or a "purely aesthetic" phenomenon, conducive to formal beauty. They are a part of a hugely-conceived theatre for the new social order.'[45] Brecht combined an intense dislike of art for art's sake with an equally intense love of the polished detail: Eisler movingly described discussing the gestic nature of Shakespeare's punctuation with Brecht in Hollywood during the battle for Stalingrad.[46]

Instead of being a stylistic device (and therefore easily outmoded), 'complex seeing' was a perceptive strategy adopted by Brecht to teach an audience how to analyse reality critically and actively, rather than 'going with the flow'. He seemed to understand very early on that the medium is the message, and that impact, up-to-dateness, and relevance, depend not just on what is said, but on how it is said. Roland Barthes called the social *Gestus* 'one of the clearest and most intelligent' concepts which dramatic theory has ever produced.[47] 'The rigid fixation of the point of view', as Brecht described movie technique in 1942, is all too familiar in the mass media in the 1980s. Any strategy which seeks to provide an antidote to the passive receptiveness engendered by the media's manipulative siren voices must be welcome, especially in the theatre, a medium where the audience still has a last chance to 'modify the performance'. Brecht's 'antidote' is political in the deepest sense. Reflecting a reaction to recent Brechtian film criticism, the playwright John McGrath stated that such high hopes for formalistic strategies amount to a 'fetishization of the sign'.[48] Nevertheless, especially for Anglophones, there is still a great need in the theatre for Brecht's critical aesthetics; they should at least be attempted before being rejected, and before being rejected they need to be understood. To revert again to Tynan's prophecy, it is worth stressing that Brecht was not obsessed with staging his own works exclusively; he thought his approach to blocking could be just as successfully used with Shakespeare (and, one assumes, with other classics) where there are many scenes requiring polyphonic lines of action. Brecht himself thought the ghost scene in Act 5 of *Richard III* was 'full of A-effects'.[49] To choose another example at random, what would a Brechtian blocking achieve with the embarrassed guests in the Banquet Scene of *Macbeth*, who are usually treated as 'background'?

The line by which Brecht liked to be remembered, 'he made suggestions', might usefully be followed, with regard to his blocking, by any working director (a really creative genius would, of course, come up with other much more relevant strategies). When advocating the use of his models, Brecht strongly warned about mindless replication, but also said his suggestions might be useful to fellow craftsmen engaged in the collective work of the theatre.[50] Directors and actors learning their craft in the competitive and hurried world of North American and British theatre need all the practical help they can get. Together with educational institutions teaching dramatic arts, they do not need the perfumed incense of Stanislavskian motivation and psychologizing as much as the plain nuts and bolts of Brechtian social gesture. Before locking the doors of the Brecht Museum and throwing away the key, there may be great benefit in first having a closer look at the exhibits.

10

Some reflections on Brecht and acting

MARTIN ESSLIN

Brecht's remarks on the art of acting are scattered throughout his voluminous theatrical writings, of which only a relatively small proportion is available in English. As a result, perhaps, not enough truly critical attention has systematically been devoted to these ideas. Yet they form a coherent body of thought, dealing with all aspects of acting, from the training of actors to rehearsal methodology and performance.

An understanding of Brecht's ideas on acting seems to me particularly important since the prevalence of the ideas and practices that go by the name of the 'method' – which claim, in my opinion wrongly, to be derived from Stanislavsky – has resulted in a decisive impoverishment of acting skills, which, above all, has made it very difficult to produce Brecht's plays in the spirit in which they were conceived.

There are two distinct aspects of Brecht's theories and ideas about acting: first, there are his ideas about the actual process of acting; and second, there is the connection he establishes between his favourite type of acting and the social significance of drama. The type of acting Brecht liked and advocated can be understood only in relation to what he was opposed to in the German theatre of his time.

Acting in the German theatre around 1920 was in a period of violent transition. The old nineteenth-century type of acting, the 'Hoftheater' or imperial court theatre style, was still alive in the provinces as well as in some of the publicly subsidized theatres. This was based on a very artificial, ritualized and emotionally false concept of 'Pathos' – a high style of declamatory, emotional delivery, with, at points of emotional climax, a false vibrato in the voice – the actors' slang for it in Vienna when I was a drama student there was a 'Bibberer'. This was based on 'beautiful' speaking, and painting the 'imagery' of the poetry with the voice.

It was in opposition to this style – which indeed could be very effective when well done, as recordings of Adolf Sonnenthal show, its greatest master at the Vienna Burgtheater, but easily degenerated into empty insincerity and cliché – that the naturalistic acting in the plays of Ibsen and Strindberg, Holz, Schlaf, Hauptmann or Schnitzler came to the fore. Great actors like Josef Kainz and Albert Bassermann developed an at least seemingly throw-away realistic style of speaking in the contemporary prose drama, with lots of hesitations, a studied neglect of 'beautiful' speech, in fact the equivalent, in acting, of the pointillist method of Impressionist painting. However, they retained, indeed emphasized, the intensity of nervous energy that had been the original basis of the 'Hoftheater' style, in effect discarding the heightened form to restore a valid emotional content. When it came to classical verse plays, actors like Kainz and Bassermann found a way of combining that realistic nervous energy with speaking against the rhythm of the verse, while somehow retaining the main beat, so that the deviations from the rhythm became themselves significant. Max Reinhardt's classical productions used these actors and developed this style. (Reinhardt had himself come out of Otto Brahm's naturalistic Deutsches Theater.)

When I was a student at the Vienna Reinhardt school from 1936 to 1938, we were trained first to translate the verse into improvised prose lines of our own making which would reproduce the meaning and psychological truth of the original text. When we had found the right tone we were then instructed to speak the verse lines at the level of private, intimate conversation. When we had the correct tone and the expression, we were told to 'enlarge' them, keeping the tone of voice but adding fuller voice power and expressive force. Brecht, who attended Reinhardt's rehearsals at the Deutsches Theater around 1925, adopted much of that method. The recordings of his rehearsals extant on East German pressings show that he used a very similar procedure, requiring his actors to translate the thoughts of the characters – for example the cardinals in *Galileo* – into their own language and then making them speak his own lines in the tone of voice thus established, but enlarged. In fact he proceeded to the objective, non-emphatic style he wanted via a stage of internalization of the emotion: that is, empathy. He reached a critical detachment via external observation and sociological analysis as the second or even third stage of the process.

Next to 'Hoftheater' declamation and naturalistic empathy, another type of acting that competed for supremacy in Germany around 1920 was the Expressionist style, which, in turn, represented a revulsion against Naturalism: the Expressionist dramatists and actors had become bored with the laborious pointillism that tried slowly to build up a psychological portrait of the characters from innumerable small touches. The Expressionists wanted to go straight to the core of the matter, to contract and condense everything into the most immediate, explosive expression. This led to even greater excesses of intensity – in fact a return to the 'Pathos' of the declamatory 'Hoftheater' style, with, however, greater stress on absolute 'sincerity'. (The acting style of the Nazi theatre in the years of the Hitler regime owed a great deal to the violence and grandiloquent 'sincerity' of Expressionist acting.) Two great Expressionist actors, Gustav Gründgens and Heinrich George, were its chief exponents.

What all these styles had in common, and what Brecht disliked above all, was their emphasis on intensity. All three styles ultimately saw the culmination of an actor's art in the *Ausbruch*, the sudden, devastating cry from the depth of the soul that in their terms constituted the climactic moments of drama.

It was this sudden and irresistible assault on the senses, during which the spectator felt that the actor on stage was going to collapse in an apoplectic fit – these *Ausbrüche* were as intense as that – that constituted for Brecht the almost obscene pressure towards empathy which made it impossible for the spectator to think critically about the character or, indeed, to 'think' at all.

However, there was a style of acting without intensity of this kind, which was already available as a model for Brecht: it existed in the popular theatre, where the actors came on with very little rehearsal, and did not know their lines too well, or improvised them. Brecht's favourite, Karl Valentin, and his sidekick straight man, Lisl Karlstadt, were of this type. There was also the cabaret, in which the performers in their sketches and songs never pretended to be characters other than themselves. There was the circus, where not only the high-wire and trapeze artists, the jugglers and equilibrists, displayed their skills with concentration (though always with the aim to show how easy it all was if you had the skill), but also the clowns 'acted' without ever pretending to be 'characters' in the ordinary sense. And on the 'legitimate' stage there was Frank Wedekind who appeared in his own plays, had come from the cabaret and was, by general consensus of the acting profession, no actor at all. Several people who knew him and had appeared on stage with him have told me: he did not act at all, he just walked on and spoke his lines into the audience. Nevertheless he was enormously impressive. Brecht loved him as a writer and even more as an actor and performer.

What all these styles of performance had in common were, on the one hand, the obviousness with which the performers displayed the fact that they were giving a performance – what Brecht came to call the *Gestus des Zeigens*, a style of performance where at every moment the performer indicated: 'Look at me, this is what I am showing you, I am exhibiting something to you, demonstrating something that I can do well. And I am pleased that I am doing well, don't you think I am good at it? *Voila!*' Thus the *Gestus des Zeigens* is always linked with the performer's self-presentation as the possessor of a special skill.

The second element common to the popular stage, the cabaret, and the circus is providing the spectator with the pleasure of admiring a special skill. This is an aspect of acting that the so-called 'method' woefully underestimates, although, of course, it is also very much present in even the most naturalistic performance. For however 'natural' an actor's acting may appear, the audience must remain conscious that the naturalness is a product of that actor's skill. Even the naturalistic actor thus has to indicate the subtle shift from 'being' to 'acting'. It is Stanislavsky himself who emphasized that in acting someone falling asleep on stage the worst thing the actor could do would be really to fall asleep. As all art is artificial, Brecht despised any attempt to try to blur the distinction between art and reality:

> The beautiful aspect of artificial things is that they are made with skill. If it is objected that 'mere' skill cannot by itself produce works of art, the use of the word 'mere' indicates that the objector is thinking of a one-sided, empty type of skill, established in just one 'field', that is missing in other fields of art, that is to say a skill that is unskilful in a moral or scientific sense. The beauty of

nature is a quality which gives the human senses an opportunity to show skill.[1]

It is in this sense that the analogy with the juggler or trapeze artist is very relevant. In his theoretical discussions about acting, Brecht's great emphasis on the elegance and aplomb with which the actor should deliver a finished product, showing clearly that it has been thoroughly rehearsed, thought out, and mastered, rather than on the 'method's' ideal of a performance, which seems to be forming itself at the moment of its being shown, draws on the circus 'artiste's' deliberate display of skilfulness.

That Charlie Chaplin was Brecht's favourite actor points in the same direction, as does his admiration for the Marx Brothers, whose acting was not greatly different from their display of skills as trick harpists or pianists. Chaplin's flick of his cane, his little gesture of satisfaction when he had evaded the horrid policeman are closely akin to the flourish with which the juggler or high-wire artist completes his act and receives the public's applause. These classical instances are paradigms of the *Gestus des Zeigens*.

But actors should not only show that they are conscious of demonstrating something. They should also express their consciousness of being objects that are being looked at:

It is . . . important that the actor should express his knowledge of the fact that he is being looked at, because the spectator can learn to behave in his daily life like someone who is being looked at. In this respect the actor is a model to be imitated. The individual derives great advantages from being conscious of being looked at.[2]

The *Gestus des Zeigens* and the awareness of being on display will save the actor from the temptation of excessive intensity of emotion, simply because not being identified with the character, and being conscious that he or she is merely showing what the character – who is emphatically not the actor – does or feels, excludes the ultimate identification which one would need for a complete *Ausbruch* of total, agonizing force.

Non-identification between the actor and the character and the suppression of empathy as the main driving force behind the actor's performance logically led to what Brecht calls the 'historicization' of the performance. The actor takes the character from the 'eternal present' that Goethe and Schiller regarded as the main characteristic distinguishing the telling of a story dramatically, as distinct from the distancing of the epic mode of narration, and places the character in a past which he or she is merely now, with skill and elegance, demonstrating. This is what the *Verfremdungseffekt* – as far as acting is concerned – is all about. The translation of this as alienation is wrong and positively harmful in its implications – non-empathic distancing is probably the nearest we can come to it in English.

But it must be emphasized that non-identification was nothing new in the history of acting. Brecht was the first to acknowledge that by his constant citing of East Asian, Indian, and Elizabethan acting. It is really only in the relatively short period when Naturalism ruled the roost – which has long passed everywhere except in the pockets of method orthodoxy in the United States – that identification and empathy were aimed at. The classical Greek theatre with its masked, sung choruses and hieratic style of delivery was distanced, non-empathic theatre of positively Brechtian dimensions; hence his attempts at calling his own ideas anti-Aristotelian are based on a complete misunderstanding of the Greeks. The *commedia dell'arte* with masks, Goethe's theatre with its elaborate rules of deportment, even the nineteenth-century 'Hoftheater' with its highly artificial intonations all used the distancing effect and the *Gestus des Zeigens*. Indeed, before the arrival of modern lighting and hydraulics the scenery itself constantly showed the audience that they were watching a highly artificial event, consciously displaying its artificiality. The really decisive point of difference between the traditional styles of acting and Brecht's ideas does not lie here, but in the uses to which he intended to put this process of non-identification and distancing.

If the *Gestus des Zeigens* in other acting styles merely signified: 'Look at me, I am showing you what Hamlet or Lear or Othello or Phaedra did', in Brecht's view it should be used to say: 'I am showing you what these characters did and I am also showing you that they may have done the wrong thing. I am inviting you to look at these actions critically.'

If the juggler's flourish at the completion of his feat says 'Haven't I done this well?', if Chaplin's flick of his cane says 'Wasn't that an elegant gag?', Brecht wants his actors' performance to indicate 'See, this is what Hamlet did; I think he might have done something else instead. I think so; what do you think? Think about it, be critical of his actions!'

You might notice that in citing examples I have intuitively chosen characters from tragedy. In fact even this aspect of Brecht's dialectical style of acting is deeply rooted in tradition.

Who, for example, would want to identify himself with Molière's Miser or Imaginary Invalid? Any actor in these roles is clearly showing the audience that the characters are deluded fools and that he would not, himself, identify with them. Similarly, the villains of Victorian melodrama clearly indicated that their cheatings and seductions and murders were anything but admirable actions that the actor himself in his private capacity would approve of. In fact by far the greatest part of any acting throughout history – all acting indeed in comedy – has always been critical, distanced acting with a clear *Gestus des Zeigens*. The way Molière played Argan going to and from his privy, the way Irving showed the pangs of the murderer's bad conscience in *The Bells*, the way the seducer twirled his moustache in hundreds of Victorian melodramas all clearly conveyed that kind of critical attitude and comment by the actor.

It was only in high tragedy that the tragic 'hero' invited empathy, or, even when he was played in a highly stylized, distanced manner, displayed the actor's identification with the character's deep moral dilemmas and heroic acceptance of them. To put this in a nutshell: what Brecht's demand for a critical rendering of the great heroic classical drama amounts to is to say, 'Let's play it not as tragedy but in the style in which, normally, comedy and even farce is acted.' In *A Short Organum* and elsewhere he makes this quite clear: about those things which in traditional theory provoke tears, the audience in his epic theatre should be laughing, and vice versa.

And in the short fragment of a dialogue *Dreigespräch über das Tragische*, Brecht himself acknowledges this observation:

> When I hear you talk like that about your way of playing theatre, I feel as though you had simply taken so-and-so-many elements out of comedy and put them in the serious play. Such distancing effects can be found in the lowest type of farce.

To which the second interlocutor adds:

> I also think that this ultimately amounts to a liquidation of tragedy . . .[3]

Brecht argues, on the latter point, that tragic effects might also be achieved by showing situations that *do* ultimately produce emotions that could be called 'tragic' – but what matters is that even these emotions are to be evoked by a comedic style of acting. But if the Brechtian, distanced, comedic type of acting has been practised from time immemorial, why did he claim such important ideological and political effects for his own epic style, and for the 'distanced', *verfremdet* relaxed style of acting he advocated?

It would be tedious to try and prove by quotation – there is far too much, and too frequently repeated evidence for it in his theoretical writings – that he saw this critical, dialectical style of acting as inherently Marxist, because each action was being shown to contain its own contradictions, and because the actor's critical attitude to the character – essentially the positive, heroic character of 'serious' drama – would provide social, political, and ideological insights which would prove powerful incentives for the audience to press for radical changes to society. Thirty years after Brecht's death I think it is legitimate to ask whether the evidence – experiential, factual, and scientific in Brecht's sense – would show that the expectation was correct. Indeed, with the conceptual tools provided by contemporary semiotics, one might ask, on a purely theoretical level, whether distanced acting would be capable of containing such signifying powers.

In discussing instances of the effects of *verfremdet* acting, Brecht tends to fall back on classical tragic heroes like Lear and Othello. A distanced, critical rendering of Lear, he argues, would show how wrong he was to give away his kingdom, the hollowness of his pretension to status, etc. A Marxist type of staging – certainly not just the actor's performance – would also provide the socio-historical background and show that this particular series of events illustrates the conditions obtaining in primitive feudalism and that there is no eternally unchanging human nature involved here, Lear is merely a product of his time.

Now I am convinced that a production of *King Lear* by Brecht or by a good director in a Brechtian style would be fascinating. But I cannot see to what extent a detached critical rendering of the role would be more efficient in making the ordinary spectator realize that Lear's actions are wrong and misguided. Even the most old-fashioned

'Hoftheater' rendering of Lear or the most naturalistic empathic rendering of the part could not leave the audience anything other than critical of that poor old man. Nor could they miss the point that Lear's tragedy would be possible only in a primitive feudal society. What Brecht was afraid of – this emerges from all his theoretical writings very clearly – was that the audience might be confirmed in the belief that human nature remains constant through all the changing dialectics of history.

Yet no amount of dialectical, critical, distanced acting could show a present-day audience that the same thing could not happen in today's society: we all know dozens of cases where children put their aged parents into old age homes or abandon them altogether. The tragedy of Lear is possible not only in late capitalist society, but also in Utopian Communistic society. I do not, for a single moment, disbelieve the Marxist idea that human nature changes through changing social conditions. I merely fail to see how a particular style of acting could make that point any more convincingly than 'Hoftheater', or Expressionistic, or indeed Stanislavskian acting.

In the case of Othello – which Brecht also loves to bring into his discussion of the issue – it is easier to suggest that male sexual jealousy, as a form of pride in a woman as a piece of personal property, is a product of a certain type of social organization. But here too, I am sure, indeed I have experienced it myself, old-fashioned traditional renderings of the part can make the same point. However you act Othello, the idea that he regards his wife as his personal property and that jealousy of this type is wrong, and, indeed, not inevitably inherent in human nature, will quite naturally obtrude itself upon most spectators. I think Brecht was quite mistaken in assuming that an old-fashioned rendering of Othello would prove that jealousy is an ineradicable human trait. Quite the contrary.

To give just one more example, one of the few in which Brecht actually illustrates his ideas about distanced acting with a concrete example of a particular passage in a play: while in America Brecht saw a play in the New York Yiddish theatre, a theatre he described as very progressive and left-wing. He does not give the title but says it was by S. Ornitz and that it tells the story of the rise of an East-side Jewish boy to the position of being a rich and successful lawyer. Brecht describes a scene in which the young lawyer is practising in the streets of New York giving cheap legal advice to his neighbours. A woman whose leg has been injured in a traffic accident complains that her case for compensation has been handled too slowly, her claim has not yet been even presented. In anguish she cries, pointing to her leg, 'It's already healing!' Brecht goes on:

> The theater, working without the V-Effect, was unable to point out the horrors of a bloody epoch in this extraordinary scene. Few people in the auditorium noticed it, hardly one of them who might be reading this would remember that exclamation. The actress spoke the line as though it were a matter of course. But precisely this, that such a complaint appears a matter of course to this poor person, ought to have been delivered as though it was the report of a messenger, returning, horror-struck, from the lowest circle of hell. But in order to do this it would have been necessary to employ a specific technique to underline the historical aspect of a particular social situation. And that only the V-Effect would have made possible.[4]

Now I can well imagine that that line could have been better spoken by a better actress. But I cannot imagine why the irony and horror of that situation should not have become obvious through any technique of acting whatever. Nor can Brecht convince me that none of the other spectators at that performance noticed the ironies of that line. After all, he noticed it – and he did not even know Yiddish very well. Moreover, the irony of the line lies in the text itself. By merely quoting the words, Brecht acquaints his readers with its full force. I cannot see what any acting element would have added to the irony of the situation and the semiotic force of the line itself. And as to 'historicizing' – if the play was staged in the costume of its period, no amount of acting could have made the historical context – New York in a period of recession or depression in the thirties – any clearer.

Of course, from a Marxist viewpoint – but from any other intelligent point of view as well – setting a play within its historical context, showing the social, political, and philosophical implications of the milieu and the conditions of the period it depicts, as well as the period when it was first performed, is important. And Brecht's contribution to having made that clear has been a powerful one. My doubt merely concerns the contribution of 'acting in a detached style' to that particular task. The staging, the direction, the design, the interpretation of the lines obviously make a much greater contribution to the meaning than the style in which the lines are delivered.

Indeed, Brecht's idea that the style of acting would induce the spectator to reflect critically upon the social and political significance of the play seems to me itself based on the idea that this critical reflection should principally happen *during* the performance. In fact a spectator who has seen a performance of *Othello* during which he has wholly identified with Othello and suffered, vicariously, all the agonies of jealousy is better, not worse, placed (as Brecht would have it) to evaluate Othello's emotions and actions critically after the performance and indeed for weeks, months, years afterwards. I still occasionally reflect on Olivier's Othello which I saw about twenty years ago; and the fact that during that performance I 'identified' with Othello has not precluded me from thinking about the causes of his jealousy in sociological and Marxist terms, nor did it convince me that human nature is always the same and unaffected by social change. And, indeed, did I really, wholly identify with Othello?

The fact, of course, is that Brecht seems to have taken the extravagantly exaggerated claims with which the advocates of Naturalistic acting advertised their method, at face value. Actually, the actor, however much he tries, can never *become* Othello, as the phrase has it, nor lose his own *Gestus des Zeigens*, his acting 'being an actor', nor does the spectator ever wholly identify with the character on the stage. Indeed, the actor, in whatever style, uses the *Gestus* of showing himself or herself to be an actor in order to impress the spectator with his or her *skill* as an actor. And as to the separation of the actor's personality from that of the character: who has ever seen Olivier, Gielgud, Dustin Hoffman, or indeed John Wayne or Marilyn Monroe without remaining always conscious of those performers' private personalities and selves, so that any performance of these actors fulfils Brecht's demand that the actor's attitude to the character remains visible. In fact it all comes down to Brecht objecting to, say, John Wayne putting a right-wing interpretation on the part while Brecht would prefer a Marxist one. But that has nothing to do with identification. A left-wing director like Brecht prefers actors with left-wing views which they express in their interpretations of their parts. It is a perfectly legitimate demand, but it does not have any value as a theoretical insight.

Which, of course, is not to say that I, personally, do not infinitely prefer the relaxed, *Ausbruch*-free, distanced type of performance to the heavy, declamatory 'Hoftheater' style, or the humming-and-hawing Naturalistic style the training for which precludes the actors who have absorbed it from developing a sense of other styles or indeed periods of history.

But that is an aesthetic reaction, not an ideological one. The proof of the pudding, as Brecht never tired of asserting, is in the eating, and the Truth is concrete.

In the thirty years since Brecht died I have attended numerous performances of Brecht's plays acted in various styles. Those that adhered to the distanced, relaxed, elegantly delivered, brilliantly lit, pellucid style, eschewing 'atmospheric' moods, that Brecht advocates were infinitely preferable to those that tried to ignore his ideas of staging. But were they also ideologically superior? Did the style of 'acting' specifically contribute to or produce more conversions to Marxism among the audience? I cannot see any evidence for that: if any ideological influence emanated from Brecht's plays – and that still has to be scientifically and experimentally proved, although I doubt if that is possible – then that influence came from the thought, the intellectual content of these plays. The style of acting can only have played a minute part in it. Of course, Brecht's plays ought to be acted in the style in which he wrote them. It is also a much more pleasing and convincing style of acting than the ones he rejected, even in many plays that are not his own. On the other hand, plays by other writers may come over better in other styles: Stanislavsky – the real Stanislavsky not Strasberg – did a lot for Chekhov. Reinhardt did a great deal for the German classics and writers like Hofmannsthal.

To demand that the director should find the right style of acting for each individual work may smack of eclecticism – but that, after all, is only another term for 'historicizing'. Brecht, however much he may have objected to that inevitable working of the dialectic of history, has become a classic. And, as he himself asserted, the classics have only *Materialwert* – they are only raw material. And that applies to their theoretical musings as well as to their poetry.

11

Brechtian theory and American feminist theatre

KAREN LAUGHLIN

In tracing the roots of American feminist theatre, critics have emphasized the importance of the Off-Off-Broadway theatre movement of the 1950s and 60s, in which many of today's feminist theatre practitioners took an active part. In the work of groups like the Open Theatre, women found political interests and experimental techniques compatible with their own.[1] Perhaps because of the obvious historical links between these groups and the feminist theatre of the 70s, little attention has so far been paid to the role of Brecht's plays or theories as models and inspiration for women playwrights.[2] Yet Brecht's work has also played a significant part in shaping the emergent feminist theatre in the United States. Individual playwrights, feminist theatre groups, and other women who have assumed leadership roles in the contemporary theatre have linked their work with Brecht's in a variety of ways.

Beyond showing an obvious appreciation for Brecht's plays, American women have found three principal aspects of Brecht's evolving theatre aesthetic particularly useful in the development of a theatre which 'privileges the experiences of women, illustrates their oppression or shows opportunities for liberation'.[3] Brecht's comments on acting and the actor–audience relationship have been incorporated in the search for a feminist acting style and related efforts to highlight the oppressive nature of gender distinctions. The argument for the 'historicizing' of dramatic events has aided women eager to reclaim and re-examine history from a woman's perspective while at the same time revealing the social and political forces at work in shaping women's destinies. And, finally, the structuring devices and narrative methods of 'epic theatre', as developed by both Brecht and Erwin Piscator, have been useful to feminists seeking to move away from realism towards a presentational style more relevant to women's experiences. In borrowing from Brecht, however, feminist theatre practitioners have often adapted his theories to suit the unique perspective and demands of feminist dramaturgy.

In her diary for 28 December 1949, Judith Malina wrote, '. . . read Brecht's *Good Woman of Setzuan*. A good play, but it's difficult to do parable propaganda theatre.'[4] Though she may have found it difficult, Malina went on to stage powerful productions of Brecht's *He Who Says Yes and He Who Says No* in 1951 and his *Antigone* in 1967. While Malina was bringing Brecht to the attention of New York theatre audiences (and of those women coming under the influence of 'new theatre' groups like Malina and Julian Beck's Living Theatre), women, who were finally beginning to assume directorial roles in American regional theatre, were putting Brecht's plays on the stage. Nina Vance, for example, opened her new Alley Theatre playhouse in Houston with Brecht's *Galileo* in 1962, while in the previous year Zelda Fichandler, a key figure in the regional theatre revolution, opened a new theatre in Washington, DC with the first American professional production of *The Caucasian Chalk Circle*.[5]

Other theatre groups have not only staged but have also adapted Brecht's plays. In 1973 the American Alive and Trucking Theatre Company adapted *The Exception and the Rule*, staging it along with their own piece, *Ally, Ally, All Come Free*. In the same year, on the other side of the Atlantic, London theatre audiences saw an adaptation of Brecht's *The Mother* by feminist playwright Pam Gems. Three years later another American group, At the Foot of the Mountain, produced *Raped: A Woman's Look at Brecht's 'The Exception and the Rule'*. The title of this piece suggests less an adaptation than a critique of Brecht's play. Yet even this example indicates the extent to which contemporary feminist playwrights and theatre groups have been not only aware of but also influenced by Brecht's work. In the words of playwright and director Roberta Sklar, who herself directed *The Good Person of Szechwan* while in graduate school, 'Like anyone I have ever known who became seriously involved with a Brecht play, I was changed by it.'[6]

Not all of the women and groups who have worked with Brecht's plays have commented so explicitly about the influence of his work on theirs. Yet both the dramatic works and the theoretical statements of several feminist theatre practitioners suggest that these groups have both adopted and adapted a Brechtian acting style. Like Brecht, they have sought a style of acting designed to reveal the workings 'as well as the machinery of society which surround the modern playgoer in his daily life, so that the playgoer will *notice* . . . and criticize and change them not simply accept them as inevitable.'[7]

American feminist theatre's debt to this aspect of Brechtian theory can be seen in Karen Malpede's comments on the work of three feminist theatre groups based in New York: Emmatroupe, established by Eleanor Johnson and Judah Kataloni in 1975; The Women's Experimental Theatre, which was founded by Clare Coss, Sondra Segal, and Roberta Sklar in 1977; and the New Cycle Theatre, founded by Karen Malpede and Burl Hash in 1977. According to Malpede, 'Each of these theatres . . . seeks a way of speaking that is also a way of hearing. The audience for each is meant to see the actor understanding . . . the new truths she or he has uttered. The shock of recognition unites audience and actors, and each group is simultaneously moved toward an emotional understanding of the next world action.'[8] In Malpede's view, then, these groups develop something very much akin to the empathy between *actor* and spectator Brecht praises in his essay on 'Alienation Effects in Chinese Acting', a relationship in which the 'performer's self-observation . . . stopped the spectator from losing himself in the character completely . . . Yet the spectator's empathy was not entirely rejected. The audience identifies itself with the actor as being an observer, and accordingly develops his attitude of observing or looking on.'[9] Malpede's comment on the participants' 'understanding of the next world action' likewise echoes Brecht's insistence that this style of acting should lead the audience to see the possibility for action in the world outside the theatre.

It is difficult to document the actual practice of such an acting style by other feminist theatre groups given the ephemeral nature of theatrical performances. Interestingly, though, a number of feminist playwrights have attempted to write the double role of the Brechtian actor – as the character and as the actor observing and judging the character's actions – into their scripts. Most frequently this involves the use of either role reversals or cross-gender casting.

Myrna Lamb's 1969 parable play, *But What Have You Done for Me Lately?*, provides an instructive early example of this technique. In this play, a pregnant man begs a female doctor to abort a fetus that has been implanted in him against his will. The double role, of course, arises from putting the man in '*the* position usually assumed to be female' and associating his response with that of the many actual 'women faced with the prospect of an unwanted child'.[10] In so doing, Lamb lays bare the social forces underlying the anti-abortion argument. The man's medically engineered pregnancy strips away the idea of motherhood as 'natural' and inevitable while his confusion and terror bring into sharp focus the hardships brought upon women by what Lamb describes as 'a society dominated by righteous male chauvinists of both sexes who identified with the little clumps of cells and gave them precedence over the former owners of the host bodies'.[11]

In *Babes in the Bighouse*, a docudrama about life inside a women's prison, Megan Terry and Jo Ann Schmidman took the Brechtian acting style a step further. In their own 1974 production of the play at the Omaha Magic Theatre, the authors cast both men and women in the roles of the female prisoners and prison matrons, an act which 'led the entire company to a more rigorous study of "women's speech patterns, their physical and emotional behaviours and just how it is to be a woman"'.[12] This technique, like Lamb's role reversal, underlines a key discovery of contemporary women playwrights: the inability of male spectators to hear and truly understand what female characters are saying and doing. As Terry and her company observed, 'men are socialized to respond to a male body and a male voice; from an early age they seem to be trained to discount what women say'. Hence the value of 'alienating' actor and character through cross-gender casting: 'by putting a man in a dress, in the same constraints as the women characters in the play, it became clear to the men in the audience what women were up against'.[13]

But in addition to simply gaining the empathy of male spectators, this technique underlines the socially constructed nature of gender distinctions, leading the audience to 'accept from the all-female context of the women's prison that our perceptions of gender are based on social roles, gestures and styles'.[14] Terry and Schmidman enhanced this revelation through the use of Brechtian *Gestus*, in a scene involving a giant hypodermic needle used to subdue a particularly rebellious prisoner. As she brandishes the needle, threatening the prisoner, Teresa, with the painful injection, the doctor urges her 'to become a lady so that we can help you'.[15] With this *Gestus* the playwrights show – in the Brechtian sense – the process of female socialization and its painful impact on the women subjected to it.

In its use of masks to highlight the distance between the actor-character and his or her social roles, Martha Boesing's *River Journal* recalls Brecht's *Good Person of Szechwan*. Boesing's play was first produced by the feminist theatre collective, At the Foot of the Mountain, which she helped found in 1974, and which also produced the adaptation of Brecht's *The Exception and the Rule* discussed above. In *River Journal*, Boesing explores the two principal roles she sees as available to women within patriarchal marriage. The play opens with a wedding ceremony, in which the protagonist, Ann, is given in marriage to a mild and loving man named Myles. Ann's sisters, Vera and Carla, give her exaggerated masks of themselves as a wedding gift. Unlike Ann, who feels trapped and unhappy in her marriage, the two sisters have little trouble relating to Myles; Carla (the nurturing 'earth mother') cooks for him and helps him keep track of his belongings while Vera (the coquette or vamp) flatters and eventually seduces him. As her situation becomes desperate, Ann finally dons the masks and takes on each sister's persona, promising, 'I'm gonna be a good wife to you, Myles. I'm gonna do it right.'[16] But a horrifying fantasy in which she kills and dismembers her sisters finally leads Ann to discover that the roles symbolized by her sisters' masks are pure invention. As a figure who combines Ann's mother and an avenging Snake Goddess assures her:

> SNAKE/MOM: They're not real, Annie. You made them up. Just like I did before you and just like all the women did and still do who live in a world ruled by men. (*Pause*.) 'Cause it's the only way we know how to survive.[17]

In terms of Brechtian 'alienation', the mask device in Boesing's play functions much as it does in *The Good Person of Szechwan*. In both instances, the mask distances the actor-character from the role he or she adopts in order to survive in the given society. The audience, then, is invited not only to recognize these roles as pure inventions (though of undeniable power) but also to examine the social conditions which have caused the characters to take on these alternative identities. For both Brecht's Shen Teh and Boesing's Ann, the masks are necessary for survival within the dominant social systems (of either capitalism or patriarchal marriage) presented in each play. But whereas Shen Teh drops the mask of Shui Ta only when compelled to do so in the trial scene, near the end of *River Journal* Ann purposefully burns the masks which cripple her in an elaborate ritual overseen by Snake. While Ann's alternatives are left unspecified (as are Shen Teh's), Boesing shows her heroine discarding the roles patriarchy has imposed on her as she moves away from her husband and towards the strongly feminine river of her play's title. Audience members, however, are still reminded of the need to duplicate Ann's act of liberation in their own lives as Boesing ends her play with a typically Brechtian call to action:

> ALL (*sing*): The die is
> cast,
> The dead no longer
> singing.
> What's done is done.
> The pendulum is
> swinging.
>
> The question is laid out
> For each of us to ask:
> Whether to hold on
> Or to drop the mask.[18]

Brechtian acting is, of course, closely bound up with Brecht's notion of historicization as a related means of distancing the dramatic events and helping the audience to see the specific and changeable conditions shaping a character's situation. In his 'Short Description of a New Technique of Acting' Brecht writes,

> The actor must play the incidents as historical ones. Historical incidents are unique, transitory incidents associated with particular periods. The conduct of the persons involved in them is not fixed and 'universally human'; it includes elements that have been or may be overtaken by the course of history, and is subject to criticism from the immediately following period's point of view.[19]

Joan Schenkar's 1979 play, *Signs of Life*, incorporates such historicization in its exploration of the power relations between men and women in nineteenth-century America. Developed and performed under the auspices of the Women's Project at the American Place Theatre, this play interweaves historical 'fact' and literary fantasy. P. T. Barnum, Henry James, James's sister, Alice, and Alice's real-life companion, Katherine Loring, are placed alongside two quasi-historical figures: an 'Elephant Woman' named Jane Merritt, modelled on the actual 'Elephant Man'; and Dr Simon Sloper, who bears the name of one of James's literary creations but wields the 'Uterine Guillotine . . . invented and named by the founder of American gynecology.'[20]

The principal action of Schenkar's drama takes place on centre stage, in a room occupied alternately by Alice James and Jane Merritt. Here we see parallel scenes demonstrating the oppressive and invasive manipulation of both women by the play's male characters. Jane is put on display as a freak by Barnum and is used by Sloper for a series of medical experiments. Alice's nervous disorder, as well as the breast cancer that eventually kills her, also brings her under Dr Sloper's questionable care, though she is able to fend off his offer to 'strike at the root of the evil' in her body by removing all of her female organs with his Uterine Guillotine.[21] She is less successful in resisting the attacks of her brother, portrayed as a kind of artistic vampire, who first plagiarizes and then burns Alice's treasured journal.[22] The parallels between Jane and Alice, both in some sense frail and dependent on the men who abuse while pretending to care for them indicate a pattern of exploitation that is woven throughout the fabric of Victorian society.

Schenkar enhances the audience's awareness of this pattern by framing these scenes with an elaborate tea ceremony taking place on the stage apron. Here Mr James, Dr Sloper, and occasionally P. T. Barnum intersperse the banal conversation accompanying afternoon tea with more passionate discussions of facts and feelings surrounding the play's female protagonists. The tea ceremony itself provides 'historical' distance from the events unfolding on centre stage in that the tea-time discussions are all set in a period after the unfortunate deaths of Alice and Jane. As they narrate many of the events in the women's lives, the three men also reveal the attitudes shaping

Victorian America's 'perverse fascination and horror toward women'.[23] With its surface restraint and gentility and its underlying intensity of negative emotion toward women, the tea-time ritual performs a key function of Brecht's 'historicizing theatre'. As it 'concentrates entirely on whatever in this perfectly everyday event is remarkable, particular, and demanding inquiry', this scene 'demonstrate[s] a custom which leads to conclusions about the entire structure of a society at a particular (transient) time'.[24]

But in addition to pointing out historically significant forces and relationships at work in the past, Brechtian historicization is of course intended to suggest the continued impact of the dramatized conditions in other historical periods. In *Signs of Life*, Schenkar seems to be aiming at just such an effect when she speaks of her desire to instil in the audience 'a constant and nervous recollection of familiarity, a shudder of recognition' at the shared 'prejudices and inclinations' of her nineteenth-century characters.[25]

This confrontation of past and present is even more forcefully conveyed in the Women's Experimental Theatre's *Electra Speaks*, which draws on Western literary history in exploring the roots of patriarchy's silencing of women. *Electra Speaks* is the third part of the Women's Experimental Theatre's *Daughters Cycle*, a trilogy of plays focussed on women within the family. But, whereas the trilogy's first two parts situate their daughters, sisters, and mothers in the present day, *Electra Speaks* turns to the ancient world and picks up the figures of Electra, Clytemnestra, Iphigenia, Cassandra, and Athena from ancient Greek literature and myth.

The play opens with a recitation of 'the old story', the story of the House of Atreus as dramatized in Aeschylus' trilogy, the *Oresteia*. Electra's recorded voice, which narrates the familiar account of the sacrifice of Iphigenia by her father, Agamemnon, and the series of murders subsequently committed to avenge previous slayings, is accompanied by 'a series of transforming physical and vocal images' that first illustrate and then question what happened to the women in the classical myth.[26] Later scenes employ a variety of additional techniques to dramatize the contradictions between the roles laid out for these women and their underlying, patriarchal assumptions. The tag 'They say,' for example, indicates the patriarchal voice's canonical version of each woman's experience: 'They say she did it for the glory of Greece', says Iphigenia. But, she continues, 'they don't say she was a young woman murdered by her father./They don't say anything about her relationship with her mother./. . . Everything is what they say./We don't know the ways in which she resisted.'[27]

Brecht's suggestion that the actor historicize his actions and remarks by speaking in the third person is given an ingenious twist here, as it is even more forcefully in the scene entitled 'Electra tries to speak'. Stuttering and gagging as she adopts the roles of 'Everybody But Herself', Electra uses the third person to narrate her painful struggle to give voice to her own experience. What Electra speaks, then, is that very struggle, and the problems faced by women in general as they confront the absence of their experience in the documents of patriarchal culture. Her concluding line, 'there's probably more she could say', spoken 'directly and clearly' to the audience, insists on the link between Electra's situation and that of the present-day spectators.[28]

But it is Athena's monologue in the play's first act which most pointedly links past and present. Just as she defended Orestes in Aeschylus' version of the story, so the Athena of *Electra Speaks* emphatically argues against the women of the House of Atreus, enumerating Clytemnestra's misdeeds and even suggesting that Orestes was pushed into murder by his sister. But Coss, Segal, and Sklar have transposed Athena into a modern lawyer who has little sympathy for women who have not played the role of 'Daddy's Girl' as she has. Her view of Clytemnestra as 'a slut', her insistence that 'no woman is raped unless she wants to be', and her parting threat, 'I tell you if that woman were alive today I'd haul her into family court', offer a powerful feminist critique of contemporary justice even while recalling the classical origins of the negative attitudes toward women implicit in it.[29]

But the historical perspective of *Electra Speaks* has an additional motive as well, one that illustrates a significant modification of Brechtian historicization to suit the aims of feminist theatre. In describing their goals for the entire *Daughters Cycle*, Coss, Segal, and Sklar speak of their desire to retrieve 'the culture that emanates from [women's] half of the human race' and 'to dismantle the past and reconstruct it with [their] own women's consciousness'.[30] Thus, even as it reveals the historical conditions shaping women's lives, *Electra*

Speaks also represents an attempt to rewrite history by making the attitudes and experiences of the women it features a part of the historical landscape. Like other feminists in the United States and abroad, the Women's Experimental Theatre turned to history not only to reveal the workings of oppressive, patriarchal structures by examining them through 'an historian's eye', as Brecht would say, but also to reclaim and reinterpret the past from a feminist perspective.

Denise Hamilton's *Parallax*, developed, like *Signs of Life*, for the Women's Project at the American Place Theatre, embodies this reinterpretation process in its very structure. In a series of vignettes, this brief, one-woman show dramatizes Daisy Bates's leadership of the bitter fight to integrate the schools of Little Rock, Arkansas. The parallax of the play's title becomes apparent through the use of projected slides and televised commentary. These juxtapose the on-stage actions of the generally forgotten Bates with media tributes to Rose Fitzgerald Kennedy, who is lovingly described as 'the matriarch of America's greatest political family'.[31] Coupled with this display of media power to create a female hero is the revelation that Bates and her husband eventually lost their beloved newspaper owing to the cancellation of advertising contracts. In the process of reminding audiences of Bates's contribution to the cause of integration, then, Hamilton invites them to recognize the role of the media and advertising in the construction of history. In addition, the contrast of Bates and Kennedy underlines patriarchal culture's power to suppress – if not castigate – women who do not fit the traditional mould of supportive, suffering mother.

As a tribute to one of history's forgotten women, however, Hamilton's play also invites us to see Daisy Bates as a role model, to admire her strength and courage even as we are angered by our recognition of the social forces at work against her. In this sense, *Parallax* illustrates a more general trend among American women playwrights, whose reworking of history often features actual women from the near or distant past. Spectators may be incited to see the historical conditions shaping these women's lives and judge the characters and their actions. But often this judgement may not be the focal point of the dramatist's work.

In *Approaching Simone*, for example, Megan Terry displays the heroic spirit and powerful will of Simone Weil in an effort to provide an alternative to masculine models of behaviour. In explaining her rationale for writing *Simone*, Terry speaks of her desire 'to come out and be as strong as I can for *other women*. They need models, they need to know that a woman can make it and think clearly in a womanly way. All the heroes are dead or killed or compromised, and women *need* heroes.'[32] Julia Miles, director of the Women's Project, appears to share Terry's view. In the preface to *Women Heroes*, a collection of plays she edited and produced, Miles speaks of the need for positive public images of women and describes her project as an attempt to 'provide an examination and celebration of the lives of notable, exceptional women'.[33] Using a variety of styles and techniques, the six plays in this volume (which includes *Parallax*) explore and often celebrate the lives of real and fictional women, including Colette, Emma Goldman, and athlete Babe Didrickson. While the title character in Brecht's *Galileo* argues 'Unhappy the land that is in need of heroes', these feminist playwrights seem to share the view of Galileo's pupil, Andrea, that heroes, or positive role models, are indeed necessary.[34] Unlike many of their European counterparts, these feminist playwrights are not afraid to 'romanticize female identity' by building strong female characters embodying women's historical accomplishments and ideals.[35]

While some American feminists have turned to history without incorporating Brechtian historicization, others have applied Brecht's experiments with a historicizing dramatic form to the presentation of more immediate or personal subject matter than the 'epic' or 'history' play traditionally allows. Noting the existence of a similar phenomenon among British feminist theatre groups, Michelene Wandor argues that, while placing 'the individual in his/her social and political context' is a useful and necessary reaction to much realistic theatre, 'the epic case can be overstated, if it results in excluding individual and emotional life from a definition of "politics"'.[36] Although this remark may imply an unfair characterization of Brecht's own plays (one thinks again of *The Good Person of Szechwan* and its clear focus on the emotional life of Shen Teh), it highlights a third significant point of exchange between Brechtian and American feminist dramaturgy. For many American women, the structuring techniques and devices of Brecht's 'non-Aristotelian' dramaturgy have played a key role in the development of a dramatic form suited to the nature and diversity of women's experiences.

Once again, the comments of Roberta Sklar are instructive. Speaking of her own elimination of linear development in the Women's Experimental Theatre's *Electra Speaks*, Sklar identifies Brecht's use of episodic structure as a source of inspiration for this work. But her application of non-linear form seems quite distant from Brecht's. Observing that 'linear sequence is almost irrelevant in *Electra Speaks*', Sklar explains, 'What interests me about episodic structure has to do with expressing the inner life . . . At any given moment things are happening sequentially as well as simultaneously . . . feelings don't happen in logical sequence . . . Episodic structure fits that understanding of reality: that, as every woman knows, life is a constant three-ring circus rather than some linear tale of adventure.'[37]

In keeping with Brecht's description of the 'epic' (as opposed to the 'dramatic') theatre, the short scenes of *Electra Speaks* break up the play's action and help bring the spectator face to face with the patriarchal assumptions underlying women's traditional role. For Sklar, however, episodic structure has an added significance, providing a means of capturing the inner life and a dimension of experience to which she feels women are particularly sensitive.

Other feminist playwrights have also adapted characteristic devices of epic dramaturgy for the presentation of an inner or extremely personal reality. Boesing's *River Journal*, for example, makes frequent use of songs, announced scene titles, and readings from Ann's journal, all of which comment on the action and move the play away from the narcotic effect of the more realistic dramaturgy to which both Brecht and many American feminists object. But the journal readings in particular, with their surreal, often violent imagery, also take us inside the dreams and fantasy life of the play's troubled protagonist. Rather than evoking a broader, historical or political context for Ann's distress (as in Brecht's description of the use of projections in *The Mother*, 'to show the great movement of ideas in which the events were taking place'[38]), these readings instead recall Adrienne Rich's belief that 'only the willingness to share private and sometimes painful experience can enable women to create a collective description of the world which will be truly ours'.[39]

Similarly, both Myrna Lamb's 'Space-Age Musical Soap Opera',

The Mod Donna, and Megan Terry's musical *American King's English for Queens* employ episodic structure, scene titles, and 'reflective and moralizing' music which become 'an active collaborator in the stripping bare of the middle class corpus of ideas'.[40] In both structure and content, these plays stand in sharp contrast to the 'culinary opera' criticized by Brecht and represent significant attempts to politicize the musical form that has become a hallmark of American theatre. Yet both plays use a blatantly domestic setting and focus on the American family rather than on more traditionally 'political' material.

The Mod Donna explores 'mod wife-swapping' which has 'turned a bit dissonant, a bit macabre' by interspersing 'Soap Opera scenes' of an absurd and exploitative *ménage à trois* with short 'commercial breaks' illustrating the dissatisfaction resulting from contemporary consumerism.[41] Central to the play is a musical number entitled the 'Liberation Song', which repeatedly asks women whether they have the courage to reject the sexist attitudes and obsessions which make whores of women in bourgeois society. No one in the play appears capable of doing so, least of all the heroine, Donna, who is ultimately rejected by the 'boss couple' who have used her to boost the level of sexual satisfaction in their marriage. But when Donna's outraged husband symbolically executes her in the final scene, the Chorus appeals to the audience; a reprise of the theme song culminates in a rousing call for 'LIBERATION LIBERATION LIBERATION' from the oppression and degradation of women implicit in modern marriage.[42]

In *American King's English*, Terry reveals the sexism inherent in American English by exploring its use in a 'typical' American family. Set in a family home, the play's short scenes dramatize the impact of phenomena such as body language or the language of business, and the confusion created for young women by the generic use of the masculine pronoun. As in *The Mod Donna*, songs reinforce the play's central question, 'Do you think like you talk, or talk like you think?'[43] Mom's medley of popular love songs, for example, shows the shallow view of marriage she has adopted from the language of romance, while Dad's subsequent rendition of 'HOME, home on the Kitchen-Queen range', effectively demonstrates how the rhetoric of advertising has correspondingly shaped his view of his wife.[44] Both songs, and others in the play, sum up Terry's awareness of the power of language to shape even our most intimate experiences.

In various ways, each of these plays embodies feminism's basic contention that 'the personal is political' and thus reorients the content of 'political theatre' as Brecht and other male political playwrights have defined it. The plays' intimate, often domestic scenes and settings tend to reflect the tight links between women's public and private lives, the intensely personal terms in which they may see what Brecht calls 'social relationships'. And whereas Brechtian theory tends to play down the inner life in favour of an 'idea of man as a function of the [external] environment and the environment as a function of man',[45] feminist playwrights have emphasized the links between inner and social realities. As Sklar observes, 'For woman, the internal reality is filled with the social suppression of womanhood.'[46] Moreover, even those feminist playwrights whose work is not necessarily focussed on the 'inner' world, frequently draw attention to the family, marriage, and the traditional work of women as a 'basic part of any political structure',[47] thus redefining or expanding the parameters of the environment that should be of interest to the political playwright.

Perhaps, though, these adaptations of Brechtian theory are in keeping with that theory itself, a response to changes in the 'given conditions of men's [and women's] life together' of which Brecht himself speaks in *A Short Organum*.[48] In the earlier essay entitled 'The Modern Theatre is the Epic Theatre', Brecht argued,

> True progress consists not in being progressive but in progressing. True progress is what enables or compels us to progress. And on a broad front, at that, so that neighbouring spheres are set in motion too. True progress has its cause in the impossibility of an actual situation, and its result is that situation's change.[49]

The evolving feminist theatre may well be progressing in a direction Brecht never foresaw and might never even have supported. But the state and understanding of political struggles outside the theatre have changed in the thirty years since Brecht's death. And, given these changes, it seems entirely appropriate that the 'neighbouring space' of sexual politics should be 'set in motion' by techniques borrowed from Brecht and adapted to the needs and aims of today's theatre women. Both Brechtian theory and American feminist theatre appear to have been enriched by this confrontation.

12

The influence of Brecht on women's cinema in West Germany

RENATE MÖHRMANN

Women artists in West Germany have an uneasy relationship with Brecht. The generation of feminist authors who raised their voices in the early seventies judged him particularly harshly. They reproached him for his failure to speak out against the oppression of women, in spite of the fact that it was his aim in life to contribute practically and theoretically to the improvement of society.

Moreover, they accused him of cultivating Wilhelminian double standards in sexual matters. A similar response also came from male authors such as Klaus Völker or Klaus Theweleit. But the response of women writers has to be interpreted differently because the modern feminist movement – unlike the women's liberation movement of the nineteenth century – made the quest for sexual identity the focal point of its protest. An author who, as Karin Struck declared in her novel, *Class Love*, 'seated the women in his rocking chairs' and 'viewed them like a herd of cows'[1] could hardly be said to have encouraged female self-awareness. 'Brecht', she says categorically, 'is a male imperialist! If the guy were still alive I would grab and shake him and ask him: why are you such a god-damned capitalist imperialist?'[2]

This attitude, however, is rarely to be found amongst West German women film-makers. On the contrary, the playwright from Augsburg still sets standards for many of them – thirty or more years after his death. This is due mainly to the fact that in the seventies women film directors considered themselves more political than did women authors of the same generation. More than in other movements during the course of film history, Western women film-makers were aiming to change prevailing social conditions through the medium of the film and to establish 'women's cinema as counter-cinema', as the English film theorist Claire Johnston has suggested.[3]

In this respect similarities with Brecht can be found. One common trait is the appraisal of the film medium. After all, it was no coincidence that active feminists in the seventies did not use literature but film to propagate their ideas. To begin with, they wanted to document discrimination against women in the office and on the shop floor, the disadvantages arising from their sex, and their depiction in the media as inferior. Therefore they needed film. 'Film offers the potential to collect documents', Brecht had already stated in 1926, a period when German intellectuals hardly took notice of the medium of film at all.[4]

The collection of documentary material marked the beginning of international feminist film work. Like Brecht, the pioneers of women's cinema evaluated the collective potential of the new medium very positively (that is, the collectivity of production as well as the collectivity of reception), and were firm in the belief that it was superior to the traditional 'individualist' reception of, for example, books. But above all they shared the basic prerequisites of Brecht's way of work: the trust that the audience can be taught; the conviction of a discerning society; and confidence in the changeability of that society.

These prerequisites also underlay the choice of the forty-five films and videotapes shown at the first International Women's Film Seminar, held in 1973 in Berlin: the films exposed social defects, and offered possibilities for change.

Claudia von Alemann presented Brecht's requirements implicitly in the title of her analysis of women's work in factory and family, *Things Have to Change*, and structures her film entirely according to his model of class warfare. This generally applies to the majority of the films presented at the seminar. They all attacked the status quo and pleaded for a change in social structure. To this category belong films such as *A Premium for Irene* by Helke Sander, *For Women – First Chapter* by Cristina Perincioli, *Productivity Scheme* by Marianne Lüdcke, *Women against the Bill* by the Nottinghill Women's Liberation Group, and *We Have Won* by a French women's film group. All these films deal with the everyday life of female workers, with the organization of strikes, the demand for equal pay, and the problem of women's double burden.

The ideological relationship with Brecht results from the fact that feminist film-makers of the early seventies saw the roots of women's oppression in the capitalist system rather than in patriarchal conditions. They could, therefore, easily transfer Brecht's models of class struggle to the specific situation of women. The exploitation of women at work – as shown, for example, by Erika Runge, Marianne Lüdcke, Helke Sander, or Claudia von Alemann in their early films – is found to be the result of capitalism. The suppression in the private sphere is considered a secondary phenomenon resulting from the same cause. For example, the husband oppresses his wife not from individual but from social motivations; he too is a victim of capitalist society. The magic formula applied in all these films is solidarity: women of the world unite against men of the exploiting class!

One aspect of his work, however, that feminist film-makers did not take over from Brecht was his talent for entertainment. As a rule their films were extremely instructive but entirely lacking in a sense of humour. Laughter appeared to be a sacrilege. The audience was sent back to school, and the solemnity of the classroom dominated the scene. The message emphasized by Brecht again and again that learning and entertainment are not contradictory was obviously ignored by the first generation of feminist film-makers. However, that changed soon enough as film production by women began to receive critical and theoretical feedback, and aesthetic considerations started to play a larger part. To make their films a more effective medium for enlightenment, women film-makers had to study how their films could make a greater impact, and not just be examples of so-called 'drawer film', that is, the well-meant didactic film which nobody wanted to see except hardcore feminists.

It was, therefore, quite consistent that Claire Johnston, in her programmatic essay, 'Women's Cinema as Counter-Cinema', put great stress on the entertainment value of film:

> At this point in time, a strategy should be developed which embraces both the notion of film as a political tool and film as entertainment. For too long these have been regarded as two opposing poles with little common ground.[5]

This corresponds exactly with Brecht's conviction of *delectare et prodesse*, his conviction that the educational must be enjoyable and that real joy and pleasure always educate.

Thus feminist cinema entered its second phase. The affinity with Brecht the ideologist is extended by the appeal to aesthetic theory. The realistic didactic film of the militant phase was superseded by the parabolic story – closely following the aesthetic model of Brecht – interrupted by songs and commentaries in order to distance the spectator from the stage events and activate his own creativity. Moreover, women's films suddenly began to be enjoyable, which in turn made them attractive to larger audiences.

Particularly when seen against the background of the prevailing tendencies in the New German Film, these traits represent a virtue which cannot be overestimated: West German cinema offers a great deal, but little to entertain. A good example of the new joy and pleasure in women's cinema is Marianne Lüdcke's film *Love and Wages* (1973). This film deals with complex matters such as the manipulation of wages, everyday life at work, and solidarity between employees. It addresses subjects such as the low wages of female workers and their difficulties within the family. However, this subject matter is no longer presented in documentary form, but as a feature film, where social reality is shown in an anti-illusory way. In this respect feminist film theory again takes up the debate on the potential of the cinematic transmission of reality. Brecht had already addressed this issue in the twenties in 'Film Needs Art' (*Der Film braucht Kunst*):

> Thereby the situation becomes so complicated that a simple 'reproduction of reality' says less than ever about reality.[6]

The debate reflects the discontinuity of cultural experience, a particular problem for women, who during the course of history rarely participated in literary groups or artistic circles. Over and over again they had to start from the beginning. What had long been settled by Brecht and the subsequent debate on realism had once more to be undergone by feminist film-makers during their own difficult process of cognition forty-five years later:

> Clearly, if we accept that cinema involves the production of signs, the idea of non-intervention is pure mystification. The sign is always a product. What the camera in fact grasps is the 'natural' world of dominant ideology. Women's cinema cannot afford such idealism; the 'truth' of our oppression cannot be captured on celluloid with the 'innocence' of the camera. It has to be constructed/manufactured.[7]

While the orientation towards Brecht during the initial militant feminist phase was of a general ideological nature, this changed in the period immediately following. A majority of feminist film-makers now detached themselves from the collective, changed over to the feature film, and developed a new, less rigid understanding of what is called political. Their relationship to Brecht changed. It became less dogmatic, more individual, and assumed more varied forms of expression. Brecht now became less of a figurehead, or a government-approved advocate for social change, and was referred to as a dialectical partner. This process is demonstrated above all in the following films by the three most renowned and most productive women film-makers in the Federal Republic of Germany today: Margarethe von Trotta's *The Second Awakening of Christa Klages* (1978), Helma Sanders-Brahms's *Germany, Pale Mother* (1980), and Helke Sander's *The Trouble with Love* (1984).

It is characteristic that each of the film-makers refers to Brecht in an entirely different way. Margarethe von Trotta refers to *Mother Courage and her Children*, and attributes the features of the mute Kattrin to her principal character, Christa Klages. In this film von Trotta is interested in the relationship between anarchy and obedience, in the possibilities open to the individual in today's society of remedying abuse. Christa Klages wants to put the *Kindergarten* she has established on a sound footing, and she therefore robs a bank.

At the time the film was first shown the reviews saw the relevance of the story to the terrorism that then prevailed in West Germany. Von Trotta herself offers a different interpretation. The young minister of the small town – a counterpart of Christa Klages – tries to interpret her behaviour, which he finds alien, as a Brechtian parable. In his Sunday sermon he compares her with the mute Kattrin. 'Pray Kattrin', her mother had advised her when the perils were great. But Kattrin had not followed her advice: she had climbed on the roof and beaten the drum. It was this act of disobedience that saved the town. In the same way Christa Klages could not limit herself to waiting patiently, but energetically intervened. One could object that the reference to Brecht is arbitrary and even perverse, for Kattrin does not commit a bank robbery but merely beats a drum, for which she is shot. But such an objection would only block the vital critical examination of Brecht, and is really only the expression of an obsolete, authoritarian perception of the work. You don't put Brecht in a museum; you have to learn how to work with him.

Such a relationship is more easily achieved by West German film-makers than by many of Brecht's literary custodians. When von Trotta elucidates the conduct of her protagonist by comparing her to a character from Brecht, and thus impresses her behaviour on the audience, she certainly is not making an actual, but rather a potential analogy. She thereby places her main character in an ideological tradition which can be traced back to Brecht. This is one – the Brechtian – perspective. At the same time von Trotta pursues a parallel perspective, a feminist one, which she quasi-dialectically relates to the Brechtian viewpoint.

This perspective must not be overlooked. It is no coincidence that von Trotta does not send her protagonist, Christa, to her death in the approved poetic manner; on the contrary she is actually interested in her second awakening. This second awakening, the learning to see afresh that all the characters in the film experience, is not based on rational insight, but happens through *eros*. This becomes obvious in the initial sequence when the bank clerk is taken hostage. The hold-up is played as if it were a love scene. A similar erotic tension exists between Christa and the vicar, and it inspires him to write his sermon about Mother Courage and the mute Kattrin. By thus eroticizing Brecht, Margarethe von Trotta obviously falsifies him. The fact, however, that she goes back to Brecht's *dramatis personae* to articulate her erotic message shows his impact on West German women film-makers.

Helma Sanders-Brahms's relationship to Brecht is a very different one. While von Trotta eroticizes Brecht, Sanders-Brahms informs him with feminist thoughts in her film, *Germany, Pale Mother*. The title of this film – shown and vehemently attacked during the Berlin Festival in 1980 – refers to a poem by Brecht entitled 'Germany'. The subject of the poem is the rising National Socialist danger and in it Brecht deplores the destiny of Germany's sons:

> O Germany, pale mother
> How you sit defiled
> Among the peoples!
> Among the besmirched
> You stand out.

Of your sons the poorest
Lies struck down.
When his hunger was great
Your other sons
Raised their hands against him.
This is now notorious.[8]

Sanders-Brahms deplores the destiny of the daughters Brecht neglects to mention. War injures not only the sons but the daughters as well, although this is seldom recorded: 'The accounts of our innumerable defeats', Petra Höhne observes, 'are nowhere documented; they just disappeared in public disasters or in private happiness. Our mothers fell silent just as their mothers before them. Who could tell our history?'[9]

Helma Sanders-Brahms tells their history. The fact that she narrates the film from the perspective of her own mother and at the same time claims to tell the story of all mothers who were young during the Second World War, attempting to achieve general political relevance while using an intensely personal approach, was criticized in West Germany, primarily by male critics. It was regarded as unbecoming for a woman. The film would have been tolerated if she had told her mother's life story as a private matter. To claim it as a political parable, and to suggest an affinity with Brecht, was considered trespassing. Brecht, it seems, belongs to the male heritage only. This was already acknowledged in 1971 by Karin Huffzky in her poem, 'My Intellectual Friends':

My intellectual friends
Are often intimate with Brecht.
On top: patting the shoulder
On the bottom: in footnotes.

I also want to be intimate with Brecht
Say I.
My intellectual friends are surprised.
You? Why that?
But don't you know that Brecht is dead?[10]

'To read against the grain' has been one of the demands of feminist film theorists. This postulate was not meant to open the door to arbitrariness. It means: possibly to discover something else behind the standard, established meanings, something that was overlooked, or something for which a new generation will develop an *apparatus criticus*. Women film-makers, who work in a different medium from Brecht, presumably have a freer relationship to his work and are obviously less reluctant to read him against the grain than are women theatre directors, at least in West Germany.

The final example, Helke Sander's *The Trouble with Love*, is closest in its dramatic structure to Brecht's epic-theatre form. Sander adheres closely to alienation techniques. Thus she prevents the spectator from confusing screen and real life. She transforms him/her from a passive onlooker to an active participant, who gains insights and evaluates them. In this way she exempts the screen – as Brecht exempted the stage – from its parasitic character: it is neither an end in itself, nor is it a simple filling of leisure time. She achieves this through specific editing techniques, through discontinuous narration, and through her ironic use of alienation, and the perpetual changing of the relationship between sound and sight.

In tragic situations, for instance, she uses opera music, and at the same time the actors play in such an exaggerated manner that the audience immediately understands that it is participating in a dramatic performance. An example of this is her use of the title of her film, *The Trouble with Love*. It satirizes the usual idea of love. Like Brecht, Sander aims at showing that love and politics, the private and public sphere, are closely related to one another. If war films deal with the absence of love, this film deals with the presence of war in love affairs.

Sander shows that idyllic situations lend themselves most favourably to the study of violence. She refuses to build up her protagonist as a figure with whom one can identify, and to offer solutions to the audience. For instance, Freia, the abandoned heroine, reproaches her boy friend for treating her with Fascist brutality. At the same time she intends to form a gang in order to attack him and thus protect her honour. This doesn't prevent her, however, from giving him the key to her house. Thus the spectator is permanently irritated and no longer able to identify with one person only. Sander aims at a dramaturgy of 'interference' with the customary processes of thinking, what Brecht called 'interventionism' (*eingreifendes Denken*). She wants to sharpen the audience's awareness of contradictions.

But where Brecht was primarily interested in social contradictions or class antagonisms, Sander focusses on contradictions in the relationship between men and women. This is her feminist extension of Brecht's social analysis. The fact that she is adding new aspects and thus treats him quite irreverently only serves to keep Brecht alive. For he should not be embalmed in the pantheon of the immortals, but is rather an active part of our present cultural life.

13

From anti-illusionism to hyper-realism: Bertolt Brecht and contemporary film

THOMAS ELSAESSER

Film-makers, especially in Europe, who profess a debt to Brecht are numerous, but his legacy has been appropriated in very different ways. For Italian directors such as Visconti, Rosi, Bertolucci, Olmi, and the Taviani brothers, Brecht's influence has been very general, and is apparent primarily in a new dramatization of history. In films like *Senso*, *Salvatore Giuliano*, *Nineteen-Hundred*, *The Tree of Wooden Clogs*, or *Kaos*, the historical process is depicted not only in the Marxist sense as the movement of conflicting class interests, but also with that sensuous apprehension of contradiction one finds in *Galileo*, a play that more than any other of Brecht's has appealed to film people.[1] Charles Laughton gave it its American première, produced by John Houseman and directed by Joseph Losey. It may even have been inspired by Hollywood biopics, judging from Brecht's praise for one of their chief directors, the German *émigré* William Dieterle.[2]

French directors such as Jean Luc Godard and Jean Marie Straub have transposed more specific Brechtian ideas into filmic terms: rethinking the question of pleasure and spectacle, developing filmic modes of spectatorial distanciation, and exploring the politics of a representational form such as the cinema in much the same spirit as Brecht reflected on the ideological implications of the traditions of bourgeois theatre. Straub, for instance, prefaced his first feature film, *Not Reconciled*, with a quotation from Brecht: 'only violence serves where violence reigns',[3] and he explicitly fashioned the acting style and verbal delivery of the protagonists after Brechtian precepts; he also adapted a prose work of Brecht, *Die Geschäfte des Herrn Cäsar*, for his film *History Lesson*. Godard's work from 1967 onwards shows an intense preoccupation with the theories of Brecht, which in *La*

Chinoise surfaces in the form of extended quotations, and culminates in such explicitly Brechtian films as *Vent d'Est, One Plus One, British Sounds*, and *Tout Va Bien*.[4]

In West Germany, virtually every director of the so-called New German Cinema makes reference to Brecht, either as a source to be acknowledged or a cultural presence to come to terms with. Of these, Alexander Kluge is the most readily identifiable Brechtian. Films like *Yesterday Girl, Artists at the Top of the Big Top, Disoriented, Occasional Work of a Female Slave, The Patriot*, and *The Power of Feelings* are typified by episodic narratives, frequent interruptions by voice-over or inserts, non-naturalistic acting, separation of sound from image, self-conscious staging of scenes, quotations from diverse sources, and, finally, their didactic-interventionist stance *vis-à-vis* contemporary social and political issues. Volker Schlöndorff directed *Baal* for television with Rainer Werner Fassbinder in the title role, and his *Poor People of Kombach* is a didactic parable in a setting not unlike that of *Mother Courage*. Rainer Werner Fassbinder's theatre work bears the mark of Brecht,[5] as does the dead-pan diction, the 'primitive epic forms' of films like *Katzelmacher, Gods of the Plague*, and *The Trip to Niklashausen* with their division of the action into individual scenes; likewise, the deliberate artifice of the situation and the didacticism of the denouement in *Fear Eats the Soul, Fox and his Friends*, or *The Bitter Tears of Petra von Kant* are reminiscent of the modelplays and 'Parables for the Theatre'. Hans Jürgen Syberberg's first film was a super-8 production of Brecht rehearsing Goethe's *Urfaust* with the Berliner Ensemble, filmed semi-clandestinely from the stalls, and his German trilogy, *Ludwig – Requiem for a Virgin King, Karl May*, and *Hitler – A Film from Germany* is, according to the director, 'a marriage of Richard Wagner and Bert Brecht'.[6] Finally, the Bavarian aspects of Brecht's humour are shared by Herbert Achternbusch and Werner Herzog. Their sense of the contradictory and grotesque elements in human behaviour, their 'blunt thinking', and satirical materialism stem from the same source as Brecht: the Munich comedian Karl Valentin and his music-hall profundity.

It would be easy to go on.[7] But to understand the role of Brecht as a source for concepts of avant-garde cinema and as a model for political film-making, and thus to assess his role today, one has to look further than the direct echoes. Not all the Brechtianisms in postwar cinema, furthermore, are true to the spirit of Brecht, and among those who have claimed him for their work, fewer inherited his questions than copied his answers, which, of course, were by then no longer answers. Not only did Brecht come to stand for a very complex set of assumptions and practices among film-makers and for film theory of the 1970s; his teachings played a crucial role in the much wider cultural shift which marked the avant-garde's final break with high modernism. To understand this break, a flashback to the 1960s is necessary, when Brecht's theoretical work was rediscovered, especially in Anglo-Saxon countries.

> Fifty years after the Russian Revolution, the American cinema dominates everywhere in the world. There is not much to be added to this fact. Nonetheless we should, each according to his abilities, start two or three Vietnams at the heart of the immense Hollywood-Mosfilm-Cinecitta-Pinewood Empire. Economically and aesthetically, on two fronts, we must fight for national cinemas, free, brotherly, comradely and joined in friendship.[8]

By the time Godard published this battlecry in 1967, the struggle for a 'political cinema' was not only fought by European directors making common cause with Third World politics but also took the form of a 'materialist' film aesthetics. The result was a powerful surge in film theory which pursued divergent paths: in Britain, for instance, the journal *Screen* argued for a return to Brecht and his theses of non-linearity and anti-illusionism, of spectatorial distanciation, and epic modes of narration.[9] Elsewhere, and especially in the United States, film theory became avant-garde theory, and identified itself more with the formalist tenets of American painting and sculpture.[10] The emphasis was on the medium itself, and not – at least in the first instance – on its ideological effects.

While minimalist and structuralist film-makers such as Paul Sharits, Hollis Frampton, Peter Gidal, and Malcolm LeGrice demonstrated the properties of the filmic signifier by a systematic destruction of the object of perception, film theory borrowed from Saussurian semiology and Russian formalism. It argued that the cinema, because intrinsically based on the discontinuity of its elementary units and materials, was a signifying system rather than a representational art. Consequently, any critical theory of the cinema needs to clarify the relations between the heterogeneous material supports of the filmic process (optics, chemistry, mechanics), but also the relation between image and image, and between sound and image. Hence the significance for theory of Brecht's concept of 'separating the elements': breaking the appearance of sensory or sensuous coherence of the spectacle by using music as counterpoint, detaching speech from the body of the actor, and marking as distinct the different sources of word and image. On the other hand, separation of the elements also meant studying the fundamental discontinuity of filmic articulation in terms of the complex, but relatively stable codes it had given rise to in the commercial cinema of Hollywood, as well as accounting for the high degree of systematicity and formal elaboration to be found in the most apparently routine products of the international film industry. This became the province of semiological analyses of cultural productions with a mass appeal: films, television programmes, but also advertisements or fashion.

The common vantage point of political film-makers who followed the lead of Godard and Straub was a more or less explicit reference to aesthetic positions of the 1920s and 1930s, when there seemed to be an obvious political function for art and cultural production in the fight against capitalism and its political crisis-management, such as German Fascism. Thus, the anti-Aristotelian theses of the late 1960s, the calls for distanciation and for textual fissures, were attempts at a return, a commemorative gesture of preserving and reviving an avant-garde tradition in the visual and performing arts, for which Brecht and Benjamin stood as the twin symbols of the possible unity between practice and theory during a historical moment of opposition and rupture.

By contrast, the modernist-formalist project, despite individual emphases, derived its unifying force from one of the aesthetic principles of heroic or classical modernism, namely the artist's moral obligation to investigate the fundamentals of each medium: just as painting is essentially 'about' painting, the true subject matter of film is film. One could call it modernism's 'semiotic programme':[11] exploring signifiers in their role of constructing rather than reproducing a referential meaning. This was as true of Cubism in France as it was of Kandinsky, and it became the fundamental credo of American art, from Abstract Expressionism to Minimalism.

In so far as Brechtian theory was also concerned with demonstrating the processes of production rather than disguising the 'work' of scenic or theatrical representation, an area of convergence seemed to occur between the political avant-garde on one side and aesthetic modernism on the other, such as had not existed historically either in literature or painting. The confrontations between Impressionism and Futurism, Symbolism and Dada (not forgetting the debates between Expressionism and Realism) had often pitted the political avant-garde against aesthetic modernism, though Brecht (in his defence of Joyce or Faulkner) and especially Benjamin (with his interest in Baudelaire, Mallarmé, Valéry) were notable exceptions.

Peter Wollen, for instance, viewed Brecht's example as crucial in arguing against specificity (the modernist credo) and for a multiplicity of intersecting discourses, against the primacy of the artwork's materiality, and for a heterogeneity of the signifying materials, against the smooth, homogeneous text of realism, and for montage. Secondly, according to Wollen, Brecht implicitly and explicitly set an agenda for what a progressive artwork should be able to do: in order to represent the non-synchronic developments in a given society, it should preserve a level of contradiction within the artwork itself, represent overdetermination, and the dynamic interplay of different levels in the social process. In the name of Brecht, cultural theory could move from text (the modernist obsession) to the definition of an audience, and the ways such an audience might be addressed: '... the question of choice of artistic means can only be that of how we playwrights give a social stimulus to our audience ... To this end we should try out every conceivable artistic method which assists that end, whether it is old or new.'[12]

Although the question of the audience was at first secondary, the coming together of a political avant-garde, a structuralist 'alternative cinema', and a theoretical 'counter-strategy' in the 1970s was ultimately due also to tactical alliances and political opposition to the dominance of Hollywood on the world markets and as a representational system. Paradoxically, and despite Godard's call to arms, anti-Hollywood film-making was defined primarily as a problem of form: deconstruction of narrative for the political avant-garde, and deconstruction of the cinema's elementary signifiers for the structural-materialists.

In the wake of this 'politics of form', avant-garde film-making became almost exclusively devoted to the critical interrogations of the twin supports of mainstream cinema: narrative and the specular seduction of the image. Politics consisted of resisting the power of images, combating their construction of a second nature, and countering the reality of their illusion with a more or less didactic discourse about the nature of filmic representation. The gesture was that of a refusal, a negation, relying on pure antagonism rather than evolving a new form of realism. It was the time of counter-cinema, of unpleasure, of anti-illusionism.

Avant-garde film-making in the 1970s had thus to confront the cinema's relation to politics on the one hand, and of modernism to popular culture on the other. As to the first, the watchword was Godard's 'the problem is not to make political films but to make films politically',[13] a Brechtian sentence down to the very formulation. To make films politically meant to challenge the strategies which contemporary popular culture, especially the cinema, had inherited from the bourgeois novel and theatre. But it also meant to engage more actively with the diverse apparati of production. If the Hollywood-Mosfilm-Cinecitta Empire was relatively far away, the different national television networks provided a more immediate target.

Modernism thus came under attack from two fronts: first, with the cinema and television accelerating the breakdown of the traditional distinctions between high-art and mass-art, theories of unpleasure threatened not only to remain frozen in a sterile negativity, but to appear elitist and anti-democratic. Secondly, modernism's concentration on the text tended to imply a neglect of the way formal means function in a given ideological context of cultural production. In both respects the legacy of Brecht proved particularly instructive and also controversial. It will be remembered that Brecht himself had, in the early 1930s, practised a strategy of interventionism (*eingreifendes Denken*) in just about every debate and through every existing medium of cultural production. These interventions, tragically, his exile robbed of their full impact, even for theory. Brecht sought in every case 'not [to] supply the production apparatus without . . . changing that apparatus'.[14] He worked in the theatre, wrote radio plays, and participated in musical life via his association with Kurt Weill, Paul Hindemith and Hanns Eisler. He was active in proletarian associations such as the *Rote Wedding*, and wrote his learning plays for factories and workers' clubs. He involved himself in film-making via Prometheus Film, and, together with Slatan Dudow and Hanns Eisler, made *Kuhle Wampe*.[15] In the theatre he wrote for various publics, or non-publics, plays as different as *The Mother* and *Saint Joan of the Stockyards*, making the years between 1928 and 1933 among the most productive of his life.[16]

West German film-makers, both on the side of the avant-garde and among the so-called author's cinema, seemed to be much more susceptible to this side of Brecht, being directly involved in institutional battles and strategic decisions,[17] than to his value for film theory. Notwithstanding the international acclaim that some of them received in the 1970s, they situated themselves, with the very notable exception of feminist film-makers, outside the debates and issues that dominated Anglo-American avant-gardes and film theory during the same period. Because of the governmental sources of finance that directors and producers depended on, but also because of an increasing access to television, German film-makers adopted more self-consciously interventionist stances and confronted the question of the spectator in more practical terms: taking up social issues as their subject matter, and targeting sections of the public who could be addressed as special interest or pressure groups.

Intervening in the apparatus and not merely supplying it with a product thus became one of the most Brechtian aspects of the New German Cinema, crystallizing around the representation of the working class, of working-class subjects (*Arbeiterfilme*), and the strategies and compromises these entailed.[18] On the other hand, television further marginalized film-makers who wanted to develop new or non-narrative forms: television caused a sort of withering away of Brechtian counter-cinema as envisaged by Godard since, even state-run broadcasting corporations have a commissioning policy, which, while quite broad-minded in terms of issues and the expression of minority views, tolerates only a limited amount of formal experiment.

In the case of the workers' films, it meant adopting a Brechtian spirit, rather than following him to the letter: showing conditions not merely as they are (Naturalism) but from the perspective of their changeability, historicizing them (which could sometimes be close to a certain bravely Utopian optimism, by assuming that the dialectic operated in favour of greater enlightenment and progress). Such old chestnuts of the Realism debate as a work's Utopian tendency, and the notion of the positive hero were widely argued in university media seminars, but also in the house journals of television stations such as Cologne's powerful WDR. Significantly it was Ernst Bloch as much as Brecht who provided the key words (*Der aufrechte Gang, Das Prinzip Hoffnung*), not least because film-makers working in television inherited a typically Blochian problem, namely, how to revitalize or redeem the revolutionary potential of apparently retrograde but emotionally still powerful narrative forms: disciples of Bloch (such as Christian Ziewer) carried the day over the hard-line Brechtians (such as Harun Farocki). Bloch's writings also represented a more conciliatory stance *vis-à-vis* mass entertainment and popular culture than the teachings of Adorno at one end of the radical spectrum, and Brecht's at the other. Brecht's own attitude to tradition was very differentiated. He wrote, for instance: 'The manifestations of the proletariat in the domain of culture, its apprenticeship, its intellectual productivity do not go on on some ground exterior to bourgeois culture ... Certain elements of culture are common to both classes.'[19]

From a general European vantage point, however, the relation between mainstream cinema and the avant-garde in the late 1960s and early 1970s was radically and absolutely antagonistic in both theory and practice. Debates borrowed their metaphors from the vocabulary of the class-struggle, and – as in the quotation from Godard – from the Third World Liberation struggles. Since the mid 1970s, it is this very assumption of pure antagonism which has been questioned. For, while Brecht offered a more genuinely political strategy in one kind of battle, his precepts were scrutinized on another front, so much so that by the early 1980s Brecht seemed a figure who had closed an epoch, as well as opened up new perspectives.

In the province of theory, a sign of an impending change in the way writers came to think about the politics of representation was the use of Lacanian psychoanalysis to displace the Brechtian concepts of distanciation/identification with a different kind of opposition. Lacan's system of the Imaginary and the Symbolic stipulates a necessary connection between these terms rather than an opposition.

Stephen Heath, for instance, attempted to compare the Freudian concept of fetishism to Brecht's notion of distanciation by pointing out that distance is not the same as separation, the necessary condition of voyeuristic pleasure: 'identity in separation, the very geometry of representation'.[20] Following Christian Metz and Jean Louis Baudry, Heath argued that Hollywood exemplifies a cinema ruled by the Imaginary (identification, mirroring, control of and through the image), with pleasure deriving from the spectator's illusory discursive mastery over such narrative processes as point-of-view, camera perspective, and the positions of knowledge within the fiction. By analysing the function of narrative in centring the spectator and investigating how filmic images are encoded according to a rigidly binary logic, these theorists sought to demonstrate the workings of the structures underpinning the effects of the filmic Imaginary, hinging as it often does on a sexually differentiated opposition between seeing/seen, subject and object of the look.[21] Interest was focussed again on classical narrative (*Cahiers du cinéma*'s widely discussed deconstruction of John Ford's *Young Mr Lincoln*,[22] Raymond Bellour's work on Hitchcock's *North by Northwest*,[23] Stephen Heath's article on Welles's *Touch of Evil*,[24] Laura Mulvey's on Hitchcock and Sternberg).[25] Classical narrative came to connote less and less the practice against which avant-garde film-makers had set themselves, and more a 'system' of representation, a 'logic' of the signifier with implications for cultural production in general. Hollywood practice seemed to provide the key to how bourgeois society constructs such crucial social markers as sexual difference and subjectivity, and therefore how ideological coherence is maintained. Narrative cinema became not only the dominant form of film-making, but, more fatally, it came to stand for the master-discourse by which meaning was encoded in the 'social text' generally, across a wide field of visual representations, of symbolic action, and the spaces of intersubjectivity. In fact, the desire for spectacular stagings of events seemed to be transforming even politics: an observation which is one of the starting points of the post-modernist dilemma.

The main impact of the Lacanian model of false consciousness (the necessary relation between recognition and miscognition) and identity (not *cogito, ergo sum*, but 'I think where I am not, I am where I do not think') was that it led to a revaluation of the Imaginary: a sense of its pervasiveness and inevitability, but also of its potentially progressive political function, in the form of a play, masquerade, and 'style'. Pleasure, in other words, became a political issue. Brecht's own critical rationality, and perhaps the entire project of an avant-garde cinema, especially one opposing itself to the 'reactionary' ideology of narrative, came itself under scrutiny in the name of an inquiry into the Imaginary of any practice, whether conservative or revolutionary. By questioning the subject positions which a particular body of knowledge such as Marxism or structuralism implied, the cultural theory derived from psychoanalysis cast doubt on any objectivist position. Thus, for instance, the avant-garde became vulnerable to the ideological charge of implying in its critical practice not only an imaginary subject of enunciation – be it the artist, the film-maker, or theorist as owner of normative or prescriptive discourses – but also of speaking to an imaginary addressee: the yet to be constituted revolutionary subject. In this respect, Brecht's own strategy was itself somewhat ambiguous: because the implied spectator of the Brechtian text is the spectator-in-the-know, he (Brecht's spectator is mostly conceived as male) is the ironic spectator, for whom the text provides a complex matrix of comprehensibility based on allusion and intertextuality. The theatre becomes a stage for the spectacle of knowledge-effects. But it is precisely this area of knowledge-effects as pleasure-effects which the contemporary, technologically very sophisticated media, such as advertising, have colonized.

Thus what we see today is the devaluation of once radical techniques and stances, such as distanciation or self-reflexivity. Not only have the media become vertiginously self-reflexive in the recycling of their own histories; their incessant self-parodies and intertextuality have made self-reflexiveness the sign of a closed, self-referential system, the very opposite of Brecht's 'open form' or of his concept of realism as contradiction. Secondly, the ubiquity of television, and in particular its manufacture of news and personalities as show-values, tends to subvert the very concepts of the 'real' and of the 'political'. Political events, in order to attain credibility and the 'truth of the image', must necessarily pass through the process of sometimes intense specularity, with the paradoxical effect that, in order to become recognizable as political, events have to be staged as spectacle.

For instance, once the many conflicts and contradictions of a class-society or of gender-based discrimination are replaced in the mega-media-television text by a manipulation of subject-positions and spectator-presences (action replays of disasters, the ideology of live television, with its incessant appeal that 'this comes to you as it happens', 'you can participate'), any terrain outside visual discourses becomes non-existent, because non-representable.

Even the war in Vietnam seems in retrospect to have been on both sides a battle for the control of enemy territory only in order to produce for the world at large images of such horror and fascination as might transgress the limits of the imaginable itself. And when a President of the United States can order his Air Force to intercept a plane in mid air, as a message to terrorists that 'you can run but you cannot hide', international politics has succumbed not only to a movie scenario, but one where superpowers and terrorists alike use violence in order to create images, and images in order to send messages: politics as the semiotics of violence.

Positing a pure antagonism in the realm of social action has been characterized as a 'politics of otherness' in which opposition is already limited and contained by being caught in the mirror of the practice against which it sets itself – an impasse in critical thinking, which Baudrillard called 'the implosion of antagonisms' and Fredric Jameson in a slightly different context has described as 'politics dominated by the categories of the Imaginary':

> to stage the relationship in terms of so radical an opposition is somehow covertly to reintroduce Imaginary thinking itself into a thought which was apparently attempting to overcome it.[26]

This dominance of the Imaginary gave rise to such pessimistic thinking about the cinema's progressive potential as Jean-Louis Baudry's 'Ideological Effects of the Basic Cinematographic Apparatus',[27] and helped to usher in the 'Second Film Semiology', which forcefully challenged the structural-materialist avant-garde, as well as Brechtian strategies of distanciation and self-reflexivity when applied to film. Constance Penley, for instance, detected in the practice of 'foregrounding the signifier' a fetishism of the cinematic apparatus which merely displaces the male-centred discourse of Hollywood representation in favour of an equally male-centred obsession with self-regulatory, closed systems:

The minimalist enterprise seems to offer a particularly pure and extreme example of the quest for an unproblematic centre of significance, a unified and coherent subject, a position of pure mastery, a phallus which is not decomposable ... The minimalist film-work, then, serves a defensive function for the spectator, assuring the subject control over his own body across an identification with the camera (as carrier of his look) which then reorganizes space, time and signification according to the needs of his own narcissism.[28]

Similarly, Paul Willemen detected in contemporary uses of Brecht's techniques a thoroughly un-Brechtian formalism:

In the light of Benjamin's warning that 'In every era the attempt must be made to wrest tradition away from a conformism that is about to overpower it', the reduction of Brecht to a repertory of techniques constitutes [just] such an example of modernism threatening to overpower an avant-garde attitude.[29]

Virtually all initiatives to win a cinema-going audience for alternative uses of the cinema and new forms of filmic realism suffered major setbacks with the commercial recovery of Hollywood. In so far as spectators returned to the cinema – and in most Western countries the mid 1970s registered an upward trend in box office receipts – it was to watch Hollywood block-busters. With enormous profits for the industry came capital investments in new technology, notably computerization, special effects, and improved sound reproduction. Technical innovations, such as the Dolby system, were themselves the consequence of new promotion and marketing strategies. By borrowing from related entertainment industries like the music business, Hollywood was able to attract a different generation of spectators, whose pleasures derived from the thrill of film technology itself: these were better served by hyper-illusionism and simulation than by anti-illusionism or distanciation. Special effects, displayed in horror movies and sci-fi epics like *Star Wars*, *Close Encounters*, *Alien*, or *Blade Runner*, to a certain extent 'deconstruct' classical narrative cinema by shifting the pleasure of representation from verisimilitude and realism to fantasy and the self-conscious, self-referential play of illusionist codes, while eight-track stereo or Dolby sound systems are not innovations that create a greater realism for the ear, as much as they 'foreground' the presence of a separate sound space and the existence of purely imaginary sound 'effects'. One might even argue that both the modernist and the political avant-garde anticipated the nature of the change, but misread its direction, and its social consequences. Not a counter-cinema superseded Hollywood, but a 'new' Hollywood whose development was neither governed by the modernist telos of the medium's self-realization through self-reflexivity, nor by the political logic of opposition and confrontation. Instead, it followed the capitalist logic, which demands the penetration of new markets in the wake of the energy generated by the complex interplay between technological innovation, advertising, and saleability. By this criterion even avant-garde techniques could find profitable uses, and as a consequence the critical dimension of film theory and film practice was in crisis, overtaken by the dynamic of transformation and change that realized the agenda of self-reflexivity, but devoid of radical political potential, and with sometimes staggering popular success.

Whereas it was once almost commonplace to regard any form of cinematic illusionism as inimical to political functions other than propaganda, recent theory, such as Derrida's critique of 'logocentrism', Lacan's view of the phallus as the 'transcendental signifier', Foucault's critique of binarism as the discourse of power, has provided arguments which can in some sense be construed as a defence of the subversive potential of the Imaginary. And it is true that the hyperactivity unleashed in the body politic by the images of Vietnam, or of mass starvation in Ethiopia indicates that the intensity of presence solicited by visual representation largely outstrips any attempts at discursive containment. Images, it would seem, are always in excess of the narratives they serve: they have, as it were, a traumatizing effect, even though they are manufactured, and are seen to be so. And, despite being 'false', they have the power to move and to shock, thus undermining significant aspects of Western philosophy and metaphysics. In the present context this raises an important point: what would Brecht's views have been of the image and of its powerful falsehood: did he have a theory of representation? And, if not, do we need a critique of the critique of illusionism?

In the age of post-modernism, or of post-modernist theory, Brecht's remarks on cinema, photography, and the media, like other critiques from a traditional left-political perspective, have not been invalidated, but their appeal to a reality outside representation, outside the world of signs, has become problematic as a critical stance. The questions which the ubiquity of images raises are the following: can there be true representations, and 'correct' representational systems (see Barthes's comments in *Diderot, Brecht, Eisenstein*),[30] and is there such a category as truth, once we are dealing with nothing but images and representations?

Obviously, any answer must remain largely hypothetical. But there is at least some historical evidence which suggests that Brecht was if not unable, then unwilling to contemplate the full implications of the cinema's particular suspension of the opposition between truth and falsehood. I am referring to Brecht's collaboration in Hollywood with Fritz Lang, another Weimar exile, which resulted in the anti-Nazi propaganda film *Hangmen Also Die*,[31] a fictional treatment of the assassination of Heydrich. For Lang, the film becomes an occasion for constructing a scenario around different kinds of lies and falsehoods; the fight for moral truth is entirely conceived within the deceptive realm of images, which is to say that the moment of truth of an image is always another image. Hence the film's narrative development proceeds by nothing but a series of false doors, false bottoms, traps for the mind and for the eye. Gilles Deleuze has recently discussed Lang and Brecht in this sense on the theme of 'The Powers of the False':

> For Lang, there is no longer truth, but only appearances. The American Lang becomes the greatest film-maker of appearances. Everything is appearance, and this new system transforms the ability to judge, though it doesn't suppress it. Appearances are not deemed to be lies because they give way to some deeper truth, but simply because they turn out themselves to be not-true: a character makes a slip, like giving away that he knows German when he is supposed to be a Czech nationalist.[32]

Lang's relativism, according to Deleuze, is 'Pythagorean', where justice is at most the 'better' point of view, and where appearances decide in favour of the better cause or the morally superior character. Such a perspective, from the vantage point of the Image, allows one to understand the encounter between Brecht and Lang and also their misunderstanding in a new light. What the two had in common was that truth cannot be apprehended directly in and through the image.

Instead, judgement is passed to the spectator, who is merely given the means to perceive the image or the scene as constructed, as 'given to be seen'.

What in Brecht, however, is a matter of sharpening a conflict to the point of producing a contradiction, is in Lang a determination to demonstrate the necessary fallibility of appearances. What interested Brecht in the fable of *Hangmen Also Die*, for instance, is that the young woman who urges the Heydrich assassin to give himself up in order to save the hostages is quite prepared, a few moments later, to sacrifice another innocent, the woman greengrocer, in order to remain undetected herself. Brecht wants the spectator to see the contradiction between two value systems or, rather, he is interested in the dependence of an emotional reaction on the social context. What fascinates him is the reversibility of the situation around a moral dilemma, but it is a scene which could equally well be dramatized on stage.

Lang, on the other hand, is interested in how a man like the conspirator and Heydrich assassin behaves, since he has nothing but disguises, and since his situation is a false one whichever way he plays it. In the film, he deliberately and desperately engineers a play of falsehoods, not in the hope of staying alive, but in order to serve the cause as long as he possibly can. Sometimes, as in the scene with the lipstick marks which are applied too perfectly to convince the police inspector of a passionate *tête-à-tête*, he loses, and sometimes he wins, as in the scene where the wounded man behind the curtain starts dripping blood, which the hero quickly disguises by 'accidentally' spilling the glass of wine he was about to offer the inspector. Good triumphs only because it has another layer of appearances to bring into play. This alienation effect can be achieved only by filmic means and the specific resources of the cinema.

There seem to be two fundamentally different attitudes to the cinema. For Brecht, from the point of view of the producer, the cinema was at best a socially more convenient support for documenting the staging of theatrical performances, and at worst (seen from the point of view of its realist potential) a technically very defective apparatus of distanciation because it permitted no division between play-text and performance-text. For Lang, on the other hand, images constitute a reality in themselves, and any critique of reality situates itself at the level of the image: thus the search for truth can only be the play of the different *mises-en-scène* of falsehood. It may well be an open question, within the context of the cinema and our audio-visual culture, which of the two conceptions is today the more Brechtian.

14

The influence of Brecht

ERIC BENTLEY

I shall name three fallacies.

Begin at the beginning. A new star is found in the heavens. Stars, in astrology, have influence. New star, new influence. A recent instance is Samuel Beckett. A whole battery of astrologers have established that he has a prominent place in the heavens. They deduce from that that he has influence. They are correct. They even prove they are correct. I read an essay just the other day making it quite clear that the plays of younger dramatists are the quintessence of Beckettism. What I'll call the First Fallacy is the assumption – the taking it for granted – that this is a good thing. The plays that are full of Beckettry are not equally full of talent. So what is the question before us? It is whether these plays would have been worse or better without Beckett's influence. Unanswerable. How could one ever find out? Luckily, all I need for my argument here is the fact that the influence of Beckett is not, in any of the evidence, *shown* to be a good thing. It is possible that some of the Beckett epigones would do better left to their own devices. Or influenced by someone else. To go further than this, one would have to look in detail at particular examples and their whole context. The next conclusion to reach is that the reason for celebrating Beckett's alleged influence has, in the last analysis, little to do with celebrating the authors influenced. The aim is to celebrate Beckett. Beckett has influence because he is big. And he is big not least because he has influence. So what is wrong? Primarily, I suppose that, when we thought we were talking about literature as such, we find we were talking only about public relations. We were talking only of the way in which the astrologers call further attention to their star. No doubt they have every right to do this. But, contrariwise, we have every right to object to the confusion of one subject with another.

The second fallacy of influence lies in the fact that the word is not clear, and that it is not clear because it is a blanket term, and the blanket covers far too large a bed. What *is* influence? When Jesus appeared in the sky and said, 'Why persecutest thou me?', Saul of Tarsus, a Christian-baiter, became the Christian saint, Paul. That's influence: impact unmistakable and total, Saul taken over by Jesus. If only literary influence were as clear and simple! Some scholars have thought it *was* as clear and simple. If Poet A says the sky is blue, and Poet B, later, says the sky is blue, these scholars see what happened as the influence of A on B. The second fallacy of influence is the assumption that *post hoc* must be *propter hoc*. Which is still a fallacy when the examples given are complex. Those who do not allow for the possibility of this kind of error are allowing neither for accidental coincidence nor for natural affinity and confluence. Did Charles Darwin influence Alfred Russel Wallace or vice versa? The two men put forward the same theory of evolution at the same time. Science was converging on the same conclusion from two sides. Does this never happen in the arts? Something very like it is happening all the time in the arts. Here it is not usually a convergence on an idea. It is more often that the influences of A, B, C, D become so mixed that it is unreasonable to cite any one as *the* influence.

What about cases when *post hoc* is *propter hoc*, cases when, for one reason or another, we know that words were transferred from an earlier text to a later? If such transfer be automatically called influence, we have a third fallacy, the fallacy involved in assuming that if Writer A draws on Writer B, B is necessarily influencing A. Writers you quote do not necessarily influence you, they are necessarily being made use of, being exploited, by you. In such cases influence is only a possibility. Did the quotations in T. S. Eliot's *The Waste Land* influence Eliot in the writing of his poem? It is possible that in some degree they did. What degree, though? One cannot take the measure of it. One certainly has no sense of other minds bearing down on Eliot and changing his course. One definitely has a sense of *his* changing *their* course: the quotations *are* influenced by their context in Eliot's poem.

It is appropriate to introduce Bertolt Brecht's name at this point. In the songs to *The Threepenny Opera* was he influenced by François Villon? The songs are, to a considerable extent, based on Villon ballades. In so far as the spirit of those ballades is carried over into German by Karl Klammer the translator and Brecht the adapter, Klammer and Brecht are surely being influenced by Villon. All translators and adapters are obviously influenced by their source. Yet there is a fallacy – Fallacy Three – here if we assume that the word influence covers the case even approximately. One can argue that the young Brecht, and not only in *The Threepenny Opera*, was influenced by Villon, but one can argue, at least as persuasively, that he was not so influenced, but that he merely made use of Villon when it was convenient and amusing to do so. What people take to be the spirit of Villon in such work could in fact be simply the spirit of Brecht which had much in common with that of Villon. In this case Villon came in handy but was probably not necessary to the formation of Brecht's spirit and style. Finally, as far as Fallacy Three is concerned, when what we have is a source on which a writer is drawing, it is *gratuitous* to speak of influence, the word *source* covers the case. So I shall not speak of the influence of John Gay on the *The Threepenny Opera*, much less that of Nordahl Grieg on *The Days of Commune* – 'much less' because, if Grieg's play were an influence and not just a source, it would be a negative influence, it would have influenced Brecht, not to say what Grieg said, but to say the opposite. In a crass, literal sense, provocation *is* a form of influence. You are powerfully affected by what powerfully provokes you. And words are free – you can use them as you choose. But negative influence is sufficiently different from the positive kind as almost to require a separate word. For the prime function of influence is positive. It is to inspire.

Every inspired writer is inspired, in part, by other writers. This is probably as it should be. It is certainly as it is. And the same thing is true in the other arts. Beethoven liked to have the scores of Handel and Mozart to hand. He was influenced by them. It is therefore legitimate to ask of any artist: who influenced him? The answer should have, at the least, biographical and historical interest, even if it does not reveal any secrets of the art that results. It can be amazing how unerringly an artist finds the predecessors who can and will influence him. They will not always be the greatest. What the artist looks for is not merit on any terms but assimilable merit, congenial, relevant merit: merit that happens to meet his need of the moment.

Sometimes a major talent is influenced by a minor one. It can be asked: how could influence like that be called inspiration? Let's take a problematic case: the influence of Eugène Scribe, and Scribean drama generally, on Henrik Ibsen. It could be argued that Scribe did not inspire Ibsen but merely provided him with a formula. But this is unfair to Scribe, who came to Ibsen, so to speak, possessed of much more than a mechanism. If the cleverness of an Agatha Christie or an Alfred Hitchcock were just a mechanical formula, then anyone who learns a little of that, shall we say arithmetic, could write a Christie novel or direct a Hitchcock film. Scribe had talent of their sort. It has its own *je ne sais quoi*. To take over something of its real quality, and not just the externals of a method, one has to be inspired by it. (If inspiration is too romantic a term for your taste, call it an infection that one has to catch.)

Brecht and influence. First, the influences *on* Brecht. I do not propose to enumerate them. The ground has been gone over many times, perhaps too many times. What of the ground that has not been gone over quite so often? Writers acquire their status by having the influences on them noted and approved. It places them in a Tradition. You or I, after all, can pay someone to prove that you or I are descended from William the Conqueror. A writer can find scholars to prove his descent from Homer or the *Urvater* of his choice. Such games become boring only when scholars continue them after they have ceased to be needed. Ceased to be needed by their author, that is. They may still be needed for the scholars' academic advancement. But the boredom inflicted on the reader will now rub off on the author. He is now that most *passé* of all creatures, a leader of a former avant-garde, hero of yesterday's tomorrow.

Side-stepping, then, the main body of information about literary influences on Brecht, let me make one or two possibly marginal comments. First, influence of the great. Brecht was little influenced by the greatest names in German-language drama: Lessing, Goethe and Schiller, Hebbel and Grillparzer, even Kleist. Ibsen had no positive influence on him, nor did Chekhov or Pirandello. But Bernard Shaw's influence is marked on *Saint Joan of the Stockyards*.

It is not limited to use of source material. And it is in part negative: Brecht is reacting against Shaw.

About Brecht, Shaw, and Shakespeare. In his youth, Shaw had had to deplore the influence of Shakespeare on the English stage. He embarked upon an anti-Shakespearean campaign in order to free that stage for modern drama. People laughed, but the laugh was on them: G. B. S. knew what he was about. The dramatist Brecht emerged in a different place and at a different date. It was his privilege, as it was not Shaw's, to let Shakespeare *inspire* him. A professional enthusiasm for Elizabethan theatre in general probably had more to do with Brecht's so-called epic forms of the twenties than anything further afield, such as Chinese or Japanese theatre of which, even later, he knew much less than the thousands of Western students who today can see Peking Opera and Kabuki and Noh.

The final result of all the polemics and all the scholarship about influences on Brecht is that these influences have come to be overstressed. I have already suggested how that could come to be. First, there was a needed polemic to legitimize Brecht and establish his place in a dynasty. Secondly, there was the need of scholars to publish articles and their way of elaborating points and repeating facts *ad nauseam* before a halt is called. It is an irony that discourse which begins as an effort to raise Brecht's status ends by lowering that status. For to overestimate a writer's dependency on other writers is to underestimate his independence, his individual strength, his originality. I am reminded of discussions of Brecht's plagiarisms and near-plagiarisms. Critics who take pleasure in pointing these out are so carried away that they fail to note how Brecht made his borrowings his own. In *The Threepenny Opera* he might use whole lines of Klammer, but the song as a whole could only have come from one hand, his own. I am also reminded of discussions of Brecht's politics. Both critics who want to show him very much the Marxist and those who want to show the reverse direct our attention to what Brecht had in common with others, Communists or non-Communists, and not to the individuality of his thinking and his writing, his own persona as a poet.

What of the influence of Brecht's collaborators on Brecht? No one was more inclined than he was, in conversation at least, to credit this collaborator or that. Yet in the text that results from collaboration what one hears is one voice, recognizable only from the other works of the one poet, Bertolt Brecht. And these other works had other collaborators.

It is known that the play *Happy End*, except for the songs, was written by Elisabeth Hauptmann. I see no problem therein. She wrote in the Brecht manner, and not surprisingly came up with second-string Brecht. Some of my colleagues believe that she wrote most of *The Measures Taken*. I have no special competence to judge the facts, but any one of us has the right to say that, if she did do so, all that is thereby proved is that she could write better Brechtian prose than *Happy End*. And we have some questions waiting for any scholar who might prove that x number of lines in *The Measures Taken* did in fact come first from the typewriter of Elisabeth Hauptmann. For instance, before she went to that typewriter, what discussions had she had with Brecht? Given his capacity to be Svengali to any Trilby, couldn't he have told her what to write, perhaps even verbatim?

Note what has happened to my argument now. Asking what influence Hauptmann might have had on Brecht, I find myself declaring that *he* had an influence on *her*. Someone may retort that, being his *Freundin*, she must surely have had an influence on him. But this is not literary influence. I see no evidence that the literary persona of Elisabeth Hauptmann had any influence at all upon Brecht's own writing, whereas it is obvious that *Happy End*, if not written by Brecht, was written by a Brecht epigone.

Those, if any still live, who believe in the possibility of collective authorship can find little comfort in the works of Brecht. *Mitarbeiter* are acknowledged, if in small type and on a separate page, but nowhere is the presence of a second personality felt in the finished work. If the claim that Frau Hauptmann wrote Brecht has a future, it can only be accompanied by the theory that she learned to write like him. He was a dibbuk, if you will, and spoke from inside her.

I come finally to the influence of Brecht on posterity. This is to speak again of Public Relations. At an early stage of a great writer's career, his Public Relations Director may well decide to establish that he is not as iconoclastic as he seems. He is in a great tradition. He is great among great predecessors. Thus the music of Schoenberg is shown, not to be arbitrarily new, but to spring from Wagner and Bruckner and other worthies. But, later, Schoenberg's Public

Relations Director must do an about-face. The greatness of the same music must now be established by the fact that it is welcome to the bright spirits of the younger generation. An appeal to the Fathers gives place to an appeal to the Sons. It is understandable, then, that people who wish to pay tribute to Brecht should cite his influence. Their tribute seems to increase Brecht's importance. But they have fallen into the trap of my First Fallacy, and have forgotten that the influence of a good author can be bad. The influence of Shakespeare was bad at the time when Shaw declared it so: his case for liberating the London stage from Shakespeare was a sound one, and incidentally did not invalidate his case for a Shakespeare differently seen, as by William Poel.

The influence of Shakespeare. The word *influence* is vague in itself and is made vaguer by its object: influence of what part of Shakespeare, what feature of Shakespeare, what connection of Shakespeare's? When we try to answer this question, another question opens up. Is it Shakespeare himself who is having the influence, or things that have grown up around him, for instance, the Victorian style of producing him? Even if we decide it is the latter, we still have to ask if Shaw, attacking the production style, by necessity of polemic rather than logic, didn't have to tackle Shakespeare too? G. B. S. used the famous phrase 'Better than Shakespeare' about himself, though with a question mark that people then omitted. Even the omission belongs to the polemic. The thrust of the whole argument was that Shaw really *was* better – for the London stage at the time – than Shakespeare.

Back to Brecht. Influence of Brecht is influence of *what*, exactly, in the Brecht *œuvre*? The influence of his dramatic theories on theatrical producers? The influence of the Berliner Ensemble? The influence of Marxism as championed by Brecht? These questions, so different from each other, get mixed up – utterly confused – in our discussions of them.

At least one of the questions brings an abrupt change of subject. I have been treating the subject of Influence as that of the influence of one writer upon another, the inspiring of one author by another. This is a matter of writer psychology. Energies of one writer pass over into another. But when we talk of influence on audience, that is something rather different. An audience as such will not be inspired to artistic creation. When we say it is influenced, we mean that something from the work of art will stay with it, will not be water off a duck's back. There is an impact which, on the one hand, and most obviously, is emotional and, on the other, and more mysteriously, is spiritual and intellectual.

How *much* influence can any art have on its audience? The only limit, emotionally, is the limit of each recipient's own emotions. A big work will touch his heart as deeply as his heart can be touched. Spiritually and intellectually, he can feel stimulated, challenged, enlightened. It is even conceivable that his opinions can be changed, which would be influence indeed. In the theatre, this seldom happens. In any art, it seldom happens and is seldom the aim. If minds are changed by anything but circumstances, they are changed by the principal idea carriers: philosophers, theologians, even politicians. Dante, one can confidently assume, has not changed as many minds as Aquinas: if it is possible for anyone to convert you to Catholicism, a priest or a philosopher is more likely to do it than a poet. If you *think* a poet has done it, you may well be deceiving yourself: the poet probably came along after the real persuading, if any was needed, had been done. Thus, if someone is going to become a convinced Marxist, he is likely to be convinced by Marx himself, and not to the same extent by Marxist poets. If you ask me if Brecht had an influence on the *world*, politically, I would answer: very little, and that not always influence of the kind he sought. The influence of words, after all, is often, in all contexts, quite different from what is intended.

Brecht's influence on theatre? Certainly very marked, not only in Germany, but in France and England. But is this a good thing? Who can say? Besides, what is good? I'm sure we are not agreed on that. In politics, we are not. Are we agreed in other areas? Yes, we probably could agree that British Shakespeare production changed sharply after the visit to London of the Berliner Ensemble in 1956. Most of us think it changed for the better. It adjusted itself anyway to *us*, the audience of the later twentieth century: especially in becoming earthier, gutsier, what Brecht called more realistic.

In England he influenced playwrights, too. Was *this* good? Probably Edward Bond would tell us it was good for him, but, for my part, I don't know if it was. These things are hard to gauge. Who knows what Edward Bond would have been without Brecht? Maybe less dryly didactic and better. But I don't know that. A writer, when influenced at all, is often influenced in several ways at the same time. Brecht may have made Bond better in one way, worse in another. Since one doesn't have an uninfluenced Edward Bond to compare with our Edward Bond, we come here to historical *ifs*, ever a frustrating and futile category.

What of Brecht's influence in America? Much that is called Brechtian in the US, well ... Brecht can't be blamed for it, or can be blamed only for writing his theoretical essays. Students – teachers even more – love it when an artist has a theory. It keeps them busy, possibly earns the teachers money and promotion and confirms them in a belief that the arts are there to illustrate theories of the arts. A play is there to be a tragedy, or to be naturalistic, or to be epic theatre.

It is widely assumed that Aristotle announced the three unities, and that Sophocles then sat down to write *Oedipus Rex*. Brecht must have thought of epic theatre in about 1916 and then written *Baal* to exemplify it. Within their chosen field – vocabulary – what academics most enjoy is playing with words. Epic theatre: two words to conjure with. *Gestus* and *Verfremdung*: two more – and even better because they have no English equivalents. Thoughts that are really deep can be expressed only in German. Hegel established that long ago, and Brecht's theoretical essays provide further evidence. This way American scholars are kept busy writing whole paragraphs – pages – chapters – on what any single German word means. The same words provide translators with food for feuds. So, alas, Brecht's theoretical writings have had an influence in America: a bad influence.

What about his poems and plays? Poetry works on people so quietly and internally one can hardly speak of its influence till it is fruitfully seen, if it ever is, in later poetry. American poetry has not become Brechtian. Nor has American drama, though I am far from insisting that it should have. When Brecht's influence is seen, if it is not the influence of his essays, probably misunderstood, it is the influence of the externals of his theatrical technique. For it is easy enough to ban coloured light, to expose the lighting equipment, et cetera. One even hears actresses mimicking the mannerisms of Lotte

Lenya or coming on real butch, arms akimbo, legs spread, as Mother Courage, hoping that this is 'Brechtian'. (I have seen the style of a cabaret singer ruined by the effort to be 'Brechtian'.)

Nor is it just the essays that are misunderstood. Everything is misunderstood. When *The Threepenny Opera* opened in New York in 1954, I asked why the actors kept bumping into each other. Inevitably I was told: 'that's Brechtian, deliberate roughness of texture, closeness to real life, the result of *das plumpe Denken*'. I am not exaggerating: I am describing, without distortion, what influence ends up as, namely, the influence of what had not been said in the first place. No fallacy here, just error. But important because it is something that has happened before and can happen again.

What remedy, short of putting an end to all human stupidity? One thing that would help is to reduce human belief in influence, specifically the influence of the great. Greatness does not impart greatness. It creates epigones: many little fish swimming around the one big fish. Epigones hope for reflected glory. But glory reflects rather dimly and becomes much less glorious. It is legitimate for the small to try to grow but, in many situations, their purpose will be less well served by following on than by breaking away. Disciples have to find the energy to become rebels – or, better, voyagers.

Richard Wagner had many epigones, and a break with Wagnerism then became appropriate. Henrik Ibsen had many epigones, and a break with Ibsen became appropriate. And now, because Brecht has had all the adulation, all the cult following that any writer could ever aspire to, a break with him, and what he stood for, has become appropriate. This is by no means to say the adulation was undeserved. Today Wagner and Ibsen have no epigones. Wagner and Ibsen are the gainers. The greatness is all theirs. Our view of the big fish is no longer obscured by shoals of little fish. So it can be tomorrow with Brecht if those who are now dependent on him can change course and emulate his independence.

Notes

1 INTRODUCTION

1 Elizabeth Wright, *Postmodern Brecht: a Re-Presentation* (London and New York: Routledge & Kegan Paul, 1989) 124.
2 'Ein Gespräch zwischen Wolfgang Heise und Heiner Müller', *Brecht 88. Anregungen zum Dialog über die Vernunft am Jahrtausendende*, ed. Brecht-Zentrum der DDR (Berlin: Henschel Verlag Kunst und Gesellschaft, 1987) 193 (my own translation).
3 *Ibid.* 193–4.
4 Werner Hecht, in *Forum für Brecht*, ed. Brecht-Zentrum der DDR (Berlin, 1988) 40.
5 Peter von Becker, 'Wer hat das Recht am Brecht? Zum neuesten Streit ums Erbe des reichen B.B.', *Theater heute* 1 (1980): 16–19.
6 Personal interview with Ekkehard Schall; see Pia Kleber, *Exceptions and Rules: Brecht, Planchon and 'The Good Person of Szechwan'* (Frankfurt-on-Main, Bern, and New York: Peter Lang Verlag, 1987) 84.
7 Andrzej Wirth, 'Vom Dialog zum Diskurs', *Theater heute* 1 (1980): 16–19.
8 Brecht-Zentrum der DDR, *Brecht 88* 194.
9 *Ibid.*
10 *Ibid.* 194–5.
11 Wright, *Postmodern Brecht* 113. See also Wirth, 'Vom Dialog' 16.
12 A point made by Janelle Reinelt in her paper on Caryl Churchill presented at the International Conference BRECHT: THIRTY YEARS AFTER, Oct. 1986.
13 Bertolt Brecht, *Gesammelte Werke*, ed. Elisabeth Hauptmann, 20 vols. (Frankfurt-on-Main: Suhrkamp Verlag, 1967) 18: 139–209.
14 For a description of Pina Bausch's staging of *The Seven Deadly Sins*, see Wright, *Postmodern Brecht* 119–20.
15 Heiner Müller, 'Brecht zu gebrauchen, ohne ihn zu kritisieren, ist Verrat', *Theater 1980*, Yearbook of *Theater heute*, 134–5.

16 Brecht-Zentrum der DDR, *Brecht 88* 194.
17 See the conversation between Heiner Müller and Wolfgang Heise in *ibid.* 194–5.
18 Wright, *Postmodern Brecht* 75.

2 QUESTIONS CONCERNING BRECHT

1 See pp. 32–4, below.
2 'Appendices to the Short Organum', *Brecht on Theatre: The Development of an Aesthetic*, ed. and trans. John Willett (London: Methuen, 1964) 277.
3 Karl Marx, *Grundrisse der Kritik der Polititischen Ökonomie* (Berlin: Dietz Verlag, 1953) 154.
4 Karl Marx and Friedrich Engels, 'Manifest der Kommunistischen Partei', *Marx/Engels Werke* (Berlin: Dietz Verlag, 1961) 4: 482.
5 Karl Marx, 'Die heilige Familie', *Marx/Engels Werke* 2: 98.
6 Karl Marx and Friedrich Engels, *Kleine Ökonomische Schriften* (Berlin: Dietz Verlag, 1955) 143.
7 Vladimir Lenin, *Aus dem Philosophischen Nachlass* (Berlin: Dietz Verlag, 1961) 134.
8 In Bertolt Brecht, 'Man Equals Man', *Collected Plays*, ed. and trans. John Willett and Ralph Manheim (London: Methuen, 1970) vol. 2, pt 1, 31.
9 Bertolt Brecht, *Gesammelte Werke*, ed. Elisabeth Hauptmann, 20 vols. (Frankfurt-on-Main: Suhrkamp Verlag, 1967) 12: 488.
10 Hanns Eisler, *Fragen Sie mehr über Brecht* (Darmstadt and Neuwied: Hermann Luchterhand Verlag, 1986) 67.
11 'A Short Organum for the Theatre', *Brecht on Theatre* 180.
12 'Economising, therefore, does not mean the giving up of pleasure, but the development of power and productive capacity, and thus both the capacity for and the means of enjoyment. The capacity for enjoyment is a condition of enjoyment and therefore its primary means; and this capacity is the development of an individual's talents, and thus of the productive force. To economise on labour time means to increase the amount of free time, i.e. time for the complete development of the individual, which again reacts as the greatest productive force on the productive force of labour.' *The Grundrisse*, ed. and trans. David McLellan (New York: Harper and Row, 1971) 148.
13 *Spektrum* (October 1984) 18.
14 '*Historicizing* involves judging a particular social system from another social system's point of view.' Second Appendix to *The Messingkauf Dialogues*, ed. and trans. John Willett (London: Methuen, 1965) 103.
15 'A Short Organum' 201.

16 'Einleitung zur Kritik der Politischen Ökonomie', *Marx/Engels Werke* 13: 641.
17 Nicolai Hartmann, 'Systematische Selbstdarstellung', *Kleinere Schriften* (Berlin: Verlag Walter de Gruyter, 55) 1: 11–12.
18 Bertolt Brecht, *Stücke*, ed. Werner Hecht, Jan Knopf, Werner Mittenzwei, Klaus-Detlef Müller (Berlin and Weimar; Frankfurt-on-Main: Aufbau-Verlag; Suhrkamp Verlag, 1988) 5: 105–6. The passage appears only in this earliest version of the play, the 'Dänische Fassung'. (Translator.)
19 *The Messingkauf Dialogues*, trans. John Willett (London: Methuen, 1965) 102.

3 THE ORIGINS, AIMS, AND OBJECTIVES OF THE BERLINER ENSEMBLE

1 'Can the Present-day World be Reproduced by Means of Theatre?', *Brecht on Theatre: The Development of an Aesthetic*, ed. and trans. John Willett (London: Methuen, 1964) 274.
2 *Ibid.* 275.
3 *Ibid.* 274.
4 'On Experimental Theatre', *Brecht on Theatre* 132.
5 'Theatre for Pleasure or Theatre for Instruction', *Brecht on Theatre* 76.
6 'On Experimental Theatre', *Brecht on Theatre* 135.
7 '*Theaterarbeit*: an editorial note', *Brecht on Theatre* 239–40.
8 Bertolt Brecht, *Gesammelte Werke*, ed. Elisabeth Hauptmann, 20 vols. (Frankfurt-on-Main: Suhrkamp Verlag, 1967) 20: 308.
9 *Gesammelte Werke* 16: 710.
10 *Les Lettres françaises*, 30 June 1955.

5 PRODUCTIONS OF BRECHT'S PLAYS ON THE WEST GERMAN STAGE, 1945–1986

1 Friedrich Wolf corresponded with Brecht on a series of questions; this correspondence Brecht edited into a Dialogue which appeared in Wolf's journal, *Volk und Kunst* I (1949), and later in Brecht's *Theaterarbeit* (1952): 'Formprobleme des Theaters aus neuem Inhalt', *Brecht im Gespräch*, ed. Werner Hecht (Frankfurt-on-Main: Suhrkamp Verlag, 1975) 79.
2 *Ibid.* 138.
3 *Der Untergang des Egoisten Fatzer* (Frankfurt-on-Main: Suhrkamp Verlag, 1976) 50.

4 *Ibid.* 3.
5 Ingeborg Bachmann, 'Brecht', *Werke*, 4 vols. (Munich and Zurich: R. Piper, 1978) 4: 366.
6 Bachmann, 'Literatur als Utopie', *Werke* 2: 271.
7 'Going down Early to the Void', *Poems, 1913–1956*, ed. John Willett and Ralph Manheim (London: Methuen, rev. edn. 1987) 431.
8 Jürgen Flimm, 'Baal', *Theater heute* 4 (1981): 4.
9 Heiner Müller, 'Keuner ± Fatzer', *Brecht Jahrbuch, 1980*, ed. Reinhold Grimm and Jost Hermand (Frankfurt-on-Main: Suhrkamp Verlag, 1981) 21.
10 Heiner Müller, 'Brecht gebrauchen, ohne ihn zu kritisieren, ist Verrat', *Theater 1980*, Yearbook of *Theater heute* 135.

7 CROSSING THE DESERT: BRECHT IN FRANCE IN THE EIGHTIES

1 I applied to Brecht's French publisher, L'Arche. They sent me to the Society of Authors. They told me that they did not have comprehensive statistics on the plays acted or on the number of performances. To obtain the figures I had first to apply to the Brecht Estate. Then I had to be permitted to consult the box-office returns in order to obtain the information I was looking for. It would have been a task for a research librarian. I gave up and had to settle for my own, incomplete, archives.
2 Paris: B. Grasset, *c.* 1979.
3 Paris: Editions Publisud, 1985.
4 Paris and Geneva: Editions Slatkine, 1986.
5 Phil Casoar, 'New Weill, New Wave', *Libération* (31 December 1985).
6 'De *Palazzo* à *Puntila* – un entretien avec le CDNA', *Silex* 7 (Grenoble, 2ème trimestre, 1978): 18.
7 *Ibid.* 19.
8 *Ibid.* 18.
9 Bertolt Brecht, 'The Life of Galileo', *The Collected Plays*, ed. John Willett and Ralph Manheim (London: Methuen, 1980) vol. 5, pt 1, 138.
10 See Alain Philippon, 'Les Champs magnétiques: entretien avec Claude Régy', *Les Cahiers du cinéma* 387 (September, 1986): 37.
11 We recall that it is the title of a study of Brecht by Guy Scarpetta in *Promesse, pratiques: textes, lectures* 28 (Tours: Automne, 1970).
12 Bertolt Brecht, 'Can the Present-day World Be Reproduced by Means of Theatre?', *Brecht on Theatre: The Development of an Aesthetic*, ed. and trans. John Willett (London: Methuen, 1964) 274.
13 *Ibid.*
14 Georges Banu, 'Entretien avec le Collectif de Gennevilliers', *L'Herne:*

Bertolt Brecht, ed. Bernard Dort and Jean-François Peyret (Paris, 1979) cahier 1, 24.

15 Georges Banu, 'Entretien avec Antoine Vitez', *L'Herne: Bertolt Brecht* 1, 44.

16 'A Short Organum for the Theatre', *Brecht on Theatre* 205.

17 'Adieu à la pièce didactique', Hamlet-machine *précédé de* Mauser *et autres pièces*, trans. from the German by Jean Jourdheuil and Heinz Schwarzinger (Paris: Les Editions de Minuit, 1979) 68.

8 'HIS LIBERTY IS FULL OF THREATS TO ALL': BENNO BESSON'S HELSINKI *HAMLET* AND BRECHT'S DIALECTICAL APPROPRIATION OF CLASSIC TEXTS

1 T. S. Eliot, 'Tradition and the Individual Talent' (1917), and 'The Function of Criticism' (1923), *Selected Essays 1917–1932* (New York: Harcourt, Brace & Co., 1932) 3–11, 12–22; see Robert Weimann, 'The Concept of Tradition Reconsidered', *Structure and Society in Literary History: Studies in the History and Theory of Historical Criticism* (Charlottesville: Univ. Press of Virginia, 1976) 57–88, and Terry Eagleton, *Criticism and Ideology* (London: New Left Books, 1976) 146–51.

2 See Ann Wilson, 'The Politics of the Script', *Canadian Theatre Review* 43 (Summer 1985): 174–9.

3 Bertolt Brecht, 'Formal Problems Arising from the Theatre's New Content', *Brecht on Theatre: The Development of an Aesthetic*, ed. and trans. John Willett (London: Methuen, 1964) 229.

4 *Theaterarbeit, 6 Aufführungen des Berliner Ensembles*, ed. R. Berlau, B. Brecht, C. Hubalek, P. Palitzsch, and K. Rülicke (Frankfurt-on-Main: Suhrkamp Verlag, 1961) Appendix. Plays by Brecht were: *Mutter Courage und ihre Kinder* (1949); *Herr Puntila und sein Knecht Matti* (1949); *Die Mutter* (1951); *Die Gewehre der Frau Carrar* (1952); and *Der kaukasische Kreidekreis* (1954). The others included M. Gorki, *Wassa Schelesnowa* (1949); N. F. Pogodin, *Das Glockenspiel des Kreml* (1952); A. Seghers, *Der Prozess der Jeanne d'Arc zu Rouen, 1431*, adapted by Brecht and Besson (1952); E. Strittmatter, *Katzgraben* (1953), directed by Brecht; and J. R. Becher, *Winterschlacht* (1955), directed by Brecht and Wekwerth.

5 Of these, the following were 'adapted by the Berliner Ensemble': J. M. R. Lenz, *Der Hofmeister* (1950); G. Hauptmann, *Der Biberpelz* and *Der roter Hahn* (1951); M. Hayneccius, *Hans Pfriem oder Kühnheit zahlt sich aus* (1954); Molière, *Don Juan* (1954); Lo Ding, Tschang Fan, Tschu Dschin-nan, *Hirse für die Achte* (1954); G. Farquhar, *Pauken und*

Trompeten (1955); Yuan Miau-Tse, *Der Tag des grossen Gelehrten Wu* (1955). At Brecht's death, the Ensemble was also working on adaptations of Shakespeare's *Coriolanus* (*Coriolan*, 1964) and Synge's *Playboy of the Western World* (*Der Held der westlichen Welt*, 1956). Also performed at the Berliner Ensemble during Brecht's life were: Kleist, *Der zerbrochene Krug* (1952); Goethe, *Urfaust* (1952); and A. Ostrovsky, *Die Ziehtochter oder Wohltaten tun weh* (1955).

6 'Formal Problems', *Brecht on Theatre* 229.

7 Heiner Müller, 'To Use Brecht without Criticizing Him Is to Betray Him', *Theater* 17 (Spring 1986): 32.

8 Weimann, 'The Concept of Tradition Reconsidered', 87: 'It is this capacity for relating the living past and the life of the present, the ability to interconnect them and make them interact, that constitutes the historical dialectics of tradition.'

9 'Classical Status as an Inhibiting Factor', *Brecht on Theatre* 272.

10 See John Rouse, 'Brecht and the Contemporary Actors', *Theatre Journal* 36 (Mar. 1984): 25–41.

11 Bertolt Brecht, *The Messingkauf Dialogues*, trans. John Willett (London: Methuen, 1965) 54, 38.

12 'Emphasis on Sport', *Brecht on Theatre* 7.

13 Arrigo Subiotto, *Bertolt Brecht's Adaptations for the Berliner Ensemble*, Dissertation Series – Modern Humanities Research Association, 8 (London: Modern Humanities Research Association, 1975) 108. See also pages 109 and 150.

14 'Classical Status', *Brecht on Theatre* 272.

15 See Michael Patterson, *Peter Stein: Germany's Leading Theatre Director* (Cambridge University Press, 1981) 15–29; Louis Althusser, 'The "Piccolo Teatro": Bertolazzi and Brecht', *For Marx*, trans. Ben Brewster (London: Allen Lane, 1969) 131–51.

16 John Fuegi, *The Essential Brecht* (Los Angeles: Hennessee and Ingalls, 1972) 131; Reinhardt Stumm, 'Kritik durch Artistik: Benno Bessons Start am Théâtre de la Comédie in Genf', *Theater heute* 24 (Jan. 1983): 12. This paragraph draws on information from: *Theaterarbeit*, Anhang; Interview and chronology, *L'Avant-scène théâtre* 741 (Jan. 1984): 6–8; Manfred Wekwerth, *Schriften* (Berlin: Henschelverlag, 1975) 27, 76–9; Henry J. Schmidt, 'Brecht's *Turandot*: "Tuis" and Cultural Politics', *Theatre Journal* 32 (1980): 302–93.

17 *Den Tragiska berättelsen om Hamlet, Prins av Danmark*, trans. Allan Bergstrand, adapted by Clas Zilliacus, Lilla Teatern, Helsinki, Finland, 28 Sept. 1979 (première). Besson used Shakespeare's original title (First and Second Quartos) in publicity posters and the programme. This was

Besson's third production of *Hamlet*: he had mounted the play at the Deutsches Theater in 1977 in an adaptation by Heiner Müller and Matthias Langhoff and the same year in French at the Théâtre de l'Est Parisien and at Avignon: see Michael Hays, 'Besson's Hamlet', *Theatre* 10 (Fall 1978): 63–5. In 1983 Besson directed *Hamlet* twice more: at the Comédie de Genève and at Zurich's Schauspielhaus; see Gilles Sandier, 'Entre le bon et le mauvais il s'est malgré tout passé des choses à Avignon', *Quinzaine littéraire* 263 (1977): 20; Reinhardt Stumm, 'Kunststück über ein Stück Kunst', *Theater heute* 24 (Dec. 1983): 35–7.

18 See Helen M. Whall, 'The Case Is Altered: Brecht's Use of Shakespeare', *University of Toronto Quarterly* 51 (Winter 1981–2): 131. References to William Shakespeare, *The Tragicall Historie of Hamlet, Prince of Denmarke,* follow William Farnham's edition (Baltimore: Penguin, 1957).

19 Bertolt Brecht, *Arbeitsjournal*, ed. Werner Hecht, 2 vols. (Frankfurt-on-Main: Suhrkamp Verlag, 1973) 1: 210.

20 Bertolt Brecht, *Poems, 1913–1956*, ed. John Willett and Ralph Manheim (London: Methuen, rev. edn. 1987) 311. See also Bertolt Brecht, 'A Short Organum for the Theatre', *Brecht on Theatre* 202; and Brecht's letter to Eric Bentley on the reading of *Hamlet* offered there, rpt in *Playwrights on Playwriting*, ed. Toby Cole (New York: Hill and Wang, 1960) 101.

21 'A Short Organum', 202.

22 Brecht added the following epilogue to his 1931 Radio Berlin production of *Hamlet* (rpt and trans. in Whall, 'The Case Is Altered', 132):

And so, carefully exploiting the echo of chance drums,
Taking in greedily the battlecry of unknown butchers,
Finally free, by such a chance, of
His so human and reasonable inhibitions,
He slaughters, in one horrible frenzy,
The King, his mother and himself.
Thus he justifies his successor's claim,
That had he been put on,
He would have proved most kingly.

23 *Arbeitsjournal*, 1: 210.

24 'A Short Organum', 189.

25 Ezio Toffolutti, Programme Note, *Den Tragiska berättelsen om Hamlet, Prins av Danmark*, Lilla Teatern, Helsinki, Finland, 28 Sept. 1979 (première); see Ulla-Britt Edberg, 'Benno Besson regisserar Brecht . . . och hela Dramaten vibrerar', *Svenska Dagbladet* 30 Jan. 1981; Ulla-Britt Edberg, 'Maskspelet på Dramaten', *Svenska Dagbladet* 17 Feb. 1981.

26 See Robert Weimann, *Shakespeare and the Popular Tradition in the Theatre*, ed. Robert Schwartz (Baltimore: The Johns Hopkins University

Press, 1978) 128–33; and Robert Weimann, 'Mimesis in *Hamlet*', in *Shakespeare and the Question of Theory*, eds. Patricia Parker and Geoffrey Hartman (New York: Methuen, 1985) 276–7. Weimann, who acted as dramaturge for Besson's 1977 Berlin production of *Hamlet*, dedicates *Shakespeare and the Popular Tradition* 'To Benno Besson and Manfred Wekwerth, my friends of the theater who have come closest to a modern Shakespeare in the popular tradition' (p. [v]).

27 In 'Classical Status' Brecht suggests that the boredom of tradition and sensational eclecticism are two modes of theatrical reproduction endemic to the productive relations of bourgeois theatre under monopoly capitalism; in *Brecht on Theatre* 272–3.

28 Bengt Jahnsson, 'Originell Hamlet', *Dagens Nyheter* 11 Oct. 1979.

29 'A Short Organum', 183.

30 Jahnsson, 'Originell Hamlet'.

31 Benno Besson, Director's Programme Note, *Den Tragiska berättelsen om Hamlet, Prins av Danmark*, Lilla Teatern, Helsinki, Finland, 28 Sept. 1979 (première).

32 Besson, Director's Programme Note, *Den Tragiska berättelsen*.

33 See 'A Short Organum', 203.

34 Hamlet's speech, 'so oft it chances in particular men' (I.iv.23–38), and Claudius' speech to Laertes, 'Not that I think you did not love your father' (IV.vii.109–25), were printed in the programme, underscoring the insidious uses made of paternal authority in the world of the play.

35 Benno Besson (interview), *L'Avant-scène théâtre* 741 (Jan. 1984): 7.

36 'The Concept of Tradition Reconsidered', 87.

9 BLOCKING BRECHT

1 *Curtains* (London: Longmans, Green and Co., 1961) 390.

2 *The Theory of the Modern Stage* (Harmondsworth: Penguin Books, 1968) 217.

3 Malcolm Hay, '*Mother Courage* and the RSC', *Plays and Players* Oct. 1984: 18.

4 Martin Hoyle, 'Mother Courage and her Children', *Plays and Players* Dec. 1984: 18–19; W. J. Igoe, *The Month* Feb. 1985; Francis King, 'Length and Brecht', *Sunday Telegraph* 11 Nov. 1984: 18; see also Irving Wardle, 'Doomed to the Treadmill', *The Times* 8 Nov. 1984: 11; Roger Copeland, 'The Renaissance is over', *American Theatre* June 1985; Benedict Nightingale, 'On the Warpath', *New Statesman* 16 Nov. 1984: 35–6; Peter Dormer, 'Looking between the Lines', *Designer's Journal* Jan. 1985: 52–4.

5 11 Nov. 1984.
6 *American Theatre* June 1985: 10.
7 Malcolm Hay, '*Mother Courage* and the RSC', *Plays and Players* Oct. 1984: 20, and 'Judi Dench: Mother Courage', *Plays and Players* Nov. 1984; Richard Allen Cave, 'Saddled with her Own Bravura', *The Times Higher Education Supplement* 23 Nov. 1984: 18.
8 Michael Billington, 'Courage with Great Daring', *Guardian* 19 Nov. 1984.
9 Ria Julian, 'Brecht and Britain', *Drama* (1st Quarter, 1985): 6.
10 *The Times* 8 Nov. 1984; *Plays and Players* Oct. 1984: 20.
11 *Plays and Players* Oct. and Nov. 1984.
12 *Drama* (1st Quarter, 1985): 4.
13 Bertolt Brecht, 'Masterful Treatment of a Model', *Brecht on Theatre: The Development of an Aesthetic*, ed. and trans. John Willett (London: Methuen, 1964) 209–15; see also 'Does the Use of the Model Restrict the Artist's Freedom?' 222–5, and 'Classical Status as an Inhibiting Factor', 272–3, *ibid*. For foreign directors' problems with Brecht see also Werner Hecht, *Sieben Studien über Brecht* (Frankfurt-on-Main: Suhrkamp Verlag, 1972) 171.
14 See Brecht's 'Fourth Appendix to the Messingkauf Theory', *The Messingkauf Dialogues*, trans. John Willett (London: Methuen, 1965) 105. See also Gita Honegger and Joel Schechter, 'An Interview with Ekkehard Schall and Comments by Barbara Brecht', *Theater* Spring 1986: 35, where Barbara Brecht insists that 'Brecht isn't a style, it's a method.'
15 *Drama* (1st Quarter, 1985): 6.
16 Jerzy Grotowski, 'The Actor's Technique', interview with Denis Bablet, *Towards a Poor Theatre* (London: Methuen, 1968) 205.
17 See Max Grube, *Geschichte der Meininger* (Stuttgart: Deutsche Verlag-Anstalt, 1926) 51–8.
18 Bertolt Brecht, 'Grundarrangement', *Gesammelte Werke*, ed. Elisabeth Hauptmann, 20 vols. (Frankfurt-on-Main: Suhrkamp Verlag, 1967) 16: 749–50.
19 See the notes to John Willett's trans. of *Mother Courage and her Children* (London: Methuen, 1980) 106–7.
20 'Fragen über die Arbeit des Spielleiters', *Gesammelte Werke* 7: 755–6.
21 *Ibid*. 16: 756.
22 See John Willett, *Brecht in Context* (London: Methuen, 1984) 129–50; for Brecht's approach to montage with special reference to *Kuhle Wampe*, see Roswitha Mueller, 'Montage in Brecht', *Theatre Journal* 39. 4 (Dec. 1987): 473–86.
23 Trans. Eric Bentley and Desmond Vesey (New York: Grove Press, 1960) 99.

24 'A Short Organum for the Theatre', *Brecht on Theatre* 201.
25 'The Modern Theatre is the Epic Theatre', *Brecht on Theatre* 37. For Brecht and Eisenstein see Antony Tatlow, *The Mask of Evil* (Bern and Frankfurt-on-Main: Peter Lang, 1977) 168–72, 239–40; and Roland Barthes, 'Diderot, Brecht, Eisenstein', *The Responsibility of Forms*, trans. Richard Howard (New York: Hill and Wang, 1985) 89–97.
26 Franco Ruffini, 'Horizontal and Vertical Montage in the Theatre', *New Theatre Quarterly* 11, 5 (Feb. 1986): 29–37. For another approach to Brecht and Brueghel see Luigi Squarzina, 'Brecht and Brueghel: Mannerism and the Avant-Garde', in *Beyond Brecht/Über Brecht hinaus: The Brecht Yearbook*, ed. John Fuegi *et al.*, 11 (Detroit: Wayne State Univ. Press, 1982) 123–43; see also Willett, *Brecht in Context* 140.
27 See André Bazin, *Jean Renoir*, trans. W. W. Halsey II and William H. Simon (New York: Simon and Schuster, 1973) 88–90.
28 See Arno Paul, 'Theater', in *Berlin 1910–1933*, ed. Eberhard Roters, trans. Marguerite Mounier (New York: Rizzoli, 1982) 206–66.
29 *Gesammelte Werke* 18: 279–80.
30 Bertolt Brecht, *Arbeitsjournal*, ed. Werner Hecht, 2 vols. (Frankfurt-on-Main: Suhrkamp Verlag, 1973) 1: 399–400.
31 Herbert Blau, *The Impossible Theater: A Manifesto* (New York: Macmillan, 1964) 194–5.
32 Trans. Willett, 111.
33 Angelika Hurwicz, 'Bemerkungen zu den Proben', in *Brecht's Theaterarbeit: Seine Inszenierung des Kaukasischen Kreidekreises*, ed. Werner Hecht (Frankfurt-on-Main: Suhrkamp Verlag, 1985) 41–7.
34 Hurwicz, 'Bemerkungen zu den Proben' 43.
35 See Eric Bentley, 'The Brecht Memoir', *Theater* Spring 1983: 21.
36 'The Brecht Memoir' 21. See also Willett, *Brecht in Context* 208: 'Everything in Brecht's work was saying something – every sentence, every movement , every musical phrase or pictorial element in the set . . .' The importance of significant detail in Brecht's productions was first examined by Roland Barthes in 'Sept photos-modèles de *Mère Courage*', *Théâtre populaire* 35 (1959): 17–32.
37 Trans. Willett, 136.
38 Trans. Walter Herries Pollock (New York: Hill and Wang, 1957) 32–3.
39 *The Messingkauf Dialogues* 75–6.
40 'Alienation Effects in Chinese Acting', *Brecht on Theatre* 94.
41 For 'discontinuous playing' see Werner Hecht, *Sieben Studien über Brecht* 152–3; further described in detail by Joachim Tenschert in a Masterclass, BRECHT: THIRTY YEARS AFTER Conference, University of Toronto, 25 Oct. 1986.

42 Jim Hiley, *Theatre at Work: The Story of the National Theatre's Production of Brecht's 'Galileo'* (London: Routledge and Kegan Paul, 1981) 133.
43 *Gesammelte Werke* 7: 762.
44 'A Short Organum', *Brecht on Theatre* 204.
45 'A Short Organum', 235.
46 Hans Bunge, *Fragen Sie mehr über Brecht: Hanns Eisler im Gespräch* (Munich: Rogner and Bernhard, 1976) 68–9.
47 *The Responsibility of Forms* 93.
48 At a Roundtable, 'Brecht and Playwriting Today', BRECHT: THIRTY YEARS AFTER Conference. For Brechtian film criticism and aesthetics see Martin Walsh, *The Brechtian Aspect of Radical Cinema*, ed. Keith M. Griffiths (London: British Film Institute, 1979); Stephen Heath, *Questions of Cinema* (London: Macmillan, 1981) 16–17; and especially Dana Polan, 'The Politics of a Brechtian Aesthetics', in *The Political Language of Film and the Avant-Garde* (Ann Arbor: UMI Research Press, 1985) 79–99, for an excellent summary of current Brechtian film aesthetics.
49 *The Messingkauf Dialogues* 58.
50 'Masterful Treatment of a Model', *Brecht on Theatre* 209–15. For the question of replication and Brecht's attitude, see Pia Kleber, *Exceptions and Rules: Brecht, Planchon and 'The Good Person of Szechwan'* (Frankfurt-on-Main, Bern and New York: Peter Lang Verlag, 1987) 94–5.

10 SOME REFLECTIONS ON BRECHT AND ACTING

1 Bertolt Brecht, 'Der Messingkauf', *Gesammelte Werke*, ed. Elisabeth Hauptmann, 20 vols. (Frankfurt-on-Main: Suhrkamp Verlag, 1967) 16: 645–6.
2 *Ibid.* 573.
3 'Über eine nichtaristotelische Dramatik', *Gesammelte Werke* 15: 309–10.
4 'Der Messingkauf', 630–1.

11 BRECHTIAN THEORY AND AMERICAN FEMINIST THEATRE

1 Both Roberta Sklar and Megan Terry, for example, were associated with the Open Theatre in the 1960s and acknowledge the impact of the outlook and techniques developed with this group on their subsequent work. See Megan Terry, interview, *Interviews with Contemporary Women Playwrights*, with Kathleen Betsko and Rachel Koenig (New York: Beech Tree Books, 1987) 380, and Roberta Sklar, 'Roberta Sklar:

Toward Creating a Women's Theatre', interview with Cornelia Brunner, *The Drama Review* 24.2 (1980): 30–1.

2 Helene Keyssar's *Feminist Theatre* (Houndmills, England: Macmillan, 1984), for example, notes that the current wave of 'feminist drama had its most immediate roots in the political and aesthetic disruptions of the 1960s' (p. 1). Though she goes on to cite Stanislavsky, Gertrude Stein, and others as influential figures, Brecht's name never appears in her discussion of the 'Roots and Contexts' of feminist theatre. Elizabeth J. Natalle's *Feminist Theatre: A Study in Persuasion* (Metuchen, NJ: Scarecrow, 1985) is only slightly more helpful since she merely lists Brecht and Piscator alongside Aristophanes, Ibsen, and Shaw as playwrights who, like the feminist theatre groups she studies, have used the stage 'to advocate a point of view' (p. 1).

3 This is Sue-Ellen Case's definition of the feminist approach to theatre as cited in Linda Walsh Jenkins and Susan Ogden-Malouf, 'The (Female) Actor Prepares', *Theater* 17. 1 (1985): 66. There are nearly as many definitions of feminist theatre as there are feminist theatre practitioners. Case's phrasing, however, sums up the salient features of many of these. See the introduction to Dinah Luise Leavitt, *Feminist Theatre Groups* (Jefferson, NC: McFarland, 1980) for a fuller discussion of the problems of defining this phenomenon.

4 Judith Malina, *The Diaries of Judith Malina: 1947–1957* (New York: Grove Press, 1984) 94.

5 Dorothy B. Magnus, 'Matriarchs of the Regional Theatre', *Women in American Theatre: Careers, Images, Movements*, ed. Helen Krich Chinoy and Linda Walsh Jenkins (New York: Crown, 1981) 221, 223.

6 'Roberta Sklar: Toward Creating a Women's Theatre', 28.

7 Timothy J. Wiles, *The Theater Event: Modern Theories of Performance* (Chicago: University of Chicago Press, 1980) 71.

8 Karen Malpede, 'Feminist Plays and Performance: Ending the Violence We Have Known', *Women in Theatre: Compassion and Hope*, ed. Karen Malpede (New York: Drama Books, 1983) 233.

9 Bertolt Brecht, *Brecht on Theatre: The Development of an Aesthetic*, ed. and trans. John Willett (London: Methuen, 1964) 93.

10 Keyssar, *Feminist Theatre* 104.

11 Myrna Lamb, 'But What Have You Done for Me Lately? or Pure Polemic', *The Mod Donna and Scyklon Z: Plays of Women's Liberation* (New York: Pathfinder, 1971) 158.

12 Keyssar, *Feminist Theatre* 73.

13 Megan Terry, *Interviews with Contemporary Women Playwrights* 394.

14 Keyssar, *Feminist Theatre* 74.

15 Megan Terry and Jo Ann Schmidman, 'Babes in the Bighouse', *High Energy Musicals from the Omaha Magic Theatre* (New York: Broadway Play Publishing, 1983) 202.
16 Martha Boesing, 'River Journal', *Journeys along the Matrix: Three Plays* (Minneapolis: Vanilla Press, 1978) 62.
17 *Ibid.* 72.
18 *Ibid.* 78.
19 *Brecht on Theatre* 140.
20 Joan Schenkar, 'Signs of Life', *The Women's Project: Seven New Plays by Women*, ed. Julia Miles (New York: Performing Arts Journal Publications, 1980) 310.
21 *Ibid.* 346.
22 Vivian Patraka notes James's 'artistic vampirism' and points to the parallels between James and Sloper in her 'Notes on Technique in Feminist Drama: *Apple Pie* and *Signs of Life*', *Women & Performance* 1.2 (1984): 68.
23 Patraka, 'Notes on Technique in Feminist Drama' 67.
24 'Alienation Effects in Chinese Acting', *Brecht on Theatre* 97–8.
25 Schenkar, *The Women's Project* 313.
26 Clare Coss, Sondra Segal, and Roberta Sklar, 'Electra Speaks', *Union Seminary Quarterly Review* 35.3 and 4 (1980): 226. The full text of 'Electra Speaks' is unpublished; this piece contains substantial excerpts from the play as well as an introduction by the authors and forms the basis for my analysis.
27 *Ibid.* 240–1.
28 *Ibid.* 253.
29 *Ibid.* 237–9.
30 *Ibid.* 223.
31 Denise Hamilton, 'Parallax (In Honor of Daisy Bates)', *Women Heroes: Six Short Plays from the Women's Project*, ed. Julia Miles (New York: Applause, 1986) 61.
32 Megan Terry, *Approaching Simone* (Old Westbury, NY: Feminist Press, 1973). Terry's comment appears on the dust jacket of this volume.
33 Julia Miles, 'Introduction', *Women Heroes*, vii.
34 Bertolt Brecht, *The Life of Galileo*, trans. Desmond I. Vesey (London: Methuen, 1963) 108.
35 See Elin Diamond, 'Refusing the Romanticism of Identity: Narrative Interventions in Churchill, Benmussa, Duras', *Theatre Journal* 37.3 (1985): 273–86, for a discussion of three European alternatives to the valorization of female identity implied in this search for heroic women.
36 Michelene Wandor, *Understudies: Theatre and Sexual Politics* (London: Methuen, 1981) 87.

37 'Roberta Sklar: Toward Creating a Women's Theatre' 27.
38 'Indirect Impact of the Epic Theatre', *Brecht on Theatre* 58.
39 Adrienne Rich, *Of Woman Born: Motherhood as Experience and Institution* (New York: Norton, 1976) 16.
40 See 'On the Use of Music in an Epic Theatre', *Brecht on Theatre* 85, 86. For Brecht's critique of the 'culinary opera' see also 33–42.
41 Lamb, 'The Mod Donna', *The Mod Donna and Scyklon Z* 31–2.
42 *Ibid.* 139.
43 Megan Terry, 'American King's English for Queens', *High Energy Musicals* 8.
44 *Ibid.* 34–5.
45 'Alienation Effects in Chinese Acting', *Brecht on Theatre* 97.
46 'Roberta Sklar: Toward Creating a Women's Theatre' 30.
47 Sarah Bryant-Bertail, 'Women, Space, Ideology: *Mutter Courage und ihre Kinder*', *Brecht, Women and Politics*, ed. John Fuegi, Gisela Bahr, and John Willett (Detroit: Wayne State University Press, 1983) 45.
48 *Brecht on Theatre* 182.
49 *Brecht on Theatre* 40n.

12 THE INFLUENCE OF BRECHT ON WOMEN'S CINEMA IN WEST GERMANY

1 Karin Struck, *Klassenliebe* (Frankfurt-on-Main: Suhrkamp Verlag, 1973) 137.
2 *Ibid.*
3 See Claire Johnston, 'Women's Cinema as Counter-Cinema', *Movies and Methods*, ed. Bill Nichols (Berkeley, Los Angeles, and London: University of California Press, 1976) 208–17.
4 Bertolt Brecht, 'Über Film 1922 bis 1933', in *Gesammelte Werke*, ed. Elisabeth Hauptmann, 20 vols. (Frankfurt-on-Main: Suhrkamp Verlag, 1967) 18: 139.
5 Johnston, 'Women's Cinema' 217.
6 Brecht, 'Über Film' 161.
7 Johnston, 'Women's Cinema' 217.
8 Bertolt Brecht, 'Germany', *Poems, 1913–1956*, ed. John Willett, Ralph Manheim, Erich Fried (London: Methuen, 1981) 218–19.
9 Petra Höhne, 'Deutschland, bleiche Mutter', *Medium* 5 (1980): 37.
10 Karin Huffzky, 'Meine intellektuellen Freunde', *Süddeutsche Zeitung* 15 Mar. 1975.

13 FROM ANTI-ILLUSIONISM TO HYPER-REALISM: BERTOLT BRECHT AND CONTEMPORARY FILM

1 See James K. Lyon, *Bertolt Brecht in America* (Princeton: Princeton University Press, 1980).

2 See Bertolt Brecht, 'Wilhelm Dieterles Galerie grosser bügerlicher Figuren', *Von Deutschland nach Hollywood: William Dieterle 1893–1972* (Berlin: Internationale Filmfestspiel, 1973) 5–7.

3 From *St Joan of the Stockyards*. In a note Straub adds that he discarded everything satirical and psychological from the novel in order to make 'a kind of film oratorio': Richard Roud, *Straub* (London: Secker and Warburg, 1971) 40.

4 For a more extended discussion of Brecht's influence on modern cinema, see Martin Walsh, *The Brechtian Aspect of Radical Cinema*, ed. Keith M. Griffiths (London: British Film Institute, 1979), and James Roy MacBean, *Film and Revolution* (Bloomington and London: Indiana University Press, 1975).

5 See Yaak Karsunke, 'Die Anfänge', in P. W. Jansen and W. Schütte eds., *Fassbinder* (Munich: Carl Hanser Verlag, 1975) 8–9.

6 See Hans Jürgen Syberberg, *Syberbergs Filmbuch* (Frankfurt-on-Main: Fischer Taschenbuch Verlag, 1979) 304.

7 More detailed examples can be found in Hans Bernhard Moeller, 'Brecht and "Epic" Film Medium', *Wide Angle* 3.4 (1979): 4–11.

8 Jean-Luc Godard, *Godard on Godard*, ed. and trans. Tom Milne (New York: Da Capo Press, 1986) 243 (translation modified).

9 See especially *Screen* 15.2 (Summer, 1974), and 16.4 (Winter, 1975/6).

10 See Peter Wollen, 'The Two Avant-Gardes', *Readings and Writings: Semiotic Counter-Strategies* (London: Verso, 1982) 92–104.

11 *Ibid.* 95.

12 Bertolt Brecht, 'Formal Problems Arising from the Theatre's New Content', *Brecht on Theatre: The Development of an Aesthetic*, ed. and trans. John Willett (London: Methuen, 1964) 229.

13 Colin MacCabe, *Godard: Images, Sounds, Politics* (Bloomington: Indiana University Press, 1980) 19.

14 Walter Benjamin, 'The Author as Producer', reprinted in Victor Burgin, *Thinking Photography* (London: Macmillan, 1982) 22.

15 See *Screen* 16.4 (Winter, 1975/6): 5–33.

16 See, for instance, John Willett, *Brecht in Context* (London: Methuen, 1984) esp. chapters 6–9.

17 The 'New German Cinema' owes its existence in part to a very elaborate state funding and subsidy system. See Thomas Elsaesser, 'The Postwar

German Cinema', in Tony Rayns ed., *Fassbinder* (London: British Film Institute, 1976) 1–16.

18 For a discussion of Brecht's influence on German postwar film and television production, see Richard Collins and Vincent Porter, *WDR and the Arbeiterfilm* (London: British Film Institute, 1981) 97–102, 118–63.

19 Quoted by Stephen Heath, 'Lessons from Brecht', *Screen* 15.2 (Summer, 1974): 123

20 *Ibid.* 107.

21 See also Laura Mulvey, 'Visual Pleasure and Narrative Cinema', *Screen* 16.3 (Autumn, 1975), as the key formulation of the Lacanian argument, applied to the cinema and gendered subjectivity.

22 'John Ford's Young Mr Lincoln', translated in *Screen* 13.3 (1972): 5–44.

23 Raymond Bellour, 'Le Blocage symbolique', *L'Analyse du film* (Paris: Editions Albatros, 1979) 131–246.

24 Stephen Heath, 'Film and System, Terms of Analysis, Part I', *Screen* 16.1 (Spring, 1975): 7–77, and 'Film and System, Terms of Analysis, Part II', *Screen* 16.2 (Summer, 1975): 91–113.

25 See note 21.

26 Fredric Jameson, 'Imaginary and Symbolic in Lacan', *Literature and Psychoanalysis*, Yale French Studies 55–6 (1977): 380.

27 Translated by Alan Williams, in *Film Quarterly* 28.2 (1974/5): 39–47.

28 Constance Penley, 'The Avant-Garde and its Imaginary', *Camera Obscura* 2 (1977): 24.

29 Paul Willemen, 'An Avantgarde for the Eighties', *Framework* 24 (1983): 56.

30 Roland Barthes, *Image, Music, Text*, trans. Stephen Heath (New York: Hill and Wang, 1977) 69–78.

31 See also Jean-Louis Comolli and François Géré, 'Two Fictions Concerning Hate', *Fritz Lang: The Image and the Look*, ed. Stephen Jenkins (London: British Film Institute, 1981) 125–46.

32 Gilles Deleuze, *L'Image-Temps* (Paris: Les Editions de Minuit, 1985) 181.

Index